State and Local Government

2012-2013 Edition

State and Local Government

FEDERALISM

LEGISLATURES

GOVERNORS

COURTS

BUREAUCRACIES

POLICY CHALLENGES

2012-2013 Edition

Edited by Kevin B. Smith

University of Nebraska, Lincoln

SAGE | CQPRESS

Los Angeles | London | New Delhi
Singapore | Washington DC

Los Angeles | London | New Delhi
Singapore | Washington DC

FOR INFORMATION:

CQ Press

An Imprint of SAGE Publications, Inc.

2455 Teller Road

Thousand Oaks, California 91320

E-mail: order@sagepub.com

SAGE Publications Ltd.

1 Oliver's Yard

55 City Road

London EC1Y 1SP

United Kingdom

SAGE Publications India Pvt. Ltd.

B 1/I 1 Mohan Cooperative Industrial Area

Mathura Road, New Delhi 110 044

India

SAGE Publications Asia-Pacific Pte. Ltd.

3 Church Street

#10-04 Samsung Hub

Singapore 049483

Acquisitions Editor: Charisse Kiino
Editorial Assistant: Nancy Loh
Production Editor: Brittany Bauhaus
Copy Editor: Megan Markanich
Typesetter: C&M Digitals (P) Ltd.
Proofreader: Sarah J. Duffy
Cover Designer: Candice Harman
Marketing Manager: Jonathan Mason
Permissions Editor: Adele Hutchinson

Printed in the United States of America.

A catalog record of this book is available from the Library of Congress.

9781452258959

This book is printed on acid-free paper.

Certified Chain of Custody
Promoting Sustainable Forestry
www.sfiprogram.org
SFI-01268

SFI label applies to text stock

13 14 15 16 10 9 8 7 6 5 4 3 2

Contents

About the Editor

Kevin B. Smith is professor of political science at the University of Nebraska, Lincoln. He is the author or coauthor of *Governing States and Localities, 2nd Edition, The Ideology of Education,* and numerous scholarly articles on state politics and policy. He is also a former associate editor of *State Politics & Policy Quarterly.* Prior to becoming an academic he covered state and local politics as a newspaper reporter.

Preface

State and Local Government takes an annual sounding of the most important political trends and policy challenges facing subnational governments. For the fourth year in a row, the dominant issue for state and local governments is coping with the fallout from the biggest economic recession since the Great Depression of the 1930s. For the first time since they were plunged into budgetary crisis, however, state and local governments are doing more than simply trying to get through the mother of all budgetary rough patches. They are beginning to contemplate what comes next.

After 2009, state and local governments were in such dire economic straits that the federal government became their single largest revenue source. Federal stimulus dollars plugged big budget gaps for subnational governments but also precipitated a power shift. The federal dollars reflected federal policy priorities, and strapped as they were for cash, state and local governments had to respect those priorities even at the expense of their own. The stimulus dollars are in the process of drying up. More than that, the federal government is sinking in its own sea of red ink and preparing to bail madly. One of the first things many expect the federal government to toss over the side is funding for vulnerable state and local programs. If such a fiscal reversal occurs, does it mean that states and localities will reassert some of the policy independence lost to Washington in the past four or five years?

No one knows the definitive answer to that question, but there are signs states and localities are beginning to pursue more freedom of action. With the economy stabilized—in a lucky few states it's actually booming—states and localities are looking to do more than survive the present. They are once again looking to the future and, as some of the readings in the volume will show, are determined to navigate their own course. They are reshaping their relationships with public employees, aggressively pursuing new revenue sources, and in general trying to drag themselves out of the twentieth (in some cases the nineteenth) century and into the twenty-first.

Following the format of previous editions, this book samples the political and policy landscape of states and localities by drawing on the best writing from a wide variety of published sources. These include publications familiar to long-term readers like *Governing* magazine and *State Legislatures*, but the readings also draw from academic journals, magazines, independent think tanks, and government associations. Where appropriate, we have edited these (mostly by redacting the technical methods sections) to ensure they remain accessible to as broad an audience as possible.

As always, the readings are all new to the current edition and organized by key institutions, processes, and policy areas. All of the introductions have been updated to reflect the content of the new selections and also to account for the political and policy changes that define the dynamic world of state and local politics.

Putting together this volume requires the efforts of many people, and special thanks are owed to the excellent editorial team at CQ Press: Charisse Kiino, Nancy Loh, Brittany Bauhaus, and Megan Markanich. We hope that you find what follows informative and thought provoking.

Federalism and Intergovernmental Relations

These days, the complex set of relationships shared by federal, state, and local governments can be summed up with a simple question: Okay, so now what? During the past four years, intergovernmental relationships have been dominated by money—or to be more accurate, the lack of money. As the economy tipped into the biggest recession in five generations, the federal government became the primary revenue source for states and localities. That money, though, was aimed largely at federal rather than state and local policy priorities. With federal stimulus dollars drying up and subnational governments managing to take a step or two back from the financial abyss, many states and localities are starting to reevaluate how power and responsibilities were reordered by the economic crisis. At least in the short term, it seems unlikely that intergovernmental relationships will be reset to the prerecession norms. Yet many are not particularly enthusiastic about states and localities continuing in a role of semi-willing partners to their national counterpart, stuck putting their energy into federal rather than their own policy preferences because that's where the money is. So the big question is, what happens next? If the economy starts to pick up, can states and localities increasingly go their own way? Or does the path built with federal dollars during the past few years keep increasing the federal government's power relatively to states and localities? No one is really sure.

The readings in this chapter do not simply take a snapshot of a period when intergovernmental relationships are poised to change. They provide some idea of what form those changes might take. The first essay, by Peter Harkness, compares the current state of affairs with an earlier era when tough economic times presaged a big shift in state–federal relations. State revenues surged after the recession of the early 1980s, which coincided with a broad political movement seeking to devolve power and policy responsibility to the states. In short, coming out of that recession, states were set up to become important and independent domestic policy innovators. Will the same thing happen this time? Harkness suggests that history might not repeat itself, but pushed by the administration of President Barack Obama, federalism is definitely moving in a new direction.

The second essay, by Pamela Prah, highlights some of the uncertainty and frustration associated with changes in federal spending. Though certainly doing better than they were a few years ago, state budgets are still pretty fragile. Then again, the federal government is not exactly in good fiscal shape either. As partisan squabbles break out in the nation's capital about how to cut the federal deficit, states increasingly wonder how they will be affected. When the federal government does not have a clear budget plan, it turns out it is tough for states to have a clear budget plan.

The third essay by Alan Greenblatt shifts focus from state–federal relations to state–local relations. While states are often not happy with what they perceive as high-handed treatment from the feds, they are not above dishing out some of that treatment to local governments. One response to tight budgets has been to give local governments increasingly greater program responsibilities. That's something that local governments often welcome, as they believe they are better positioned to tailor services to a local constituency. What is less welcome is that while states are passing off programs, they are also passing off the bill for those programs. That's a bill that local governments are sometimes having a hard time paying.

The final essay, by Lisa Soronen, examines a series of cases examined by the U.S. Supreme Court in 2012. It might seem a little unusual to have this sort of focus on a federal institution in a book about state and local government, but the content of these cases reminds us that the U.S. Supreme Court is the ultimate umpire of federalism. Judicial review—essentially the authority to determine what the U.S. Constitution does or does not allow—means the Supreme Court ultimately gets to decide who wins power struggles between state and federal governments. And that is exactly what the court is doing in the four cases here: essentially deciding where the power of the federal government ends and the rights of states begin. Court rulings on these cases will provide a partial answer to the big question of what's next for federalism in the United States.

1

What Brand of Federalism Is Next?

By Peter Harkness

The relationship between states and the federal government is about to change. The question is whether that change will be driven by cooperation or coercion.

I n *Governing's* first issue almost 25 years ago, John Herbers, who had just retired as a national correspondent for The New York Times, wrote a cover story heralding the advent of a largely unplanned, unpredicted new federalism, where more responsibility and authority were being devolved down to the states and their localities as the Reagan administration reduced the federal imprint on American governance.

State and local management capacity had improved substantially, he wrote, since Washington had relied on those bureaucracies to manage federal money rather than expand its own. States and localities raised as much in new taxes as the administration had cut. And perhaps most surprising in the context of what we are experiencing today, there had been "a sharp decline in ideological or partisan divisions among state and local public officials, a result of the growing belief among Democrats and Republicans alike that certain public outlays for social and economic programs are likely to save money in the long run."

Indeed, coming out of the recession of 1980–82, states in the subsequent four years grew their revenues by one-third, to $228 billion. And that didn't include mushrooming cash inflows from nontax sources like lotteries, which had expanded into a majority of the states.

Because the national economy was humming along quite nicely and the tax base had significantly expanded, state and local governments experienced what would be an almost three-decade run of solid increases in tax revenue—interrupted slightly by two mild recessions.

From *Governing*, January 2012.

The political side of it didn't go quite as Herbers had imagined. Many states took a leadership role on national policy matters from the time *Governing* launched through the end of the Clinton presidency in January 2001. The most prominent trophy on their mantel probably was the national welfare reform law in 1996 that grew out of programs started by Republican governors in Michigan and Wisconsin. Relations with the feds during that period were sometimes a bit rocky, but there was little doubt that Washington and the country were headed in the same general direction.

The surprise came later, with the election of the George W. Bush administration, which showed no interest in following the traditional conservative, states-rights script. What followed was the No Child Left Behind education law, the Real ID Act, a wave of pre-emptions of state regulations and thinly disguised mandates (which supposedly had been banned). Meanwhile, the White House Office of Intergovernmental Affairs was a sham—a purely political operation manned by junior staffers whose sole interest was promoting the administration's policies rather than working with state or local officials. Washington lobbyists pushed for more centralization, with the idea that their industries could cut a better deal at the federal level and avoid a patchwork of statutes and regulations. It was what Don Borut, executive director of the National League of Cities, called "coercive federalism," or when he was being more blunt, "shift-and-shaft federalism."

Plenty has changed since the Bush years, of course. The Great Recession has weakened the revenue base of most states and localities, and a rising tide of partisanship and ideological rigidity has swamped both Washington and many of the states. The mixture has been toxic.

In this atmosphere, the Obama administration has pursued a very unique mixture of collaborative and coercive strategies in dealing with states and localities,

making it hard to define just what kind of federalism we're seeing. The health-care, education and financial regulation reform bills, the climate change proposal and the massive financial stimulus bill all represented an aggressive use of federal power, some of it unprecedented and some pre-empting state regulations.

But there was a difference: Collaboration and sensitivity to state prerogatives was built into the mix. In an analysis in the publication *Publius* by political scientists Paul Posner and Tim Conlan of George Mason University, the authors noted that "the most significant feature of Obama's approach to intergovernmental relations thus far may be his hybrid model of federal policy innovation and leadership, which mixes money, mandates and flexibility in new and distinctive ways." Under this "nuanced federalism," plenty of carrots are mixed in with the sticks. Even with the health-care reform plan, they noted, progressive states were allowed to exceed minimum federal standards and conservative ones could avoid participating in almost any facet of the system, using the feds as a backstop.

By most accounts, both from the federal officials who ran it and the state and local officials they worked with, the massive Recovery Act stimulus effort was an extraordinarily successful collaboration between all three levels of government. States enjoyed unusual flexibility in how they spent much of the billions in funding the act provided, and Washington was able to rely on a state and local infrastructure to get the cash out the door fast.

So what brand of federalism will we see next? Will it be the kind John Herbers foresaw as *Governing* was launched? Or will a mixture of this crippling recession, massive cutbacks in discretionary federal spending, and continued political dysfunction at the national and state levels render the system paralyzed?

I'm hoping for the former, but can't say that I'm too optimistic.

2

Washington and the States: A Year of Uncertainty and Foreboding

By Pamela M. Prah

Everyone knows the federal government is going to be sending fewer dollars to the states. But what is going to get cut? Planning in the states is tough when that question is not getting answered.

A long siege of deadlock and dysfunction in Washington has left states frustratingly unclear what to expect from the federal government in the coming year. About the only thing they know for sure is that it is not going to be a year of generosity.

In fact, it's likely to be quite the opposite. As a result of last summer's deal to raise the federal debt ceiling, and the consequent failure of the congressional "super committee" to decide on budget cuts, states are bracing for automatic across-the-board cuts in education, social welfare and other programs for the upcoming 2013 fiscal year. Those cuts would come atop federal cuts in 2011 and 2012, not to mention the continuing wind-down of federal stimulus aid.

Partisan standoffs between Congress and President Obama aren't just related to the budget. Long overdue legislation setting federal policy for states on key issue areas remains stuck, making it difficult for states to know what to expect in 2012 and beyond. "For states, the uncertainty creates planning and budgeting problems in both the immediate and long run," says Dan Crippen, executive director of the National Governors Association. "Governors will soon present budgets to their legislatures without knowing if, and in what form, programs such as transportation, ESEA (education) and TANF (welfare) will be reauthorized."

AUTOMATIC CUTS KICK IN

Republicans made good on their promise to rein in spending when they took command of the U.S. House after the 2010 elections and gave Washington divided government. And a huge GOP target was

From *Stateline.org*, January 2012.

the amount of federal money sent to the states, which in the past has accounted for one-third of state revenue.

Last year, states had to wait almost until Christmas— six months into fiscal year 2012 for most of them—to find out how big a chunk Congress was taking from key discretionary programs such as low-income housing, Head Start and worker training. The overall result was nearly $5 billion fewer federal dollars for state programs, or a 2.7 percent cut from fiscal 2011, according to Federal Funds Information for States, which provides federal funding data to state lawmakers and governors.

Those cuts came on top of already-large reductions in certain programs the previous year—cuts that were largely overlooked because states were still getting so much support at the time from the federal stimulus program. "States got hit hard in FY 2011, which isn't widely appreciated," says FFIS Executive Director Marcia Howard. Taken together, states will have seen a 7.2 percent decrease in federal aid for major programs between 2010 and 2012, nearly $14 billion in all. "The compounding of these cuts is getting to be significant," Howard says.

Michael Bird, senior federal affairs counsel at the National Conference of State Legislatures, says the cumulative drop in federal funds is the most significant in recent memory. "I can't think of a time when the cuts were as deep as these."

But deeper ones are coming.

The failure of the congressional "super committee" to come up with a plan to reduce the federal deficit set up automatic across-the-board federal spending reductions. While those cuts wouldn't begin to take effect until January of 2013, states have to budget now for a fiscal year that in most cases starts in July of 2012.

Assuming no change in the rules by Congress, the cuts are to be split evenly between defense and domestic spending, except for entitlement programs, including Medicaid, which are spared. States such as Maryland, Virginia and Texas, with economies heavily dependent on military bases, defense contractors and armed forces procurement, could see their tax revenues shrink significantly because of these cuts. "I don't think there is any

question that we are going to have to tighten our belts," says Republican state Representative Dan Flynn of Texas.

But all states would feel the squeeze from an across-the-board cut in domestic programs. While the exact amount of the cuts that would come from this so-called "sequestration" process won't be known until next year, FFIS used an 8.8 percent figure to provide rough estimates for states to plan by. In dollar terms, cuts of that magnitude would result in a reduction of more than $9 billion from fiscal 2012 levels. In California alone, nearly $1.3 billion is at stake for work study programs, special education, juvenile justice grants and many other programs.

"Clearly the poorest people and families in the country are not the focus of concern in the Congress—which is my biggest worry," says Ruth Kagi, a Democratic state representative from Washington State.

MORE UNCERTAINTY AHEAD

But future cuts to domestic spending could be even deeper than the current agreement calls for. Already, there is rumbling on Capitol Hill that defense should be relieved from bearing half the burden. "We'd like to get it changed," says Republican U.S. Senator John Hoeven. If defense programs were shielded from cuts, it could mean that states would see an even bigger reduction in federal funds for domestic programs. Hoeven, who spent a decade as governor of North Dakota, says he sympathizes with states' plight. "We have to find savings and that obviously will have an impact on states. . . . That's just part of getting the deficit under control."

But where will the savings come from? The states probably won't get a whole lot more clarity on that question before they have to write their budgets for the coming year. Nick Johnson, vice president for state fiscal policy at the Center on Budget and Policy Priorities, a liberal think tank in Washington, D.C., predicts that presidential politics will push big decisions off until after the November elections. He thinks the most likely decision time for further state spending cuts may be a lame-duck session in late November or December.

Election-year politics will likely derail any major reforms in federal tax or entitlement policy. But states can't even count on knowing for sure what tax rates to expect in 2013. Reduced federal income tax rates first enacted under President George W. Bush, and later extended, are set to expire at the end of 2012. Some states, such as Maryland, are assuming these tax breaks will in fact end—a result that in Maryland's case would have both positive and negative effects on the state's revenues. But none of them will know for sure until the presidential election is over, and perhaps not for some time after that.

The one bright spot is that revenues are up for states, although the amount is not anywhere near enough to replace the billions states got from the federal stimulus package. The latest data from the National Conference of State Legislatures show that over the last four years, states closed more than $500 billion in budget gaps. However, for early 2012, NCSL reports, "new gaps are practically non-existent."

STATES MAKE CONTINGENCY PLANS

Some states aren't waiting to hear just how big the federal cuts will be. Massachusetts is counting on a 10 percent reduction in federal funds. That could mean deeper cuts to safety net services and education programs like METCO, which sends inner city kids to schools out in the suburbs. "It's really frustrating," says Sean J. Fitzgerald, chief of staff to Democratic state Representative Jay R. Kaufman. "METCO and other well-deserving programs have already seen cuts and the fear is there will be more," but he says the uncertainty makes it hard to plan.

In Utah, agencies have gone through an exercise to figure out what they would need to do if federal funds were cut either by 5 percent or by 25 percent. Utah is often touted as one of the best-managed states and one that is least reliant on federal funds. But that's not a great deal of comfort to Republican state Representative Ken Ivory, who introduced the state legislation requiring the contingency plans. "That's like being called the best-looking horse in the glue factory," he says.

Ivory, like many others at all levels of government, says the entire relationship between the states and the federal government is out of whack. "We've got to have the partnership discussion and clearly define the lines," he says. "This is your job. This is our job."

But virtually no one on either side of the ideological divide thinks that will happen anytime soon. "Republicans talk about limiting the growth in the size of the federal government, but have little to say when it comes to the scope of the federal government's activities,"

Figure 2.1

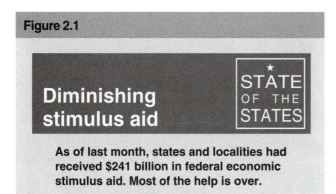

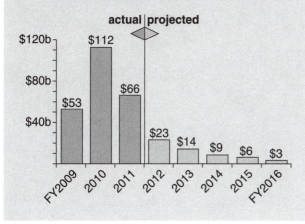

Source: U.S. Government Accountability Office

says Tad DeHaven, a budget analyst at the Cato Institute, a libertarian think tank.

In the meantime, even if election-year politics gets in the way of substantial changes in the relationship between states and the federal government, states would at least like Washington to stop the political brinkmanship. "Make a decision," says Warren Deschenaux, the chief fiscal analyst for Maryland's nonpartisan Department of Legislative Services. "Tell us what's coming so we can deal with it."

3

States Handing Off More Responsibilities to Cities

By Alan Greenblatt

States are giving local governments more and more program responsibilities. They are not giving them more money to actually run those programs.

Jerry Brown is dusting off one of the oldest plays in his book. Back in 1975, during his first term as governor, Brown had appeared before the California State Association of Counties (CSAC) to talk about realignment—the term of art in California for devolution, or changing the way responsibilities are split between the state and localities.

Now that he's back in the governor's office, Brown is putting some of those ideas into action. He returned to CSAC on his first full day in office to promote a realignment package that would make counties responsible for running a much larger share of public safety and social service programs. Proposition 13—the property tax law that passed during Brown's first term—"took away the power of counties to tax, for the most part," Brown said at CSAC in January. "It sent the decisions up to Sacramento. So we want to redistribute all that."

County officials are welcoming the chance to take charge of certain programs, while expressing great concern about handling others. Unsurprisingly, the big question is money—whether the state will send enough cash to localities to fund the missions it expects them to carry out. "There's a lot of anxiety," says Jean Kinney Hurst, a legislative representative with CSAC. "We're talking about $6 billion worth of programs, many of which counties have never done before."

Similar anxieties are being expressed elsewhere around the country. Other states may not be holding the same overt policy debate about whether localities should take on a larger load, but the question is nonetheless being posed in the form of budget cuts that leave localities more on their own. "There's a potential," says Ellis

From *Governing*, April 2011.

Hankins, executive director of the North Carolina League of Municipalities, "for local elected officials to have to pick up more of the burden and increase the taxes to pay for more public services."

There's nothing new in this. States always cut aid to local governments in recessions. During the ongoing state budget crunch, the cuts have grown so deep that many officials at the local level are complaining that states are doing to them what Washington does to the states—passing on more mandates even while cutting funding.

"We want to make sure that, at a minimum, states don't try to balance their budgets on the backs of cities by mandating that local governments do what historically has been done by states," says Don Borut, executive director of the National League of Cities. "And we don't want the states preempting or putting restraints on how cities can raise money."

Devolution by budget cut is happening all over the country. Very few states still have a line item called "aid to localities." But program responsibilities—and finances—are all mixed up between the state and local levels across a broad range of program areas, including health, public safety and the big cost driver of education.

States have slashed billions over the past couple of years that otherwise would have gone to local governments. In Massachusetts, for example, Gov. Deval Patrick has proposed cutting direct municipal aid for the fourth year in a row. His package would bring the total cut to more than $481 million, or 37 percent. Beverly, Mass., Mayor William Scanlon says such cuts are "really painful," because state aid is the second largest share of his city's revenue. But cuts in total state aid to localities —education has been better protected than municipal aid—aren't out of line with levels of Massachusetts' spending cuts overall. Scanlon says he recognizes that the governor and legislators have had little choice in the matter. "The state's revenues have fallen off the table," Scanlon says. "If I was in their shoes, I'm afraid I would do what they've done."

What Scanlon and other mayors object to, however, is the state backing out on prior promises—failing to return what are really local revenues. Massachusetts established a program back in the 1970s to encourage police officers to continue their education by increasing their salaries when they receive degrees in higher education. The state promised localities it would pick up 50 percent of the tab. Under that formula, the state's share for the coming year stands at nearly $60 million, but Patrick's budget only provides $5 million. Court decisions suggest that localities may be on the hook for the rest.

Similar stories can be told all over. North Carolina Gov. Bev Perdue wants to slash the local share of lottery proceeds from 40 percent to 10 percent. And her budget would shift the $57 million cost of school bus replacements onto counties, a responsibility they have never had before. In all, the overall cost shift to counties is $345 million. In Michigan, where much local taxing authority was taken away decades ago in favor of a local share of state sales taxes, the state over the past decade has cut $4 billion that, by statute, should go to local governments.

Michigan Gov. Rick Snyder not only wants to cut remaining revenue sharing by a third this year, but wants to make localities earn the money. State aid, under his proposal, would be contingent on their putting in place measures to save money, including consolidation of services and winning concessions on wages and benefits from their workers.

Last month, Snyder pushed a bill that would make it easier for the state to intervene in municipal and school district finances by creating "emergency fiscal managers" with broad authority. Snyder said he didn't want the state to have to take over local budgets but that his legislation would create an early-warning system when localities are getting in trouble.

It has become a common tack. Governors promise more flexibility on certain rules or help with pensions or employee health costs in exchange for less money overall, and demand that localities change workforce rules and consolidate certain services—or merge with their neighbors altogether. Governors haven't gotten far over the past decade with most of their proposals that local governments consolidate, but they are now wielding a much bigger financial stick. "The fiscal constraints are now coming to bear on localities," says John Krauss, director of the Indiana University Public Policy Institute, who helped run a local government reform commission for Gov. Mitch Daniels.

"Resources are becoming scarce, things change and you can't do it the same way," Krauss continues.

"Localities are now seeing that it is probably wise to have merger and intergovernmental agreements. Those are taking off."

Krauss argues that consolidation at the local level is "logical," and notes that many of the ideas his commission recommended echo back to a governmental reorganization report from 1932. But local officials are understandably wary of reorganization that is pushed from above. They naturally worry about having to pick up any financial difference, particularly where they are operating under constraints—often imposed by their states—in terms of their own ability to increase taxes.

But they also worry about equity issues. Some local governments are better off financially than others. As more and more responsibility falls primarily or wholly on local governments, states may be abdicating their role in seeing that a certain level of service is made available to all residents, regardless of the jurisdiction in which they reside. For some services, such as education, states are required to see that disparities based on ZIP code are not too wide.

That's certainly the case in California, which is a pioneer state when it comes to school-equity lawsuits. Because of a 1988 ballot initiative, the state is required to spend at least 40 percent of its general fund revenues on K–12 education. A lot of the money the state spends on education comes out of locally collected property taxes, which the state vacuums up and then redistributes.

Education is just one way state and local finances are hopelessly entangled in California. There are dozens of others. A discussion solely about how revenues from vehicle license fees are shared between Sacramento and localities could go on for many long and tedious hours. Even local officials who are nervous about Brown's proposals give him credit for trying to sort through the mess. There's a lot to be said for citizens' being able to know who's responsible for raising the money and spending which funds for which programs. But given the convoluted nature of the way money is taxed at one level of government—and then chopped up and redistributed to other levels of government—it's often impossible to know who to thank and who to blame. "One of the reasons why California got so screwed up," says former California Assembly Speaker Robert Hertzberg, "is the unintended consequences of the jury-rigged attempts to get money to the locals."

Hertzberg is a strong backer of Brown's realignment proposal. He recognizes, however, that the word "realignment" is code to local governments that they will have to pick up more responsibilities without getting more money to pay for them. Brown initially proposed offering localities funding to cover their new responsibilities for five years, but has since said he will find a way to provide more permanent funding. "It's a long discussion that starts with, 'There better be enough money,'" says David Finigan, a Del Norte County, Calif., supervisor.

Finigan has reason to be wary. Brown's whole idea is predicated on the hope that voters will approve a tax package to pay for it in a special election in June. And past realignment debates in Sacramento haven't all come through with the kind of money that Brown is promising. A 1991 realignment of social services left counties about a billion dollars short.

Cities are already livid that Brown wants to eliminate nearly $2 billion in local redevelopment funds. The state of California has long been notorious for dipping into local coffers, either by using sticky fingers to hold on to tax dollars the state is supposed to hand down, or by "borrowing" local revenues. Local officials in California have twice succeeded in recent years in convincing voters to pass propositions designed to block such behavior on the part of the state. "There has been a long-standing history of distrust in the relationship between the state and local governments in California," says CSAC's Hurst. "Unless you put things in the constitution, you can't rely on anyone's word or handshake agreement."

Los Angeles District Attorney Steve Cooley warns that Brown's proposed realignment will "wreak havoc" and be a "public safety nightmare." He notes that jails in his county are already at or near capacity limits imposed by federal courts. County supervision of paroled rapists and murderers, he says, would mean some convicted felons will serve little or no time in custody due to insufficient bed space.

But many other local officials in California aren't opposed to the idea of realignment—in principle. Just as states have long argued that they can run programs more efficiently than the feds if given adequate support and flexibility, Finigan says that localities can handle most of the programs Brown has put on the table "better and cheaper" than the state.

Hertzberg now co-chairs California Forward, a policy group that has advocated better alignment of services and level of government. He says it's unfortunate that the idea has been distorted by the unending arguments in California about how revenue streams flow up and down and diverge between the state and localities. He recognizes that money has to follow program responsibility in order for realignment to work, but argues that realignment is a necessity in order for localities and regions within the state to operate in a more responsive way.

It's possible that Brown's ideas—ambitious as they are—represent only a first step in this regard. It will be challenging enough to put counties in charge of parole, for instance. But the current debate about public safety and social services may only be the opening of a long discussion that will eventually incorporate even bigger issues such as education and the tax code.

If it's done right—and isn't just a cost-cutting maneuver—many local officials in California believe they can offer more efficient coordination of services. As things stand now, though, counties struggle to knit together closely related programs that nonetheless are funded through separate state revenue streams, each with its own set of mandates.

Some counties have figured out how to do this already. Kids who are at risk of being removed from their homes, for instance, might fall under the purview of any of three different agencies, depending on whether the problem is parental abuse, drug use or involvement in crime. Each of these programs comes with its own set of state money that goes to either the county health, human services or probation department. Quite often, the problems of at-risk kids are intertwined. But this has often led to situations where local agency officials point fingers at one another and argue, "This kid belongs to you, it's a substance abuse issue," or "No, the primary problem is the criminal activity." Taking kids out of their homes is an expensive proposition and no one wants to be stuck with the bill.

About a decade ago, officials in San Mateo County, Calif., decided it was pointless to try to shift responsibility between departments. Officials from different agencies began meeting on a weekly basis, getting to know the kids and their problems, and trying to coordinate the whole panoply of services that they might need. It didn't always go smoothly at first, but over time the agencies learned to work together. The result has been a 50 percent reduction in the number of kids removed from their homes. "Kids who stay in their homes, so long as they get the right services, do a whole lot better in the long run," says County Health System Chief Jean Fraser.

Fraser recognizes that her county has resources others might not be able to draw on. The county is made up largely of affluent suburbs just south of San Francisco and has 700,000 residents—as many as the state of Vermont. But she argues that it's even more important for poorer counties to have greater flexibility in expending the limited resources at their disposal.

Already facing budget shortfalls of their own, it's difficult for local officials to contemplate the prospect of taking on further program responsibilities. Many of the programs Brown is expecting them to take over come laden with mandates from either the state or federal level—or both. And in many other states, localities are being asked to do more without seeing real help in terms of delivery on promises of greater flexibility, or even serious debate about what responsibilities best lie with which level of government.

The issue, of course, is whether California will remain committed to funding the responsibilities Brown hopes to pass down—an ever-present source of anxiety for local officials in California, as it is for their counterparts in other states. If the commitment is there, Fraser sees real promise in the notion of freeing counties to design programs in ways that best meet the needs of their own residents. "From our perspective, the idea of having more flexibility about what we do is really exciting," she says. "We're raring to go."

4

States' Rights At Center of Trilogy of Cases Before Supreme Court

By Lisa Soronen

The U.S. Supreme Court is the ultimate umpire of the federal system. It is about to make some calls that will decide the power of state and federal governments on some big-league policy questions.

From *Capitol Ideas*, March/April 2012.

It is a rare Supreme Court term where the issue of federalism is raised in all of the most prominent cases. In the Affordable Care Act litigation, the Arizona immigration case and the Texas redistricting case, however, states' rights are the central question with which the Court must contend.

What makes these three cases different from even the prominent federalism cases of the last few decades is that they all involve politically charged topics—health care, immigration and voting—and concern issues that directly impact the lives of your average American, health care in particular. As usual, the implications of the Court's decisions in these cases may extend well beyond the specific facts litigated.

AFFORDABLE CARE ACT

The Court is considering four questions in the Affordable Care Act case—two of which address federalism head on.

First, they will decide whether the individual mandate—which requires almost all Americans by 2014 to obtain health insurance or pay a fine—violates the Commerce Clause. One of the reasons the 11th Circuit concluded the individual mandate is unconstitutional is that insurance and health care are traditional areas of state concern.

Second, the Affordable Care Act requires states to expand Medicaid coverage or lose all federal Medicaid funding, not just additional federal funding that will cover the cost of the expansion. The Court will decide whether the Medicaid expansion is permissible under the Spending Clause or fails the coercion test because states are essentially compelled to participate in Medicaid.

Whether the Court considers the requirement to buy health insurance interstate commerce or the Medicaid expansion coercive will impact both legal doctrines in contexts well beyond the individual mandate and Medicaid. The argument that Congress can regulate inactivity—not buying health insurance—is novel. Likewise, the Court has only twice ruled on the coercion in the Spending Clause context, making any ruling—much less a ruling regarding a program as big as Medicaid—significant.

ARIZONA IMMIGRATION

In this case, the Supreme Court will decide whether four provisions of Arizona's immigration statute are preempted by federal law. Arizona argued in its certiorari petition that Senate Bill 1070 "authorizes cooperative law enforcement and imposes sanctions that consciously parallel federal law." But the Ninth Circuit disagreed, concluding that all four provisions of Senate Bill 1070 are pre-empted by federal immigration law.

Regarding police being required to determine if a person is in the United States legally, the Ninth Circuit concluded that the federal Immigration and Naturalization Act allows state and local police to aid in immigration enforcement only under the supervision of the attorney general.

Regarding state criminalization of failing to carry immigration papers, the Ninth Circuit concluded this requirement is pre-empted because Congress did not provide for state participation in this section of the Immigration and Naturalization Act, though it did in other sections of the law.

Regarding Arizona criminalizing employment for undocumented immigrants, the Ninth Circuit noted that the INA only sanctions employers.

Regarding police officers being allowed to arrest a person who is likely subject to deportation, the Ninth Circuit concluded this section is pre-empted because "states do not have the inherent authority to enforce the civil provisions of federal immigration law."

Other states have adopted state immigration laws similar to Arizona's. These laws, too, may be pre-empted by federal law, depending on how the Court rules in this case.

TEXAS REDISTRICTING

The issue in the Texas redistricting case was whether and how much a federal district court must defer to a state legislature's drawing of electoral maps when the federal district court creates interim electoral maps. Due to population growth, Texas gained four U.S. House of Representative seats requiring the Texas state legislature to redraw its electoral maps. The state legislature's redistricting plan would likely allow Republicans to gain three of the four additional seats.

Per the Voting Rights Act, Texas's redistricting plan must be precleared to make sure it wasn't discriminatory on the basis of race or color. While preclearance of Texas's plan was still being litigated in a D.C. federal district court, the candidate filing period for 2012 election was closing imminently. So the federal district court in San Antonio drew an interim redistricting map. The court's interim map would likely give Democrats two of the new seats and, according to Texas, substantially changed all but nine of the 36 districts. Texas sued, claiming the federal district court should have deferred to the state legislature's electoral map when drawing up an interim map.

The Supreme Court's opinion in this case was favorable to the Texas legislature. The Court vacated the federal district court's interim maps. It instructed the district court to "take guidance from the State's recently enacted plan in drafting an interim plan. That plan reflects the State's policy judgments on where to place new districts and how to shift existing ones in response to massive population growth."

CONCLUSION

The Supreme Court has already issued an opinion in the Texas redistricting case. It will issue an opinion in the Affordable Care Act and Arizona immigration cases no later than the end of its term in June. Not all the cases from this term affecting state and local government have been as prominent, controversial or partisan as these three cases. The State and Local Legal Center has filed or will file amicus briefs in three other cases . . . , all of which will likely have a greater impact on local government than state government.

Elections and Political Environment

The political landscape always changes from election to election. There are new faces running for office, different economic and political issues dominate the debate, and partisan fortunes rise and fall. Rarely, though, has the political landscape changed as much and as quickly as it has in the past couple of years. The change was precipitated by the so-called red tide of Republican victories in 2010. As a result of that election, the GOP did not simply pick up the keys to twenty-eight governors' mansions and complete party control of twenty-five legislatures for 2011. They also got the opportunity to shape the elections for 2012 and far beyond.

One of the most obvious ways this was accomplished was in redistricting. Republican timing in surging to legislative power at the state level was impeccable. In 2011, states began redistricting on the basis of the 2010 census. As this is an activity controlled mostly by state legislatures, Republicans found themselves well positioned to shape state legislative and congressional political boundaries to their advantage for a decade. Republicans also began in 2011 to make good on all those campaign promises they had made in 2010. Some of this agenda turned out to be highly controversial—attempts to reign in the bargaining power of public unions in Ohio and Wisconsin, for example, prompted a passionate backlash. Other favorite items on the Republican to-do list that sparked conflict were numerous attempts to change the rules and rights of voting; for example, there was a notable uptick in legislative activity on voter ID and registration laws.

The readings in this chapter focus on the consequences of past elections and the policies and laws that have consequences for future elections. In both cases, the end result can be much more than the ephemeral sorts of things associated with each electoral cycle: the new faces, new issues, and new partisan alignments that are part and parcel of the regular democratic political reshuffling. Some of the consequences considered in this chapter's readings are so long-lasting that they may help shape the electoral landscape—perhaps even determine the outcome of elections—for decades into the future.

The first reading is a series of excerpts of the Brennan Center for Justice report authored by Wendy Weiser and Lawrence Norden. The topic of Weiser and Norden's report is an analysis of the changes in voting laws during the 2011 state legislative session. For the better part of a century, legislative changes at the state and federal levels have generally been oriented toward making it easier for citizens to vote. In 2011, Weiser and Norden find that trend was reversed. State legislatures considered, and in many cases enacted, a broad variety of voting restrictions and regulations that could make it harder for as many as 5 million citizens to vote (particularly affected are the young, minorities, the poor, and those convicted of felonies).

While Weiser and Norden's report looks at how state governments are taking it upon themselves to proactively change electoral environments, the essay by Edward Smith provides insight into changes to the electoral landscape that legislatures have little control over. Elections are often driven by demographics, and demographics in many states are changing rapidly. Baby boomers are headed for retirement, population is shifting from rural to urban communities, racial and ethnic minorities are increasing as a proportion of the electorate, and increasing numbers of voters have fallen into low-income categories. These changes, all documented by the decennial census, portend not just a change in policy focus for states but a permanent reshaping of the political environment.

Finally, John Gramlich takes a snapshot of the Republican victors of 2010 as they headed into the 2012 elections. What he finds is that many Republican officeholders are moderating the stands they ran on in 2010. The bruising political battles fought in 2011 to implement the GOP agenda might be the result of a good faith effort to deliver on 2010 campaign promises, but some of those promises looked less sellable two years on. The campaign of 2012, like all elections, was promising to be different, raising some new issues and reflecting some hard-won lessons.

5

Voting Law Changes in 2012

By Wendy R. Weiser and Lawrence Norden

Government has spent a century making it easier for citizens to cast a ballot. In 2011, that all changed as state legislatures pursued a new agenda that increased regulations and restrictions on voting.

EXECUTIVE SUMMARY

Over the past century, our nation expanded the franchise and knocked down myriad barriers to full electoral participation. In 2011, however, that momentum abruptly shifted.

State governments across the country enacted an array of new laws making it harder to register or to vote. Some states require voters to show government-issued photo identification, often of a type that as many as one in ten voters do not have. Other states have cut back on early voting, a hugely popular innovation used by millions of Americans. Two states reversed earlier reforms and once again disenfranchised millions who have past criminal convictions but who are now taxpaying members of the community. Still others made it much more difficult for citizens to register to vote, a prerequisite for voting.

As detailed in this report, the extent to which states have made voting more difficult is unprecedented in the last several decades, and comes after a dramatic shift in political power following the 2010 election. The battles over these laws were—and, in states where they are not yet over, continue to be—extremely partisan and among the most contentious in this year's legislative session. Proponents of the laws have offered several reasons for their passage: to prevent fraud, to ease administrative burden, to save money. Opponents have focused on the fact that the new laws will make it much more difficult for eligible citizens to vote and to ensure that their votes are counted. In particular, they have pointed out that many of these laws and students— eligible voters who already face the biggest hurdles to voting.

This report provides the first comprehensive overview of the state legislative action on voting rights so far in 2011. It summarizes

From Brennan Center for Justice at New York University School of Law, 2011.

Map 5.1

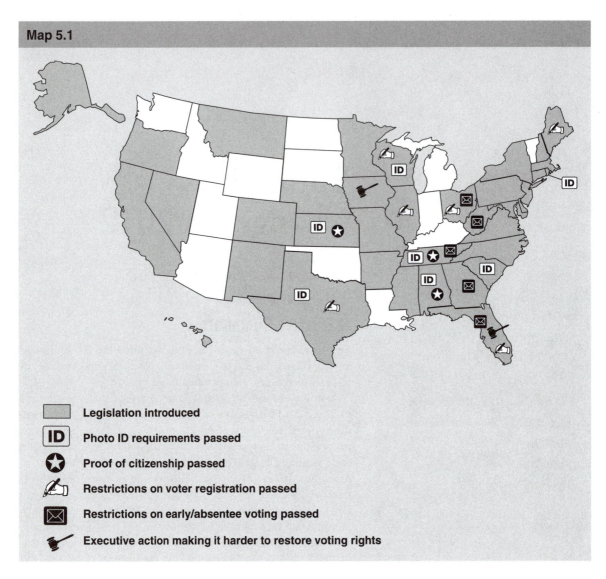

Legislation introduced

ID Photo ID requirements passed

★ Proof of citizenship passed

✍ Restrictions on voter registration passed

✉ Restrictions on early/absentee voting passed

⚖ Executive action making it harder to restore voting rights

the legislation introduced and passed this legislative session, provides political and legal context, and details the contentious political battles surrounding these bills.

VOTER IDENTIFICATION

A. Background

By far the most widespread legislative development this session involved bills to impose stricter documentary identification requirements on voters. Voter ID laws—especially those that require voters to show one of a small number of government-issued photo IDs to vote—have been the subject of intense debate over the past few election cycles, and the debate heated up this year.

Proponents of strict voter ID laws maintain that they are reasonable measures to prevent fraud by persons improperly casting ballots in the names of other registered citizens, real or imagined. They dispute that such laws will discourage voting by any group, claiming that photo IDs are needed for many aspects of modern life, including boarding an airplane or entering certain government buildings.[3] Opponents maintain that photo ID laws exclude large swaths of the electorate, since 11% of citizens—and an even greater percentage of low-income, minority, young, and older citizens—do not have state-issued photo IDs.[4] They argue that photo ID requirements are similar to a poll tax, whether or not the IDs are offered for free, because to obtain the necessary IDs citizens must produce documents that cost money, like passports and birth certificates.[5] Opponents also claim that impersonation voter fraud—the only type of fraud prevented by voter ID laws—almost never happens since our laws adequately protect against and punish such fraud.[6] Although the best available study found that strict voter ID laws reduce turnout, neither side can definitively demonstrate the extent of the effect on voter turnout, since such laws have not been in effect long enough to permit accurate study.[7] Each side also questions the other's motives.

Voter ID is nothing new—indeed, federal law requires every new voter who registers by mail to show ID before voting,[8] and a variety of states have additional common-sense ID requirements.[9] What is new, however, is the degree to which the voter ID bills that were proposed and passed this session were restrictive, excluding many common forms of photo and non-photo IDs, such as student IDs and Social Security cards, and offering no alternative mechanisms for eligible citizens without the selected IDs to cast ballots that will count. What also is new is the extent to which such restrictive bills passed this session.

Prior to the 2006 elections, *no* state required its voters to show government-issued photo ID at the polls (or elsewhere) in order to vote. In 2006, Indiana became the first state in the nation to do so. Although Georgia and Missouri passed photo ID laws at around the same time, both states' laws were blocked by courts on the ground that they interfered with the right of eligible citizens to vote—under the U.S. Constitution in Georgia's case and the Missouri State Constitution in Missouri's case.[10] In 2008, the U.S. Supreme Court upheld Indiana's voter ID law against a constitutional attack.[11] After lengthy litigation in response to which Georgia amended its voter ID law several times, Georgia's law was eventually upheld as well.[12] That law

first went into effect in late 2007, making Georgia the second state in the nation to require its citizens to show photo ID at the polls.

Thus, as of the start of this legislative session, only two states had ever imposed strict photo ID requirements on voters, and only for a short period of time. Several other states—Florida, Hawaii, Idaho, Louisiana, Michigan, and South Dakota—also requested, and still request, photo ID from their voters at the polls, but if a voter in those states does not have photo ID, she can still cast a ballot that will count after an alternative verification procedure, like a signature match or a sworn affidavit. The remainder of the states had more flexible voting identification requirements.[13]

B. Roundup of Legislative Developments

This year, at least thirty-four states introduced a record number of bills to require photo ID to vote.[14] As Jenny Bowser, senior fellow at the National Conference of State Legislatures, observed, "It's remarkable. . . . I very rarely see one single issue come up in so many state legislatures in a single session."[15]

Photo ID bills passed and were signed into law in seven states to date: Alabama, Kansas, Rhode Island, South Carolina, Tennessee, Texas, and Wisconsin.[16] (The Alabama, South Carolina, and Texas laws cannot go into effect unless and until they are pre-cleared by either the U.S. Department of Justice or a federal court under the Voting Rights Act.) Bills also passed but were vetoed in five additional states: Minnesota, Missouri, Montana, New Hampshire, and North Carolina.[17] A number of additional states—including Pennsylvania[18]—still have active photo ID bills pending in ongoing legislative sessions. In New Hampshire, legislators failed to override the Governor's veto,[19] and in North Carolina, legislators could attempt to push a new voter ID bill despite the Governor's veto.[20]

In addition, Missouri legislators passed a ballot measure to amend the state constitution to allow the state to impose photo ID requirements on voters; the measure will appear on the state ballot in November 2012.[21] (If the measure passes, legislators will have to enact further legislation before a photo ID requirement could be imposed.) Supporters of strict voter ID in Mississippi similarly introduced a ballot initiative that will appear on the November 2011 ballot.[22]

II. DOCUMENTARY PROOF OF CITIZENSHIP TO REGISTER OR VOTE

A. Background

In general, except for certain local elections, a person must be a U.S. citizen over eighteen years old to be eligible to participate in American elections. A voter typically establishes her eligibility by swearing an affidavit, under penalty of perjury, that she is a U.S. citizen of voting age and meets all the other eligibility requirements of her state (such as residency and lack of disqualifying criminal convictions).[112] A non-citizen or other ineligible person who falsely claims eligibility and either registers to vote or votes is subject to serious criminal penalties—including five years in prison and $10,000 in fines under federal law[113]—and also deportation.

Until recently, no state has ever required any voter to produce documentary proof of citizenship—or age or any other component of eligibility—to participate in elections. In 2004, however, as part of a broad-ranging ballot initiative, called Proposition 200, regulating the treatment of immigrants, Arizona for the first time passed a law requiring prospective voters to present documentary proof of citizenship in order to register to vote.[114] The Arizona law, which went into effect before the 2006 elections, specifically directs election officials to reject voter registration applications that are not accompanied by one of several specified citizenship documents,[115] thus denying those individuals the ability to vote. Until this year, this Arizona law was an outlier, unique in the country.

Arizona's proof of citizenship law sparked significant controversy from the outset. In March 2006, the U.S. Election Assistance Commission, a bipartisan federal agency charged with regulating certain election administration matters, voted to reject Arizona's request to amend the federal voter registration application form to reflect the state's new rules.[116] Shortly afterward, the law was challenged in federal court;[117] it has been wrapped up in litigation ever since. In the most recent ruling in that case, a panel of the U.S. Court of Appeals for the

Ninth Circuit held that the proof of citizenship requirement conflicts with federal law—specifically, the National Voter Registration Act of 1993.[118] The Ninth Circuit agreed to rehear that case *en banc,* and oral argument was held before a larger panel on June 21, 2011. The court has not yet issued its decision.

Georgia became the second state to pass a proof of citizenship law in 2009, requiring prospective voters to provide documentary proof of citizenship in order to register to vote.[119] This came after the Department of Justice blocked implementation of an earlier Georgia policy for checking the citizenship of registered voters as unreliable and discriminatory.[120] The Department of Justice ultimately approved of Georgia's proof of citizenship law in April 2011,[121] but the state has not yet put the law into effect.

Thus, as of the start of this legislative session, only two states had ever sought to require documentary proof of citizenship for voter registration or voting, only one had implemented such a requirement, and the legality of the requirement had not yet been resolved (and still is not resolved) in the courts.

> *As of the start of this legislative session, only two states had ever sought to require documentary proof of citizenship for voter registration or voting.*

The push for proof of citizenship requirements should also be considered in the context of the bills targeting immigrants that swept the states this year. Alabama, Arizona, Georgia, Indiana, South Carolina, and Utah are among the states that passed laws supposedly designed to restrict benefits for, and crack down on, undocumented immigrants.[122] As with Proposition 200, Arizona was the national leader in this effort, with its highly controversial H.B. 1070.

B. Roundup of Legislative Developments

This session, at least twelve states introduced legislation that would require documentary proof of citizenship to register or vote: Alabama,[123] Colorado,[124] Connecticut,[125] Kansas,[126] Maine,[127] Massachusetts,[128] New Hampshire,[129] Nevada,[130] Oregon,[131] South Carolina,[132] Tennessee,[133] and Texas.[134] Washington State introduced a resolution to request that any federal voting mandates make funding contingent upon the adoption of photo

ID and proof of citizenship requirements.[135] Three proof of citizenship bills passed: in Alabama, Kansas, and Tennessee.[136] The new Kansas and Tennessee laws go into effect immediately; the Alabama law must await approval by the U.S. Department of Justice or a federal court under the Voting Rights Act.[137] To date, Alabama has not yet submitted the law for preclearance.[138]

III. MAKING VOTER REGISTRATION HARDER

In every state but one, citizens must be registered in order to vote. Voter registration facilitates election administration by enabling election officials to more easily plan for elections, process voters, and prevent fraud. But registration requirements can also function as a barrier to many eligible voters, preventing them from participating because of technical hurdles or missed deadlines.[153]

Experts have long pointed out that the nation's outdated registration system is among the most significant barriers to voting, resulting in the disenfranchisement of millions of Americans during every federal election.[154] In 2001, the Carter-Ford National Task Force on Election Reform found that "[t]he registration laws in force throughout the United States are among the world's most demanding ... [and are] one reason why voter turnout in the United States is near the bottom of the developed world."[155] This impact has not abated: around 3 million Americans tried to vote in the 2008 Presidential election but could not, due to voter registration problems.[156]

The general thrust of the law over the past few decades has been to ease registration requirements to make it easier for eligible citizens to get on the voter rolls. The most significant advance was the National Voter Registration Act of 1993, also known as the "Motor Voter" law, which made voter registration opportunities widely available across the country.[157] More recently, states have taken the lead in modernizing their voter registration systems so that more voters are getting on the rolls and the rolls are getting more accurate.[158]

This year, the tide reversed. Instead of efforts to increase voter registration, this year new registration requirements have been instated that will make it more challenging for eligible citizens to ensure that they are registered to vote on Election Day. Voter registration regulations range from restrictions on individuals and groups who help register voters, to efforts to scale back Election Day and same-day registration, to new rules making it harder for voters to stay registered after they move.

Part 1: Voter Registration Drive Regulations

A. Background

Voter registration rates in the United States are routinely lower than they are in other democracies around the world: more than a quarter of voting-age Americans are not registered and thus cannot vote.[159] This is in part because, unlike in other democracies, U.S. state governments do not assume the responsibility of getting voters onto the rolls; instead, we rely on individual voters to ensure that they are registered. Community-based voter registration drives play an important role in encouraging and assisting other citizens to register to vote. Restrictions on voter registration drive activity have a direct impact on who has access to voter registration and who gets registered to vote.

Although community-based voter registration drives have been around in some form for decades, Congress helped expand such voter registration activity by passing the National Voter Registration Act of 1993 (NVRA).[160] Among other things, the NVRA greatly simplified voter registration application forms, required states to follow uniform rules for accepting those forms, and required them to make blank forms generally available "with particular emphasis on making them available for organized voter registration programs."[161] As a result, civic groups were easily able to obtain and circulate voter registration forms to potential voters who might not otherwise register or become engaged in the electoral process.

Voter registration drives have become an increasingly important registration method in the past decade, especially for low-income citizens, students, members of racial and ethnic minority groups, and people with disabilities. For example, in the 2004 general election, large-scale voter registration drives report assisting almost 10 million citizens to register to vote, contributing to a surge in new registrations and increased turnout in that election. In one county in Florida alone, voter registration organizations were responsible for registering 62.7% of all newly registered voters.[162] Nationally,

Census data show that Hispanic and African-American voters are approximately twice as likely to register to vote through a voter registration drive as white voters.[163]

Voting rights advocates point to increased voter registration rates, especially among minority, low-income, and younger citizens, as a positive effect of voter registration drives and a reason to expand them. They also cite recent falling voter registration rates as a reason to encourage voter registration drives. The 2010 election saw a plunge in new voter registrations, as new voter registrations in 2010 were down almost 17% from the 2006 cycle.[164] This was accompanied by a dramatic decrease in voter registration drive activity, for the first time in years. But voter registration drives have unfortunately become an increasingly controversial political topic.

Over the past few years, there has been a growing effort to push back against voter registration drives. Opponents have argued that voter registration drives are susceptible to fraud, citing allegations of fraud related to ACORN, a defunct organization that focused on registering low-income voters.[165] Presidential candidate John McCain cited allegedly fraudulent registration cards submitted by ACORN as "one of the greatest frauds in voter history in this country, maybe destroying the fabric of democracy."[166] Other opponents have argued that voter registration should be made more difficult to reflect the importance of the right to vote.[167] At the extreme end of the spectrum, some have argued that by specifically empowering low-income voters to register, voter registration drives are "antisocial and un-American."[168]

Recently, a number of state legislatures have pushed legislation to regulate and restrict community-based voter registration drives. This extensive regulation of voter registration drive activity is a unique government regulation of private political activity. These regulations have serious consequences for citizens' ability to organize and conduct voter registration drives; for example, the recent Florida law imposing a set of new restrictions on third-party voter registration activity (discussed at length below) has resulted in the volunteer-based League of Women Voters placing a moratorium on all voter registration work because the law imposes too great a burden on voter registration. The type and extent of laws governing voter registration have a direct impact on who gets to participate in the process, and who is permitted to assist them in doing so.

B. Roundup of Legislative Developments

Bills placing new restrictions on voter registration groups have been proposed in at least seven states—California (passed in both houses; awaiting governor's action), Florida, Illinois (pending), Mississippi (failed), Nevada (restrictions removed by amendment), New Mexico (failed), North Carolina (pending), and Texas.

These bills have been signed into law in Florida and Texas. Florida and Texas stand out as two states that have long histories of restricting voter registration drives, and the new laws passed in this session will make both states further outliers in limiting this activity. Neither state had reported cases of registration fraud linked to voter registration drives in the past election cycle, nor any other apparent precipitating cause for the further regulations imposed by these bills.

Part 2: Eliminating Same-Day Registration
A. Background

Prior to 2011, eight states—Idaho, Iowa, Maine, Minnesota, Montana, New Hampshire, Wisconsin, Wyoming—allowed for Election Day registration ("EDR"), meaning that citizens could register and vote at their local polling place on Election Day.[191] Maine was the first state to adopt EDR, in 1973; Iowa was the most recent, in 2008.[192] In 2007, North Carolina adopted same day registration for the early voting period, but not on Election Day.[193] Beginning in 2008, Ohio allowed same day registration for the first week of early voting.[194] (Other states provide for EDR in certain circumstances; for instance, in Connecticut and Rhode Island, voters who register on Election Day may vote for presidential candidates only.)

Voting rights advocates have long praised EDR.[195] Because it has existed in some states for nearly forty years, there is a substantial record of its benefits. States with EDR have consistently had higher turnout than states without, and the top five states for voter turnout in 2008 were all EDR states.[196] There is also evidence that EDR specifically increases turnout among young voters.[197]

Proponents of EDR point out that it greatly reduces the use of provisional ballots[198] (under federal law, provisional ballots are provided to voters when there is a question about the voter's eligibility, very often related to whether they are properly registered). Most voting rights advocates prefer the use of regular ballots to provisional ballots where possible, because a significant percentage of provisional ballots go uncounted in every election.[199]

The most common objection to EDR is that it "invites" voter fraud.[200] This has been the main public explanation provided by supporters of bills to end same day registration, though some have also argued that same day registration imposes administrative burdens on those running the polls on Election Day.[201]

Bills to eliminate same day registration in 2011 were uniformly sponsored by Republicans. The bills that passed the Montana and Ohio legislatures were unanimously opposed by Democratic legislators in the legislative chambers that voted on them.[202]

The partisan split over Election Day Registration has not always existed. When Maine became the first state to adopt EDR in 1973, the Republicans controlled both houses of the Legislature, and the proposal passed unanimously.[203]

B. Roundup of Legislative Developments

Bills to eliminate EDR or same day registration were introduced in five states: Maine, Montana, New Hampshire, North Carolina and Ohio. The bills in Maine and Ohio have been enacted, though both bills may be overturned in the coming months by ballot initiative processes currently underway in each state. The bill in Montana passed the legislature, but was vetoed by Governor Brian Schweitzer on March 4, 2011.[204] The bill in North Carolina is still pending.

IV. MAKING VOTING HARDER: RESTRICTING EARLY IN-PERSON AND MAIL-IN ABSENTEE VOTING

A. Background

For years, the growth of early voting—through in-person early voting sites and no-fault absentee voting by mail— has been dramatic, and seemed unstoppable. 2011 marks the first year that inexorable progress may have stalled. Early in-person and absentee voting have come under attack by legislatures around the country; these attacks have been particularly successful against early in-person voting.

The numbers tell the story of early voting's growth in just the last decade. In 2000, an overwhelming majority of Americans still voted at their local polling places on Election Day; less than 4% voted at early voting sites, and only 10% voted by mail. By 2008, more than a third of American voters voted early. The percentage of Americans voting at early voting sites had increased nearly five-fold, to 18%, and the percentage voting by mail nearly doubled to 19%.[228]

The primary benefit of early voting is convenience. Voters are provided more options and days during which they can vote.[229] While there is little evidence that early and absentee voting increase turnout,[230] there is strong anecdotal evidence that it makes election administration easier, reducing the crush of voters at the polling place on a single day.[231] In the past, that Election Day crush has led to hours-long lines, and resulted in the *de facto* disenfranchisement of tens of thousands of voters.[232]

Through much of its growth, early voting has had strong support from both Democrats and Republicans.[233] In 2011, most, though not all, of the new restrictions on early voting have been proposed by Republicans and adopted by Republican-controlled legislatures.

As discussed below, the reasons most often provided for restricting early voting were cost and administrative burden, though they sometimes also included arguments that the restrictions would reduce fraud.[234] Opponents of the new restrictions frequently disputed the alleged savings,[235] and many argued that the changes were really a response to the success in 2008 of Barack Obama's campaign to get the candidate's supporters—and in particular black voters—to vote before Election Day.[236]

B. Roundup of Legislative Developments

At least nine states—Florida, Georgia, Maryland, Nevada, New Mexico, North Carolina, Ohio, Tennessee, West Virginia—all considered bills to reduce their respective early voting periods this year.[237] At least four states—Georgia, New Jersey, Ohio, and Wisconsin— saw the introduction of bills to change or add new restrictions on absentee voting.[238]

Texas introduced a law that would omit early voting locations from official notices of a general or special election, but the measure did not pass.[239] In Wisconsin, a provision to eliminate no-excuse absentee voting was later removed from the state's voter ID bill.[240]

Ultimately, laws reducing early voting were passed and signed into law in five states: Florida, Georgia, Ohio, Tennessee, and West Virginia. Pending bills remain in North Carolina, Georgia, and New Jersey.

V. MAKING IT HARDER TO RESTORE VOTING RIGHTS

A. Background

Disenfranchisement after criminal conviction remains the single most significant barrier to voting rights in the United States. Nationally, 5.3 million American citizens are not allowed to vote because of a criminal conviction; of those, 4 million have completed their sentences and live, work, and raise families in their communities.[275] This disenfranchisement disproportionally impacts African-American men. Nationwide, 13% of African-American men have lost the right to vote, a rate that is seven times the national average.[276] Given current rates of incarceration, three in ten of the next generation of African-American men across the country can expect to lose the right to vote at some point in their lifetime.[277]

These voting bans are exceptional among democratic nations. The United States is one of only two countries that disenfranchise large numbers of persons for lengthy or indefinite periods after they have completed their time in prison.[278]

While the history of felon disenfranchisement laws in the United States dates to the nation's earliest days,[279] its greatest growth came in the decades after the Civil War. By 1900, thirty-eight states had some type of criminal voting restriction, most of which disenfranchised convicted individuals until they received a pardon.[280]

The last decade and a half saw a striking reversal of these restrictions. Since 1997, twenty-three states either restored voting rights or eased the restoration process; nine of these states repealed or amended lifetime disenfranchisement laws.[281] These changes occurred under both Republican and Democratic governors.[282]

Iowa and Florida saw the most recent dramatic restoration of voting rights. In Iowa, in 2005, Democratic Governor Tom Vilsack issued an executive Order ending the state's permanent disenfranchisement policy (at the time, Iowa was one of only three states with such a broad restriction on voting) and restoring voting rights to 80,000 Iowans.[283]

Like Iowa, Florida also had a notoriously severe law modified by executive action. Prior to 2007, nearly one million Floridians were permanently disenfranchised in the state; almost a quarter of them were African-American. In 2007, Republican Governor Charlie Crist amended the State's clemency rules in an attempt to streamline the restoration process for some individuals with non-violent convictions. Since restoration rules were streamlined, the voting rights of at least 150,000 Floridians were restored.[284]

B. Roundup of Legislation and Executive Actions

Last year marked the end of fifteen years of progress restoring the right to vote to formerly incarcerated persons. Specifically, the dramatic changes in Iowa and Florida were reversed. By executive action, the Governors Terry Branstad of Iowa and Rick Scott of Florida, both Republicans, returned their state policies to *de facto* permanent disenfranchisement for all citizens convicted of felonies. In Florida, this has meant that 87,000 persons who were in the "backlog" of cases waiting for restoration under Governor Crist's new rules will not get their voting rights restored.

Also in 2011, Nevada Governor Brian Sandoval, also a Republican, vetoed a bill that would have automatically restored voting rights to anyone who honorably completed a felony sentence of imprisonment, probation, or parole. The bill had received bipartisan support in the Legislature.

Five states saw bills further restricting the ability of people with criminal convictions to participate in the political process: Alabama, Maryland, South Carolina, Washington, and West Virginia. None of these bills have passed.[285]

6

Policy, Politics and Population

By Edward P. Smith

Demographics determine electoral environments. Demographics are changing rapidly in many states and in the process changing those electoral environments.

Aging baby boomers heading for retirement, a growing Latino population, swelling ranks of the poor, and a steady flight to cities and suburbs from rural areas all are trends evident from the 2010 census that will have political and policy implications for state lawmakers.

Some are obvious. Both political parties have been concerned for years about attracting the growing ranks of Latino voters. Others may not be so obvious, such as how the burgeoning numbers of older voters will respond to cutbacks in public spending.

And there are policy implications, some of which are still coming into focus as lawmakers digest the 2010 numbers and consider how they may affect their state.

Older Boomers

An aging population means an aging state workforce. That translates into a growing demand on state pension funds; more workers retiring, many of whom may be supervisors; and a need to recruit top-notch younger workers to take their places.

As well, public employees are, on average, older than the general population, and many have the opportunity to retire with pensions by age 60 or 65. This varies widely from state to state. California, for example, reported in March 2011 that 23 percent of the permanent civil service workforce was 55 or older, and another 17 percent was between 50 and 55. In New York, officials say by 2015, 44.5 percent

From *State Legislatures*, December 2011.

of current state employees will be 55 or older. Even in Utah, the state with the youngest median age, 21 percent of state workers were 55 or older in 2010.

Older workers may be inclined to stay on the job a few more years if national trends hold true. People over 65 who were still working hit a low point at 12 percent in 1998, but now it's above 16 percent.

One of the most dramatic demographic shifts of the past century has been the transformation of the country from largely rural to largely urban.

There are other reasons, however, that an aging population can put a strain on states. Medicaid, the joint state-federal health plan, costs nearly $400 billion a year; 67 percent of that money goes to provide long-term care for the severely disabled and the elderly. Buried in the census data is this germane piece of information: Those age 80 and over represent 10 percent of the older population and will more than triple from 5.7 million in 2010 to more than 19 million by 2050. These are the folks most likely to end up receiving help from Medicaid for long-term care.

Children

The census found there was a decline of 4.3 million Anglo children over the past 10 years. Those under age 18 grew only 2.6 percent over the decade, and declined in 23 states.

In the 27 states that gained children, almost all the increase was among minorities, especially Latinos. The most remarkable demonstration of that may be in Texas, which gained nearly 1 million children; Latinos accounted for 95 percent of the gain.

A growing number of those Latino children are living in poverty. There are 6.1 million poor Latino children in the nation today, compared with 5 million Anglo children and 4.4 million African-American children living in poverty, according to the Pew Hispanic Center.

The data have policy implications, including what sort of programs to support for new parents and preschool children. Research indicates preschool programs are particularly helpful for children from lower-income households who may be at risk for doing poorly in school. They also are at greater risk of mental health problems and illnesses such as asthma, hypertension, heart disease and diabetes.

Some believe states need to support programs for parents, such as home visiting and participation in child care and preschool classrooms. Such programs may help address the achievement gap and prepare these young learners for school and a strong academic future.

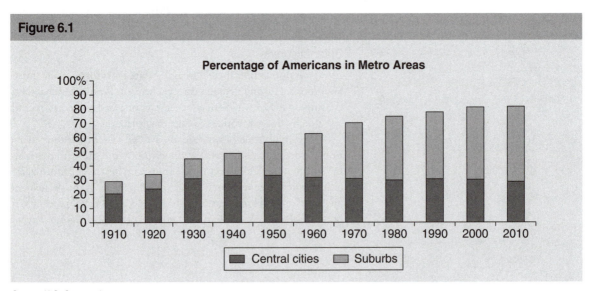

Figure 6.1

Percentage of Americans in Metro Areas

Central cities ■ Suburbs

Source: U.S. Census data.

Poverty

The Census Bureau reports an additional 2.6 million people slipped into poverty last year, bringing the number of Americans living below the official poverty line to 46.2 million, or 15.1 percent, the highest level since 1993. (The poverty line in 2010 for a family of four was $22,314.)

Medicaid is under particular pressure because of the rising level of poverty. Medicaid enrollees increased by 7.6 million people or 17.8 percent since the start of the recession, but the growth rate shows signs of slowing. Enrollment growth peaked in the period from June 2008 to June 2009, according to the Kaiser Commission on Medicaid and the Uninsured. Despite this slowdown, Medicaid exceeded 50 million people for the first time in the program's history in 2010.

The increased demand for Medicaid is accompanied by the rising number of Americans without health coverage—up from 49 million in 2009 to 49.9 million last year. The huge number of people without health insurance is largely attributable to the loss of jobs, a decline in employer provided coverage and cutbacks in benefits as health costs rose. The percentage of the nonelderly who had health insurance through their employers fell from 69.3 percent in 2000 to 58.7 percent in 2010, according to the Employee Benefit Research Institute.

Education

As the growing numbers of young Latinos enter school, state policymakers recognize their educational success is critical to providing states with a well-educated workforce and ensuring economic vitality. Improving college graduation rates has become a national and state focus to meet future workforce demands and stimulate the economy. And college graduation rates of Latinos—the largest and fastest growing minority group in the nation—is a specific focus. While the aging boomer population is largely Anglo, the rapidly growing younger population is largely Latino. Support for Social Security and Medicare for the older population will rely on a well-educated, competitive Latino workforce.

More than one in five K–12 students is now Latino. The number of Latinos enrolling in college is increasing rapidly—24 percent within the last year. This is good news, since Latino adults have the lowest educational attainment of any U.S. population group. Only 19 percent of Latinos have a degree, compared with 26 percent of African Americans and 42 percent of Anglos.

Simply enrolling in college, however, does not guarantee graduation. Only 36 percent of first-time, full-time Latino students earn a degree within six years, compared with 49 percent of Anglos.

For the United States to rise to the top of the world in the percentage of college graduates, the nation needs to graduate an additional 13.4 million students, including 3.3 million Latinos, by 2020.

Increasing the number of Latino college graduates requires a coordinated effort, including providing more preschool, middle and high school college counseling. Dropout prevention programs, simplifying college admission and transfer, and improving college affordability will also help Latino kids achieve a college education.

Rural vs. Metro

One of the most dramatic demographic shifts of the past century has been the transformation of the country from largely rural to largely urban. In 1910, 72 percent of the country lived in rural areas. Today, only 18 percent do. Everyone else lives in a city or suburb. The population in rural counties, in fact, is growing at less than half the rate of metro counties, and the most isolated rural counties—those farthest from metro areas—are not growing at all; they have declined by 1.4 percent since 2000.

This decline means less clout for rural issues in statehouses. The laws and issues that most affect rural areas—agriculture, water, natural resources and rural infrastructure development—have fewer voices to advocate for them. Laws that uphold the freedom to farm, the right to hunt and fish, and water allocation and transportation, and those that provide money to preserve rural schools and maintain country highways may lose support as fewer legislators are elected from outside metropolitan areas.

Former Arizona Senator Jake Flake once said the reason he formed a rural caucus was to educate urban legislators about rural needs. "We don't have enough caucus members to force anything, but we can enlighten our colleagues as to what is needed for the rural parts of the state." More statehouses may need such caucuses to understand rural needs.

State lawmakers will clearly face serious challenges in the next decade as they grapple with the national demographic changes revealed by the census. The growing number of elderly people and the poor will strain state pensions and Medicaid budgets. Education policy at every level will need to meet the needs of Latino students, and a population increasingly concentrated in cities and suburbs will likely be at odds with the dwindling number of people in rural areas.

After a Contentious Political Year, Republicans May Moderate Their Approach

By John Gramlich

7

Republican lawmakers dealt with some bruising political battles in 2011 as they tried to make good on the campaign promises they rode to victory in 2010. In 2012, they seek a little less conflict.

From the moment he took office last year, Florida Governor Rick Scott made clear that a new and unabashedly conservative administration had taken power in Tallahassee—just as it had in state capitals around the country following an historic election haul for Republicans in 2010.

Scott, a Tea Party–backed Republican, stood before a cheering crowd and introduced a state budget that contained more than $4 billion in tax cuts for corporations and property owners, even as it slashed funding for K–12 education. "Critics have said we can't afford to cut taxes now," Scott said. "I say they are wrong. I say we must cut taxes now."

But the plan didn't sit well with Scott's fellow Republicans, who control both chambers of the Florida legislature. They largely ignored the governor's budget and sent him their own—one with more money for schools and just a fraction of the tax cuts Scott demanded.

This year, Scott is taking a noticeably different approach. He has unveiled a second-year budget that provides $1 billion more for K–12 education. In fact, Scott is so intent on getting more school funding that he has promised to veto any budget that does not include it. "The dollars in this budget belong to all Floridians," Scott said when he introduced the plan, "and I have listened to the things they believe are important to spend these dollars on."

If Scott's new budget appears to be a political retrenchment, it is. Tallahassee observers say the governor has learned from what turned out to be a rocky first session, marred by frequent fighting with members of his own party, by some of the worst polling numbers of

From *Stateline.org*, January 2012.

any governor in the nation and, ultimately, by the departure of some of his most senior advisers.

Scott is not the only governor in the Republican class of 2010 who is treading more carefully as this year's legislative sessions begin.

In Ohio, Republican Governor John Kasich is talking a less partisan game after voters soundly rejected the signature legislative achievement of his first year in office, a collective bargaining measure restricting the negotiation rights of state workers. Kasich acknowledged after the vote that the law may have struck voters as "too much, too soon," and has since stressed his commitment to bipartisanship.

Wisconsin's Scott Walker steered through a collective bargaining restriction last spring similar in many ways to the one in Ohio—driving Democratic legislators to leave the state in an unsuccessful attempt to block its passage. As a result of the backlash, Walker is on the campaign trail two years ahead of schedule as his political opponents seek to oust him in a recall election, perhaps as early as June. Walker isn't backing away from the law he pushed through last year, but like Scott and Kasich, he is talking in milder tones than he did in 2011.

Elsewhere, Republican governors and state lawmakers who came into office last year in numbers not seen since the 1920s also may tack toward the political middle as they prepare for a presidential election year that will see about 6,000 of the roughly 7,500 state legislative seats up for grabs.

In Alabama, Republicans who passed the toughest state-level immigration law in the nation are under intense pressure to scale back the measure this year, even as the law and others like it are being challenged in the courts. Religious leaders have urged Governor Robert Bentley to repeal the law because they see it as an attack on the immigrant community; farmers and other business leaders say it hurts their livelihoods by scaring off their workers.

Sounding more conciliatory as election time approaches is not an unusual tactic: State leaders from both parties often tackle their most aggressive—and divisive—agendas in non-election years. In 2009, a time when Democrats held power in more capitals, states collectively raised $24 billion in taxes and fees. But by the time voters were ready to go to the polls in November of 2010, major tax increases were off the table in most states. "It's the cycle of governing," says Chris Tessone of the Thomas Fordham Institute, an education think tank in Washington, D.C. "When you're out of election years, you feel empowered to do really courageous stuff."

Another reason majority Republicans seem poised to pursue a less ambitious agenda this year is that voter turnout—and especially Democratic turnout—is likely to be much higher for President Obama's reelection bid than it was during the midterm elections. The GOP, now in control in more states than it has been in a long time, has more to lose. It may want to avoid giving Democrats any added incentive to come to the polls.

"The name of the game for Republicans is holding the gains they've got," says Larry Jacobs, a political science professor at the University of Minnesota. "Republicans don't want to end up with a situation they saw in Ohio, where they take a position that gets every member of organized labor and their family out to the voting booth."

MORE TO WORK WITH

As 2012 begins, Republicans actually have power in more places than they had last year. The GOP won a majority in the Mississippi House of Representatives and forced a tie in the Virginia Senate in the off-year elections of 2011, giving them total control over the political process in both states, since Virginia's Republican lieutenant governor can break legislative ties. Republicans now control both the legislative and executive branches in 22 states, double the number held by Democrats and nearly triple the number they held just two years ago. They have a share of the power in another 16 states.

Republicans also have the advantage of state finances that are improving for the first time in four years, rather than continuing to deteriorate. While state tax collections still have not returned back to their peak levels, budget analysts are forecasting steady revenue growth over the coming months.

Despite the improving budget news, states still have tough choices to make as they continue struggling to keep up with increased demand for services—particularly for Medicaid, the state-federal health insurance program for the poor. The National Association of State Budget Officers reported in an annual year-end analysis that Medicaid is eating up a growing share of states' budgets, and that this trend is likely to continue under the health care expansion envisioned by the federal Affordable Care Act. New revenues may have to go to Medicaid or other growing social service needs, or they may just be used to restore funding to programs that states cut deeply in earlier years.

But from a political standpoint, state leaders almost everywhere will be able to point to healthier budgets—whether or not their own policies had anything to do with them. That, in turn, is likely to reframe the political discussion in 2012. Rather than simply identifying the government services they want to cut, leaders also will need to articulate the government investments they want to make, as Scott has done in Florida.

SCHOOL FUNDING, TAX CUTS

If the tone of Republican rhetoric has changed, however, the fundamental priority for most GOP governors remains the same: reducing the size and scope of government under the philosophy that doing so will allow the private sector to flourish. The long-standing GOP priority of returning money to the taxpayers will top the agenda in several states this year, perhaps with added momentum given the improving revenue picture in many places.

Some Democrats are talking in similar terms. Democratic lawmakers in Illinois have debated cutting tax rates a year after they approved big increases in the corporate income tax and personal income tax. In New York, Governor Andrew Cuomo and his fellow Democrats have already cut personal income taxes for most taxpayers for 2012, doing so in a special legislative session before Christmas.

Republican governors in Kansas and Oklahoma want to overhaul their state tax codes to lower rates, and both have all-Republican legislatures that will debate those proposals seriously. The same is true in Idaho, where Governor C.L. "Butch" Otter wants to reduce the personal income tax to help small businesses. In all-Republican Michigan, Governor Rick Snyder—who pushed through the biggest business tax cuts in the nation last year—wants to reduce personal property taxes this year. Republican governors Sean Parnell in Alaska and Terry Branstad in Iowa are pushing forward on stalled proposals to cut taxes on oil and on commercial property, but both must find common ground with Democratic legislative leaders in order to do so.

Beyond tax cuts, many governors are likely to propose plans similar to the one that Scott is emphasizing in Florida—more funding for schools, a politically popular idea on both sides of the aisle.

In South Dakota, Republican Governor Dennis Daugaard introduced a budget that increases school funding from last year's levels and includes pay raises and a one-time bonus for teachers. As a result of improving revenues—and the ability for the state to restore some money for education and other areas that were previously cut deeply—"I see the upcoming session as being more collegial than the last session," Daugaard told *Stateline* in an interview.

K–12 education, however, will have to compete with Medicaid, which has caused a bigger strain on state budgets as federal stimulus money has expired. Republican governors, in particular, are looking for ways to trim Medicaid spending so that the money can be used elsewhere. They are calling on the federal government to give them flexibility from strict rules and, in some cases, let them remove residents from the rolls.

Both Walker in Wisconsin and fellow Republican Governor Paul LePage of Maine have proposed cutting tens of thousands of state residents from the Medicaid rolls this year, citing the program's explosive growth. LePage argues that Medicaid has grown so much that it has "cannibalized" money for other state priorities.

LABOR BATTLES RENEWED?

The most enduring image from last year's legislative sessions may be the tens of thousands of protesters who took to the streets in Midwestern states where Republicans cut negotiating rights and other benefits for public employees. A key question for 2012 is whether similar battles will be waged. Some states are already gearing up for them.

The states' pension crisis is by no means over, and California, Kansas and other states will debate proposals to rein in the cost of public retiree benefits. Kasich in Ohio and Walker in Wisconsin are reluctant to stoke union anger on the scale that they did last year, but Indiana Republicans are planning to make the state the 23rd in the nation to enact "right-to-work" legislation, banning labor unions from requiring union membership as a condition of employment.

When Indiana debated the same legislation last year, minority Democrats fled the state to deny Republicans a quorum, holding up all legislation for five weeks and nearly derailing the entire legislative session. Already this year, Democrats have resorted to the same tactic, refusing to show up for votes during the opening days of the legislative session last week and calling on Republicans to hold public hearings around the state before they push through the bill.

Republicans acknowledge that pushing right-to-work is a politically risky move. "I've challenged my members, and in fact our whole legislative body," Indiana House Speaker Brian Bosma told *Stateline* in an interview. "You can be brave, or you can be safe. . . . Given all of the concerns that we face economically today, it's time for elected officials to be brave."

Even where Republicans are pushing an ambitious agenda, however, many of them are doing so in a less confrontational way this year, wary that the voters will be watching—and that partisan finger-pointing may cause them to lose their majorities. Bosma, for instance, notes that he and his GOP colleagues made a point of putting right-to-work legislation on the agenda nearly two months before the legislative session, so that no one can claim it was a "sneak attack."

The move, Bosma says, was part of a concerted effort this year to "create a space in the statehouse where a civil debate can occur."

Political Parties and Interest Groups

Many people seem to view political parties and special interest groups as closely related creatures rather than distinct species. This perspective is understandable. They both seem to be more interested in their own interests rather than the public interest, both throw a lot of money around during elections, and both seem to spend the time in between elections pointing fingers and yelling at each other. While there is an uncomfortably large grain of truth in this popular view, it actually misses some important distinctions between political parties and interest groups and ignores some of the very real and very important services that both sorts of organizations provide to democratic politics.

First, let's clarify the difference. While political parties and special interest groups do a lot of the same things (e.g., take issue positions, support candidates) they are different in one all-important way: Political parties run candidates for office under their own label, and special interest groups do not. This has important implications, it means that while special interest groups might try to influence the government, political parties actually organize and run the government. The National Rifle Association (NRA) might raise money and endorse candidates, but those candidates appear on the ballot with a partisan label next to their name, not the NRA logo. If elected to office, a candidate will be assigned committee and other responsibilities based on partisan power in the chamber, not his or her standing with an interest group. Second, let's be clear that political parties and interest groups do a lot of good for democratic politics. Indeed, they do so much it is impossible to give a comprehensive list in a short space. They mobilize voters and encourage civic participation. They aggregate interests and transmit those interests to government. They help provide voters with clear choices and provide means of accountability (if you don't like what the Republican legislature is doing, you can throw the bums out by voting for a Democrat, and if you want to know what candidate is really supporting your Second Amendment prerogatives, an NRA endorsement is a pretty good clue).

Okay, enough of the good stuff. What about the bad stuff? Aren't political parties and special interest groups often too elitist, too self-centered, and far too cozy with one another? Well, that's certainly what many think. But as the readings in this chapter show, the story is a bit more complicated than that. For example, a common complaint about political parties is that they promise one thing on the campaign trail but forget about their promises once in government. Not so according to our first essay by John Gramlich. In the past couple of years, the Republican Party has achieved unified partisan control in a large number of states and has followed through on its campaign promises with a vengeance. It seems that what stops parties from keeping their promises is not a lack of political will or a reluctance to keep a campaign pledge but actually having the power. It is not enough to have broad commitment to a party agenda; putting that agenda into action requires strong legislative majorities and unified party control of executive and legislative branches. In 2011, Republicans enjoyed one-party control in a large number of state legislatures, and they made the most of it.

The strong winds behind the Republican Party's agenda in 2011 and 2012 was good news for certain interest groups (e.g., business interest groups) but not so good for others. Public unions, already battered and squeezed by the tight budgets of states and localities, found themselves dealing with a political party philosophically, not just fiscally, committed to reducing their benefits and their power. The result, as Alan Greenblatt details in the next essay, means a very rough couple of years for organized labor in the public sector. Historically some of the strongest interest groups in state and local politics, public unions are fighting the reductions in benefits and power lawmakers are increasingly seeking to impose.

While public unions may represent interest groups who were having a hard time in the new GOP-dominated world of state politics, a second essay by Greenblatt focuses on an interest group that is thriving in that environment. The American Legislative Exchange Council (ALEC) is a conservative advocacy group that champions free market principles and limited government at the state level. Its members include a broad cross-section of private and public sector members (including state legislators). While Republican success at the state level may have public unions in retreat, it signaled a full-scale charge for the interests championed by ALEC.

The final essay, by Louis, Jacobson takes a look at the Tea Party, an unusual political phenomenon that does not quite seem to be a political party or an interest group. The Tea Party is clearly having an impact at the state level, but exactly what that impact is and what it means is hard to say. While an increasingly high-profile element of Republican Party politics, the Tea Party does not have a consistently focused agenda and thus, it is not clear to what extent the Tea Party movement is driving the Republican agenda in the states.

8

In an Era of One-Party Rule, Republicans Pass a Sweeping State Agenda

By John Gramlich

The Republican Party took charge of many state governments in 2011. They used the opportunity to make good on some long-cherished campaign promises.

Republicans controlled all the levers of government in a staggering number of states this year—and it showed. Holding a lock on the governorship and both houses of the legislature in 20 states, GOP conservatives advanced an agenda that may change the face of state government for decades. They honored pledges not to raise taxes by enacting huge spending cuts to balance budgets in Florida and Texas. They put tough abortion limits back on the agenda, passing laws in Alabama, Kansas and Oklahoma. Most famously, Republicans in Indiana, Ohio and Wisconsin put new restrictions on the rights of public employees, whose protests made national news for a month.

Though Democrats proved powerless to stop those changes, they moved a profoundly different agenda in the 11 states where they enjoy total control of state government. Arguing that budget cuts could only go so far, Democrats pushed tax increases in Connecticut, Illinois and Maryland. Meanwhile, Vermont approved a health care law supported by liberals that could prove far more expansive in scope than the controversial overhaul passed in Congress last year.

These were the results of an historic election last November, one that created vast shifts in power in statehouses across the country. Almost all of it went in the Republicans' favor. The GOP picked up more than 500 legislative seats, winning their biggest majority of seats nationally since 1928. Republicans snatched 13 House chambers, seven Senate chambers and 11 governorships out of Democratic hands, and in Maine and Wisconsin they wrested control of all three.

From *Stateline.org*, June 2011.

Even in some states where Republicans had long held power—such as Texas—they gained such dominant new legislative majorities that Democrats could no longer rely on procedural tactics they had previously used to derail proposals they vehemently opposed.

TURNING POLITICS INTO POLICY

Suddenly, Republicans enjoyed not only a staggering amount of leverage in state legislatures but also support from discontented voters to make major changes. And in the ongoing fiscal crisis states have been experiencing, many Republicans saw not a calamity but an opportunity to actually shrink government by reducing spending. They dispatched Democratic opposition with ease as they approved major budget cuts alongside long-stalled policy changes that previously couldn't attract enough votes to pass.

In Oklahoma, where Republicans took control of both the governorship and legislature for the first time ever, the GOP achieved a huge party objective: They rewrote tort rules to limit the damages that lawsuit filers can collect.

In Florida, Republican Tea Party favorite Rick Scott replaced the independent Charlie Crist in the governor's office and oversaw a dramatic revamping of the state's Medicaid system. Essentially, Florida is converting Medicaid entirely into a managed care model of service.

Maine's new Republican leadership took concrete steps toward repealing the state's Democratic-approved experiment in universal health care, known as Dirigo Health. A spokesman for Governor Paul LePage, another Tea Party–backed executive, pledged gleefully that "Dirigo will be Diri-gone."

In Michigan, new GOP leaders made the state the first in more than 50 years to scale back state-level unemployment benefits. They reduced the length of time workers could receive benefits from 26 weeks to 20. Conservatives in Florida and Missouri soon followed.

Social legislation found plenty of success, too. Indiana, where Republicans took control of the legislature, became the first state to cut off government funding for Planned Parenthood. It was one of dozens of new GOP-supported laws around the country curtailing abortion rights. In Alabama, where Republicans retained the governor's office and took control of the legislature

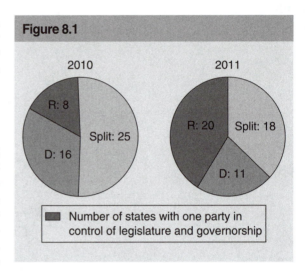

Figure 8.1

2010

R: 8
D: 16
Split: 25

2011

R: 20
D: 11
Split: 18

■ Number of states with one party in control of legislature and governorship

Note: Nebraska has a nonpartisan, unicameral legislature and is not counted.

Source: National Conference of State Legislatures. Graphic by Lauren Orsini.

for the first time since Reconstruction, lawmakers passed an immigration crackdown that goes even further than last year's lightning-rod measure in Arizona. Newly empowered Republicans required voters to show photo ID in Alabama, Kansas, South Carolina, Texas and Wisconsin, with dozens of similar measures being debated around the country.

"Frankly, we didn't stand a chance of stopping it," says South Carolina state Representative Joseph Neal, a Democrat. A year ago, South Carolina Democrats filibustered the same bill. This year, Republicans managed to push it through.

PUBLIC WORKERS TARGETED

Perhaps more than any other issue, this year's state legislative sessions are likely to be defined in the public consciousness by the GOP-led clampdown on public workers. The movement sparked furious protests that began in February in the snow-covered streets of Madison and Columbus but soon spilled over into capitals as far afield as Maine and Texas. Collectively, hundreds of thousands of people took to the streets to register their unhappiness with what they saw as a blind-side attack on unions and public employees by over-reaching Republican majorities.

Indiana, Ohio and Wisconsin—all of them run by Republicans after November's elections—passed measures limiting collective bargaining rights for public employees. Given the Midwest's long pro-union history, such measures would have been unthinkable under Democratic or mixed-party rule.

In Indiana and Wisconsin, minority Democrats took the almost unheard-of step of fleeing the state to deny Republicans a quorum to pass their legislation, though both states eventually passed measures anyway. Indiana limited bargaining rights for teachers, while Wisconsin approved a much broader limitation of bargaining rights for teachers, state workers and others. Wisconsin's new law is being challenged in court, and protesters and counter-protesters are engineering a series of highly unusual recall elections in an attempt to oust lawmakers on both sides of the issue, as well as Governor Scott Walker.

In Ohio, where Republican Governor John Kasich signed an even tougher collective bargaining measure than Wisconsin's, opponents are vowing to repeal the new law with a referendum in November. In Tennessee, where Republican Governor Bill Haslam's victory in November gave the GOP complete control of state government for the first time since 1869, lawmakers responded by eliminating many collective bargaining rights for teachers and creating a new bargaining process called "collaborative conferencing." Unions complained that it would give them a fraction of their former rights.

But it was not just collective bargaining limits that infuriated public workers. More broadly, teachers saw wide-ranging changes to K–12 classrooms as an attack on their livelihoods.

In Texas, teachers protested by the tens of thousands in March as the Republican-dominated legislature pressed forward with what is likely to be a $4 billion cut to K–12 education, threatening thousands of teacher jobs. Florida and Nevada modified teacher tenure rules, making layoffs easier.

Nationally, no new Republican governor seemed to embody the new GOP spirit more than Walker of Wisconsin. For weeks, raucous protesters massed outside his capitol office in Madison while shouting denunciations of his collective-bargaining bill. But Walker rejected

any assertion that his party took the public by surprise, arguing instead that elections have consequences—and that the GOP was simply delivering on the mandate it was given in November.

"This is not a shock," Walker told The Associated Press in February when he announced his plan to cut collective bargaining rights. "The shock would be if we didn't go forward with this."

TAXES OUT, SPENDING CUTS IN

Underpinning the tough Republican approach toward public workers was the states' long-running budget crisis, which remained the dominant issue in most states and which the GOP responded to with deep spending cuts—not only to the public workforce, but to health care, K–12 schools and a host of other programs.

One of the reasons for the Republican insistence on spending cuts is the fact that 11 new GOP governors refused, even before taking office, to consider tax increases this year. By and large, all 11 of those Republicans delivered on their no-tax promise, although Nevada Governor Brian Sandoval agreed to extend previously approved sales and business tax increases. Guided by their tough position against taxes, and spurred on by what they saw as voter distaste toward big government, Republicans in many states made deep cuts, sometimes even when they had other options available. An expected $4 billion cut to public schools in Texas, for instance, comes despite the state having more than $6 billion in its rainy-day fund. The cuts often hit vulnerable populations the hardest, underscoring a belief among many in the GOP that the nation's social safety net has become too sprawling and costly. A small group of conservative Missouri state senators, for example, forced Democratic Governor Jay Nixon's hand and brought about a reduction in state-level unemployment benefits, arguing that government can't pay for month after month of assistance to the long-term jobless. Republicans in many states slashed funding for mental health services and lobbied the federal government to turn Medicaid into a block-grant program, potentially allowing states to spend far less on health care for the poor.

At the same time that they were making budget cuts to social programs, Republicans were friendly to business, announcing in press conferences and in news releases that, after years of Democratic policies, their states were now "open for business."

Under partial or total GOP leadership, Arizona, Florida, Indiana, Kansas, Michigan, Missouri, Nevada and Wisconsin all cut business taxes. In Maine, LePage's administration took aim at environmental regulations that he said were unnecessary and a burden on businesses. In Pennsylvania, where Republicans took control of the governorship and both legislative chambers, lawmakers have declined to hit the burgeoning natural gas industry with an extraction tax, even though Pennsylvania is the only major gas-producing state without such a levy.

FOR DEMOCRATS, SOME HIGHLIGHTS

While Republicans took complete control of the legislature and governorship in 12 new states in November, Democrats did so in just four. All of them—California, Connecticut, Hawaii and Vermont—were already overwhelmingly Democratic, and the party simply won back the governorship from Republicans. Still, the newly Democratic states show how dramatically different single-party rule can look, depending on which party holds the reins.

Connecticut lawmakers just ended a session that will likely go down as the most aggressively liberal in memory. Under Governor Dannel Malloy, who won election by just 6,000 votes in November, lawmakers signed off on the largest tax increase in state history, became the first state in the nation to require private companies to provide paid sick leave for workers, and decriminalized the possession of small amounts of marijuana, among plenty of other measures that left minority Republicans just as furious as their Democratic counterparts in the Midwest.

Malloy's election marked the first time since 1991 that Democrats held both the legislature and the governorship at the same time. As Larry Cafero, the House Republican leader, sees it, the Democrats overreached. Cafero says he asked House Speaker Christopher Donovan during the session why Democrats were moving so quickly on such sweeping legislation—such as paid sick leave for workers—and received a blunt answer: "Because we can."

In Vermont, Democratic Governor Peter Shumlin pushed for and won legislation calling for a statewide, single-payer health care system—the inverse of the free-market insurance approach that Republicans have been pushing in other states, and one that proved too controversial for Democrats in Congress to include in their own health care law last year.

California, meanwhile, is still mired in fiscal trouble as legislative Republicans have torpedoed Democratic efforts to extend previously approved tax hikes. But Democrats have found success on other matters. Among them: The state is likely to join other Democratic strongholds, including Connecticut, Illinois and Maryland, in extending more tuition assistance to illegal immigrants. That stands in sharp contrast to the immigration crackdowns passed by Republicans in Alabama and Georgia this year, where lawmakers have escalated enforcement against undocumented residents in the absence of federal action.

Dan Smith, a political science professor at the University of Florida, says it is indisputable that Republicans were the big winners in 2011 legislatures, based on the laundry list of legislative victories they claimed. At the same time, he says, the huge differences in the laws approved in Republican- versus Democratic-run states underscores just how consequential state-level elections can be.

"This is the two Americas," Smith says, "in stark contrast."

9

Are the Unions Winning the Fight?

By Alan Greenblatt

Public unions historically are some of the more influential special interests in state and local government. Not anymore. Tight budgets and Republican rule put organized labor in the public sector on the defensive.

B eing a cop, George Beattie doesn't use loaded expressions lightly. But when he considers the terms San Jose Mayor Chuck Reed is dictating to city workers, the president of the San Jose Police Officers Association can't help himself. "He's basically putting a gun to our head," Beattie says. "He is saying either do what we say, or this is what is going to happen."

San Jose has suffered 10 straight years of budget shortfalls. It will certainly face another one in the new fiscal year just getting under way. Like so many other cities, San Jose is looking at retirement health and pension costs that are set to grow at a rate that threatens to swallow enormous chunks of the municipal budget.

That's why Reed has just declared a state of "fiscal emergency." He has put forward a proposal that would raise the retirement age for city workers, abolish cash payments for sick leave and recalculate how pension benefits are accrued. Because the plan changes retirement rules for both current workers and new hires, it's certain to be challenged in court—that is, if it passes muster with voters first.

Beattie claims to be certain of the outcome. "If he puts this on the ballot, and he will," the police officer says, "there's not a doubt in my mind that people will vote this in."

Reed's proposal may be onerous for city workers, but it's not really so different from what state and local employees are seeing all over the country. Due to budget constraints over the past three years, hiring and wage freezes have become common while unpaid furlough days are now nearly *de rigueur*. More than 300,000 state and local workers have lost their jobs in the past two years. This year, they may be joined by 450,000 more.

From *Governing*, July 2011.

On top of all this, elected officials in states such as Wisconsin and Ohio have directly challenged the ability of their workers to have a say in how budget cuts will affect them—by trying to strip them of their collective bargaining rights. All in all, this set of circumstances represents the biggest challenge public-employee unions have ever faced.

If the stakes were not high enough already, union leaders in the public sector are attempting to raise them even higher. The current circumstances, they say, represent a challenge to their workers—and, indeed, to government programs in general. They also consider themselves to be on the front lines of a broader battle between corporations and the wealthiest Americans on one side, with union members and middle-class workers on the other. "This is a bigger fight than just public-sector unions," says Lee Saunders, secretary-treasurer of the American Federation of State, County and Municipal Employees (AFSCME). "It's a fight about the direction of the country."

State and local retirement accounts might be more than $1 trillion in the red, but union leaders such as Saunders say it's unfair to blame government workers when legislatures failed to make scheduled payments to pension funds over the years. Better to blame Wall Street, they say, for racking up record profits even as large-scale investment losses have blown a hole through pension accounts. "Public employees are being blamed for problems they never caused in the first place," says Randi Weingarten, president of the American Federation of Teachers (AFT), who, like Saunders, says Wall Street bears greater responsibility. "There's a very coordinated, mean-spirited strategy to use a budget problem to try to divest ordinary people of any voice in the electorate or the workplace."

It's true that the Republican leaders who have sought to strip unions of their bargaining power are working hand-in-glove with advocacy groups that have deep backing from business interests, such as Americans for Prosperity and the Club for Growth. Those groups have not only argued that public-sector pension plans are too generous to be sustainable, but have also sought to portray government-employee unions as recalcitrant for trying to hold onto such benefits. "The other side has been very successful with divide and conquer—'look at the greedy unions, look at what they're getting and you're not,'" says Stephen Madarasz, a union official in New York state. "Nobody should ignore the fact that corporate America is in many cases trying to undermine the middle class."

Union leaders like to point to polls showing that most of the public supports collective bargaining rights for government workers. They also note that approval ratings for anti-union governors such as Scott Walker of Wisconsin, John Kasich of Ohio and Rick Scott of Florida have fallen into "buyer's remorse" territory. "They're really overreaching," says AFSCME's Saunders. "I believe the majority of Americans are recognizing that."

A key test of that belief will be the July 12 recall elections of several Wisconsin senators who helped push through Walker's plan to strip most unions of collective bargaining power. Union leaders also have taken heart from the results of a May special election in upstate New York, where a normally Republican district was captured by a Democrat who railed against the congressional GOP's plan to turn Medicare into a voucher program. That election spoke to the "whole notion" of pensions, Weingarten says. "People in America get that Medicare is one of the only retirement security programs they've got," she says. "They don't want it touched."

At the same time, however, plenty of polls suggest that most of the public sees the kinds of benefits that government workers get—and private-sector workers often don't—as rich and unaffordable. The unions are right to see that they are in a political fight against enemies with an agenda beyond shoring up budgets. But that doesn't mean they're bound to win. Polls indicate that support for public-sector unions is at an all-time low.

"The body blows the unions are suffering now in states like Wisconsin can be overcome if unions are able to get their base out, change the narrative somehow and defeat their political enemies in 2012," says Richard Kearney, a professor of public administration at North Carolina State University. But he notes that there has been a strong conservative tide in recent state elections. "They're facing long odds, because there is this toxic combination of business and Republicans working against them."

It's not just Republicans who are demanding that unions change with the times. Democrats such as Govs.

Dannel Malloy of Connecticut and Andrew Cuomo of New York are demanding that unions give up billions of dollars in concessions or face workers being laid off by the thousands. "Government can't blame the unions in total," says Patrick O'Connor, a Chicago alderman. "Government is what put the benefits in place. But I don't think anybody who looks at pension plans thinks they can be funded at the levels they're at."

For decades, public-employee unions have been able to associate themselves and their members with the services that the public enjoys. They've framed any cuts to their wages and benefits as an attack on the teachers of our children, the hospital workers who tend the sick, and the police and firefighters who save our lives. "The unions did control the narrative," Kearney says. "They had public buy-in."

But that kind of argument is harder to sustain when government programs are being cut across the board. Politicians make the case that by cutting worker salaries and benefits, they're not weakening public services but trying to protect them. If they don't cut worker benefits, they say, they'll have to close more pools and libraries and let the roads remain rutted with potholes. "If you're a local taxpayer," says Geoffrey Beckwith, executive director of the Massachusetts Municipal Association, "and 20 cents of your property tax dollar goes to pay for benefits that are richer than you get, and that's going to rise to 25 cents, then the public at some point is going to have a reaction that actually would do much more damage overall to the public-sector workforce."

Both chambers of the Massachusetts Legislature— which are both overwhelmingly Democratic—recently voted to block collective bargaining rights over healthcare plans at the local government level. The change was meant to address skyrocketing costs for towns and cities. Union leaders in the state said they were disappointed their nominal friends in the Legislature would make such a move. Future electoral backing would be predicated on how they came down on the measure, the unions warned, calling it an attack not only on their rights but also on the middle class itself. "You are either on the side of collective bargaining for the workers who have been willing to compromise on this issue, or you are against those collective bargaining rights and want to reward intractable, uncompromising management

advocates," Robert J. Haynes, the president of the Massachusetts AFL-CIO, wrote to legislators.

But the problem, Beckwith argues, is that the unions had been unwilling to compromise. Until now, they held veto authority over health plans offered by local governments and seldom had been willing to brook change, even at the threat of layoffs. The Massachusetts legislation would give cities and towns the ability to alter health plans, but they would have to remain at least as generous as those offered to state government workers in terms of co-pays and deductibles.

Massachusetts unions were trying to ride a wave of sympathy that carried all the way east from Wisconsin. Union leaders in Wisconsin, as elsewhere, have argued that there shouldn't be a "race to the bottom" in terms of benefits. But the reality is that 80 percent of workers in the private sector do not have defined-benefit pension plans, and fewer and fewer of them are getting health insurance coverage through employers. There may be limits as to how much traction public-sector unions can get with a solidarity argument when private-sector workers resent their members' benefit levels. "This is one of the major risks that union leaders are taking, by not recognizing that these are new times," Beckwith says. "When society overall sees a change, it's unsustainable for one segment to try to remain as an island."

Union officials and their allies note that people working in government aren't getting rich. Benefits have gone up but wages haven't, says David Madland, director of the American Worker Project at the Center for American Progress. This means public-sector worker compensation has declined as a share of state costs over the past 20 years. The average defined-benefit pension pays out less than $25,000 a year, according to AFSCME. "Public-sector unions are being scapegoated for budget problems that were mostly not of their making," Madland says. [For more on public payrolls, read "Who's the First To Go?".]

The whole idea of collective bargaining, after all, is to come up with ideas that both labor and management can live with. Union leaders complain that government officials are being high-handed when they come to the table demanding that workers either accept large-scale layoffs or serious givebacks. In New York state, for instance, Cuomo has warned his unions that if they don't come up with $450 million worth of cuts, he'll have to lay off

1,900 workers. It doesn't have to be "an either/or," says Madarasz, who is the director of communications for the Civil Service Employees Association in New York, AFSCME's largest chapter. "If both sides are approaching things in good faith," Madarasz says, "there are a thousand solutions you can come up with."

The problem, say both critics of the unions and plenty of their friends, is that for too long public-employee unions have resisted accepting the sort of changes that would help stave off financial disaster. Many mayors and governors will tell you that some of their unions "get it" and recognize that the times call for a fundamental restructuring of public employee contracts. But others have sought to preserve wage levels and benefits that were hard-won over the decades, even as the financial terrain changed and made them both fiscally and politically unsustainable.

It's difficult for union leaders to come back to their membership with packages that represent no increase in pay—or actual cuts. Union leaders face the prospect of their members not only rejecting austere contract agreements, but ousting them as well. And laid-off workers, however much they are missed, will not vote in the next union election.

In San Jose, Mayor Reed is warning that he will have to lay off two-thirds of the city's workforce if he can't achieve significant savings in retirement benefit costs. What consumed $65 million of the city's budget a decade ago already accounts for $250 million and half the city's budget shortfall. Retirement costs could rise to as much as $650 million annually over the next few years, Reed says.

In Reed's mind, it's simply a math problem. Last year, he convinced six of the city's 11 unions, representing about a quarter of its workforce, to accept a 10 percent salary cut for employees. But even if the police and fire-fighters accept that kind of cut again, he says, it will only represent half the amount that pension and retirement benefit costs have increased. "We are draining money out of services and pouring them into retirement benefits," Reed says. "However you define unsustainable, it's unsustainable."

The mayor is convinced the public will be with him. San Jose voters and taxpayers think it's reasonable, he says, to raise the retirement age, over 20 years, to 65 for most government workers and to 60 for those in public safety. Some of the unions are betting he's wrong, rallying against his fiscal emergency proposal and even importing a pro-union state senator from Wisconsin to raise the argument that Reed's plan represents an attack not only on city workers, but on the broader middle class.

Beattie, the president of San Jose's police union, is nervous that that kind of strategy won't carry the day. The San Jose Police Officers Association has hired its own auditors and forensic accountants to examine the city's books. He knows the problem is real, but he blames Reed for not giving serious weight to a pension reform proposal that the police union has come up with that would save the city $100 million over the next 15 years.

Beattie can cite plenty of examples of when his union was willing to make concessions on retirement pay formulas, increased health premium contributions and pay cuts. Reed's declaration of a fiscal emergency is "political in nature and has nothing to do with solving the problem." Still, if Reed is willing to break faith and bypass the bargaining process, Beattie thinks the mayor can win. "Right now, we're the haves," he says. "The people without jobs are the have-nots."

Union leaders nationwide are betting that the argument will play out differently. Casting themselves as the have-nots, they hope to prevail over attempts not only to cut their members' wages and benefits, but also to block their basic right to bargain collectively over compensation. "It's a political fight and it's about power," says AFSCME's Saunders. "This is a power grab, and folks want to take us out of the picture so we will be silent and they can do what they want to do."

Whether or not the charges are fair, it's clear that unions are going to have to respond to the argument that government employment grants benefits that are out of line with what's offered to workers in the private sector and unaffordable in the current budget environment. Weingarten, the AFT president, says public-sector unions are in for a "big fight," but she says she's grown more confident that they'll prevail since the political backlash against governors such as Wisconsin's Walker and Ohio's Kasich has set in.

Public employees in every state would have won mandated collective bargaining rights under the federal Public Safety Employer-Employee Cooperation Act, which came close to passage in 2008. But that bill's chances ended with the death of its sponsor, Sen. Edward M. Kennedy of Massachusetts, and the Democrats' loss of their House majority in 2010. Instead, public-employee unions are watching collective bargaining rights being chipped away, not only in the high-profile fights in the Great Lakes region, but also in other states such as Nebraska and Tennessee.

Unions may be able to turn the tide through their political efforts, with many of them, such as the International Association of Fire Fighters, shifting attention and resources away from federal campaigns and toward state contests in 2012. There are now more unionized workers in state and local government than in the private sector, but it's hard to see how they can grow either in number or strength over the coming years. "Right now, we're going to see a race between the potential impact of these policies, which will dramatically weaken union power in these states," says David Madland, the American Worker Project director, or "whether, before these policies actually kick into effect, unions can build on public support for their basic positions."

"It's sort of even odds" as to the question of whether public-sector unions will be significantly weakened over the next several years, says Rick Kearney, the North Carolina State political scientist. "People are saying it's an existential threat, and it is, if the unions can't adjust course here. They have to adapt, and they have not, as we now see they should."

10

ALEC Enjoys a New Wave of Influence and Criticism

By Alan Greenblatt

A conservative advocacy group flexes its muscle at the state level, and people start to wonder who is this group and how much power do they have.

For decades, the American Legislative Exchange Council has been a force in shaping conservative policies at the state level. Today, its impact is even more pervasive. Its legislative ideas are resonating in practically every area of state government, from education and health to energy, environment and tax policy. The group, which brings together legislators with representatives from corporations, think tanks and foundations to craft model bills, has rung up an impressive score. Roughly 1,000 bills based on ALEC language are introduced in an average year, with about 20 percent getting enacted.

Its very success, however, is beginning to prompt a backlash. While it has long been the target of ideological opponents, many media outlets are now portraying it as a kind of cabal that is secretly pulling the strings in state capitols nationwide. More recently, ALEC has become part of the broad litany of complaints among those castigating corporations for gaming democratic institutions in their favor.

ALEC officials, needless to say, scoff at such characterizations. But they recognize how potent they can be, given the growing anti-corporate populism exemplified by the Occupy Wall Street movement. For the organization, it's a bigger public relations headache than it's ever experienced before. "The hook about some conspiracy or some secret organization," says Chaz Cirame, ALEC's senior director of membership and development, "is a lot better story than one about bringing state legislators together to talk about best practices around the country."

From *Governing*, December 2011.

Regardless of the looming PR challenge, ALEC's own success is *prima facie* evidence of its growing influence. Its support for limited government and fewer regulations resonates with many state officials in the wake of the sweeping victories enjoyed by Republicans last fall. "The elections did have a huge impact in terms of membership and financial support for the organization," says Duane Parde, president of the National Taxpayers Union and a former ALEC official. "ALEC was well positioned."

These days, you can hardly think of a front-burner issue in states in which ALEC doesn't play an important role:

Health care: ALEC's *State Legislators Guide to Repealing Obamacare* has served as a template. Legislators have introduced countless bills based on ALEC language to block implementation of the 2009 federal health-care law. Approaches vary, from trying to block states from applying for federal grants to calling into question the mandate for individuals to purchase health insurance. The organization recently approved a resolution decrying the requirement that states set up health insurance marketplaces known as exchanges.

Versions of ALEC's Freedom of Choice in Health Care Act, a direct challenge to the federal law, have been introduced in more than 40 states. Measures have passed in about a dozen. Next year, such measures will go before voters in Alabama, Florida, Montana and Wyoming. "It's really no secret," state Sen. Jane Cunningham, the lead sponsor of Missouri's version, told the *St. Louis Post-Dispatch* in August. "I learned about the idea from ALEC and brought it back to Missouri."

Climate change: More than a dozen states have approved resolutions, with basic text provided by ALEC, calling plans by the federal Environmental Protection Agency to regulate greenhouse gas emissions a "train wreck" that will harm the economy. In addition, a number of states from New Hampshire to Oregon have seen legislation, based on an ALEC document, looking to withdraw from regional climate change initiatives.

Voter ID: In more than 30 states, legislation was introduced this year to mandate or strengthen requirements that voters produce state-issued photo identification. Many of the bills were based on ALEC model legislation and became law in a half-dozen states. Other bills addressed matters such as shortening voting periods and tightening registration requirements.

Immigration: Last year, NPR reported that the tough law regarding illegal immigrants in Arizona—and since copied in Alabama and other states—had been drafted months before its introduction at an ALEC meeting. The group's critics say the law, which requires local police to check the immigration status of people suspected of being in the country illegally, was another attempt to provide business for its members from the private prison industry. "This is not one of our priorities at ALEC," says Ron Scheberle, the group's executive director. "We are not taking the lead on immigration. It's someone else's idea."

Pensions and unions: Scheberle also says ALEC is "not really leading the effort" to scale back pension benefits, although the group has been doing work on limiting the types of packages offered to new hires. ALEC has also had a hand in shaping legislation designed to limit the role and organizing strength of public-sector unions.

Scheberle's demurrals are not unusual. For years, ALEC has sought to downplay its own role in affecting legislation. The fact that it has model legislation covering a particular issue is seldom announced and legislators like to say that they thought up an idea on their own, or through consultation with a variety of interest groups and not just ALEC.

But the publication of 850 model bills and other documents on a website called ALEC Exposed, which is run by the liberal Center on Media and Democracy, has made it easier to compare proposed bills with language crafted by ALEC—both for journalists and the group's ideological opponents in individual state capitols. "ALEC's fingerprints were all over [Florida's] bill prohibiting state employers from withholding union dues and requiring members to approve using dues for political campaigns," the *Sun-Sentinel* of Fort Lauderdale editorialized in August.

In addition, Common Cause, a liberal advocacy group that supports campaign finance restrictions, filed a request in July with the IRS for an audit of ALEC's books, claiming it acts more like a lobbying group than a nonprofit.

ALEC began its rise to power and influence in 1973 with a series of small steps. Its first meeting attracted just 27 members. The group initially concentrated on social issues such as abortion, but soon switched its focus to business and regulatory matters. Over time, it evolved into its current structure, which includes oversight from separate boards representing the public sector—that is, legislators—and roughly 300 corporations and other private entities. Together, legislators and private-sector members sit on nine task forces that craft model legislation that is often introduced in states.

Its current level of influence represents something of a comeback. Back in 2007, the group was hemorrhaging staff. More than two-thirds of its people left, many complaining about the imperious style of its executive director. Fundraising suffered as relationships with some private-sector donors soured. To stay afloat, the group depended on a half-million dollar infusion from one of its major backers. "Yeah, ALEC was going through a tough time then financially," says William Howell, the Republican speaker of the Virginia House and a former ALEC national chairman.

All that's changed now. Internal management and fund-raising issues have been resolved, and today, ALEC is atop the leader board. Membership is currently a heady 2,000 legislators—more than 25 percent of all legislators nationwide. This summer, Noble Ellington, ALEC's national chairman and a Louisiana state representative, could proudly say that ALEC is "enjoying one of its finer times."

It's no wonder ALEC continues to attract support from some of the nation's largest companies, including AT&T, Exxon Mobil, Coca-Cola, Pfizer and Koch Industries, a privately held energy company whose owners are also major tea party supporters. Other associations to which state lawmakers belong also attract droves of lobbyists to their meetings and rely heavily on corporate underwriting. But only ALEC gives corporate types a seat at the table with elected officials to create and shape policy directly.

Unions, environmentalists and other progressive groups have long lamented that they have not been able to set up an organization with the heft and scope to rival ALEC. "Over the years, I've watched many good alternatives fail," says Wisconsin state Rep. Mark Pocan, a Democrat. "We have just never had the resources that they do. We have a barking Chihuahua compared to an 800-pound gorilla."

Liberals not only complain that they themselves lack the kind of funding available to ALEC, they also warn that the group's backers distort the legislative process

through such heavy spending. Not only do legislators often find their attendance at ALEC meetings paid for through corporate "scholarships," but once they arrive, they are heavily wined and dined and golf-coursed by the group's private-sector members.

If they choose to fill their briefcases or iPads with ALEC model legislation and introduce similar bills back home, campaign contributions may follow. Groups such as Common Cause say that the $6 million or so that private-sector entities annually provide ALEC has been dwarfed by their campaign donations. According to an analysis released this summer by the National Institute on Money in State Politics, ALEC corporate members have devoted more than $500 million to state-level politics since 1990, with about $200 million going to candidates, $85 million to state parties and $228 million to ballot measure campaigns.

As always with money and politics, there are questions about whether corporations are able to sway legislators through their largesse, or are simply rewarding politicians for pushing sympathetic policies. No doubt both dynamics are at work. Money, of course, helps buy access to lawmakers. That's undeniably true of ALEC, where legislators pay a measly $100 for membership but corporations are dunned for $10,000, or often much more.

But ALEC's rapid growth in membership over the past year—and the 30 percent bump in attendance at its annual meeting in New Orleans in August—can also be attributed to the election of a large new class of conservative legislators. Republicans now hold more seats in state legislatures than at any time since the 1920s. Pocan, the Wisconsin Democrat, decries ALEC's pro-corporate agenda and says it presents too narrow a view on most issues, but he concedes that the vast majority of legislators who participate aren't so much swayed as already sympathetic to its brand of conservatism. "So many more legislators now are more oriented toward the ALEC philosophy, and it's a good resource for them," says Howell, the Virginia speaker.

ALEC bills itself as bipartisan and has had a couple of conservative Democrats serve as chair in recent years, but its membership is overwhelmingly Republican. Many of ALEC's setbacks this year have come when GOP-dominated legislatures have passed versions of its model legislation, only to see them vetoed by Democratic governors in states such as New Hampshire, Minnesota and Montana.

But those setbacks have been relatively few. Given its influence, ALEC now finds itself subject to angry headlines with language such as "Wolf in Sheep's Clothing" and "Vile Machinations in Minnesota." Oregon state Rep. Gene Whisnant, an ALEC Legislator of the Year, says sardonically, "We're getting a lot of attention saying we're trying to destroy the earth and everything on it."

ALEC had occasionally been attacked over the years by left-leaning publications for pairing legislators with corporations that, along with trade associations and foundations, pay most of the group's freight. But the leak of a large cache of documents to the Center for Media and Democracy triggered critical coverage, not only from lefty bloggers and magazines like *The Nation*, but from more mainstream media outlets as well.

An increasing number of legislators are being confronted by local media about the close resemblance of bills they've introduced to ALEC model legislation or about their attendance at ALEC meetings, which is often financed directly by the group's corporate members. It's become almost commonplace for many legislators to disavow having been overly influenced by the group or its model bills.

If some lawmakers demur from publicly pledging allegiance to the group or giving it credit for their more controversial ideas, many still say it's a tremendous resource in terms of converting campaign rhetoric and nascent policy ideas into legislative language. Whisnant freely credits ALEC model legislation for forming the basis of several bills he's introduced, including a law setting up a website to allow easy inspection of state expenditures and a bill, thus far unsuccessful, to abolish positions that agencies have kept vacant for more than six months. "It helps bridge that gap in institutional knowledge," says Cirame, ALEC's membership director. "Folks know they want to go to their state capitols and change things, and the question becomes how."

All politics, at the state level and beyond, is about influence. Oil companies, teachers, real estate agents and beer distributors are all looking for ways to help their cause. Some are seeking conditions that will help their businesses grow, while others are seeking to profit either directly through government contracts or through regulations that help them while harming rivals. (Over the years, many of the relatively few examples of contention within ALEC ranks have come from companies in competition with one another.)

Some groups that claim to promote the common good know they must compete not only with those who hold differing views about what's best for the state but also interests and individuals that are seeking direct gain from policy changes. ALEC often promotes policies that clearly benefit its members, including efforts to expand public-private partnerships in areas such as education. Its success on so many fronts is taken by its critics as proof that the game is rigged in favor of its private-sector members.

Just about any legislator involved with ALEC will remind you that all sorts of groups help draft bills, provide campaign cash and help fund efforts to influence legislation. "A lot of people don't understand model bills—they think of them as pernicious," says Alan Smith, a former ALEC director who is now a senior fellow with the Heartland Institute. "But bills come from every corner in this country, and they still have to go through the whole process."

Current ALEC officials say they are providing an avenue for legislators to get ideas, not only from private-sector companies but also their colleagues from other states. "What ALEC does as much as anything else is give legislators support and strength in numbers," says Howell, the former ALEC national chairman. "You're not only the one out there with that idea—this has worked in Idaho or Nebraska or wherever."

Scheberle, the group's executive director, is pleased that ALEC has seen an uptick in membership. But he claims this has less to do with the election of large numbers of conservatives to legislatures lately than to the effort his group makes to provide "solutions" to the pressing problems of the day. "[Most] legislators don't have the staff or budgets to go and hire a bunch of people, but they do need good ideas and they'll take them from wherever they can get them," Scheberle says. "If they come to our meetings and they don't come away with good ideas of things to do once they're back at their legislatures, we haven't done our job."

11

Welcome To The Tea Party

By Louis Jacobson

The Tea Party represents an increasingly high-profile voice in state legislatures. Not everyone is sure, though, what that voice is saying.

There's little doubt Tea Party groups have flexed their muscles in state legislatures this year. But as lawmakers and seasoned political observers reflect on the sessions of 2011, defining the Tea Party's precise impact in the states is tricky.

Tea Party activists pushed steeper budget cuts or more far-reaching initiatives in a number of states than Republican legislators might have sought before their Tea Party–led gains of the 2010 election, says Martin Cohen, a political scientist at James Madison University who has studied the movement. "The Tea Party, in its ability to dominate the Republican Party's agenda, has been a great success" in 2011, he says.

In Maine, a relatively moderate state in recent history, Tea Party–backed Republican Governor Paul LePage pursued an aggressively conservative agenda despite winning office with only 38 percent of the vote in a five-candidate race. He signed a budget that featured $150 million in tax cuts, phased-out a health care plan backed by Democrats and cut benefits for state workers.

In Texas, where Republicans dominate state politics, activist groups aligned with the Tea Party held establishment GOP lawmakers' feet to the fire on spending and taxes—and in a break with the past, lawmakers did not drain the state's rainy day fund, as they could have. Instead, they made cuts to education and health programs.

Despite such victories for the Tea Party and their policies, the boundary between Republican causes and Tea Party causes is often

From *State Legislatures*, September 2011.

Louis Jacobson is a staff writer for PolitiFact.

murky. This makes it difficult to pin down whether Republican policy victories in 2011 owed more to general Republican gains at the ballot box in 2010 or to specific legislative initiatives pushed by Tea Party activists.

In the GOP-controlled Missouri legislature, for instance, "the Tea Party represents a powerful and influential voice," says Ken Warren, a Saint Louis University political scientist. "But since normal Republican cuts in the budget have been going on for so long in Missouri, it is hard to say that any of these cuts occurred because of the Tea Party. In my opinion," Warren says, "the Republican Party in Missouri is naturally made up of people who have been acting like so-called Tea Partiers for a long time."

Meanwhile, a similar dynamic prevailed in Indiana, where Republicans gained complete legislative control after a takeover of the House in the 2010 election.

"The issues the Tea Party championed elected a huge Republican freshman bloc that was sympathetic to the cause, but even if there had been no Tea Party groups, the candidates would have won and been pushing the same agenda," says one political observer in Indianapolis, who asked not to be named in order to speak freely. "There seemed to be an undercurrent of sorts of trying to please, or at least not wanting to tick off, the Tea Party types, but I'm not sure that this changed the results on any vote. What it may have done is change the tenor of debate and the rhetoric."

Part of the inconsistency in the Tea Party's impact nationally stems from the movement's structure, or lack thereof. Several national groups have "Tea Party" in their names or work to encourage Tea Party–type activities—such as rallies, candidate forums and grassroots lobbying—but these groups have sometimes squabbled or gone their own way rather than presenting a unified front.

In fact, Senator Jim Banks, an Indiana Republican, notes that "several of us were supported by Tea Party factions in our campaigns, but I found that while in one county some Tea Party members might support me, in other counties they might not."

> *"The Republican Party in Missouri is naturally made up of people who have been acting like so-called Tea Partiers for a long time."*
>
> —Ken Warren, Saint Louis University Political Scientist

DIFFERENT AGENDAS

Florida became home to the nation's first official Tea Party in August 2009, but a handful of similarly named groups have jockeyed for primacy ever since, sometimes waging fiercer battles among themselves than against establishment politicians. These groups, University of South Florida political scientist Susan MacManus has written, "were quite disparate in name, origin, size, organizational structure, candidate preferences ... and top concerns."

Meanwhile, many Tea Party supporters have focused more on national politics, either in Congress or in the Republican presidential race, than on the nitty-gritty work of influencing legislatures state by state.

"In Alabama, Tea Party activists seemed decidedly more involved in national issues than state issues," says Todd C. Stacy, communications director for Alabama House Speaker Mike Hubbard, a Republican. "The Legislature passed many reforms that Tea Party activists tend to support, including measures to crack down on illegal immigration and cut excessive government spending. Tea Party or not, anyone who has long wanted to enact good-government conservative reforms in Alabama would have been very pleased with this legislative session."

Perhaps most important, the Tea Party, as a self-styled grassroots movement, has tended to encourage decentralized and locally autonomous leadership. As a result, state Tea Party groups have not taken a cookie-cutter approach to influencing legislation.

Based on interviews with several dozen political observers and participants in a range of states, State Legislatures magazine found that while Tea Party activists agreed on a low-tax, small-government agenda, activists in the movement—and the legislators who won their support—actually pursued a wide range of issues.

Some worked inside the system, others outside it. Some took up a focused agenda, others backed a more expansive one.

It's not clear whether the end of collective bargaining for state employees—the centerpiece of the conservative agenda that gained so much national attention in Wisconsin, Indiana and Ohio earlier this year—qualifies as fundamentally a Tea Party issue, as opposed to a generally Republican issue. Much the same could be said about efforts approved in a number of legislatures to tighten immigration enforcement, impose new identification requirements on voters, or restrict abortion.

Brendan Steinhauser—federal and state campaign director at FreedomWorks, a national group that has encouraged the formation of Tea Party affiliates nationwide—says his group's "biggest" issues at the state level are budgets and taxes. Other longstanding priorities include curbs on state-employee unions and expansion of school choice initiatives. In certain states, he says, FreedomWorks has encouraged smaller local issues, such as the privatization of liquor stores in Pennsylvania.

At the same time, Tea Parties tend to stay out of other policy battles popular among many conservatives. Guns, Steinhauser said, "are not in our issue set." Nor are "social issues," including gay marriage.

Still, while Steinhauser's group has some influence with Tea Party groups and activists the movement is neither hierarchical nor uniform.

"Most of the vocal Tea Party members were already conservative activists" before the movement began, and each had their own particular set of favorite issues, says Utah Senator Dan Liljenquist, a Republican. "As such, they have tried to mesh the fiscal responsibility side of the movement with their own specific non-fiscal issues."

Local tea parties "are free to address the issues they feel are important," says Debbie Dooley, co-founder of the Atlanta Tea Party and a Tea Party Patriots national coordinator. "On the national and state levels, the Tea Party Patriots stick to our core principles of fiscal responsibility, limited government and free markets.

> *"I found that while in one county some Tea Party members might support me, in other counties they might not."*
> —Indiana Senator Jim Banks

> *"What the majority of Tea Party members consider a victory is any and all legislation that guarantees more liberty and less government."*
> —Pennsylvania Representative Daryl Metcalfe

"We avoid social issues on the state and national levels," she says, but some local groups do address social issues. The Walton County Tea Party Patriots, she says, often talk about social issues at their tea parties.

Dooley's Georgia Tea Party Patriots helped kill a tax bill that would have lowered individual income tax rates but cut out charitable contributions and other deductions.

The group also successfully lobbied against a measure backed by Republican Governor Nathan Deal that would have begun setting up the health care exchanges called for in the federal health care reform law. Tea Party activists typically oppose any efforts to advance the health care law, which they strenuously oppose. The group also publicly clashed with Deal over his choice of a state party chairman. "We wanted someone who answered to the grassroots, not powerful elected officials," Dooley says.

One of the group's most notable impacts, however, was less stereotypical: An effort—unsuccessful so far—alongside odd-bedfellow allies such as Common Cause and the League of Women Voters, to push lawmakers to enact tougher ethics rules.

The Tea Party agenda in Pennsylvania, however, took an entirely different tack. A key issue the party supported [there] was the "castle doctrine," a law protecting people who use deadly force, such as firearms, to stop intruders in their home or other locations. In passing the law, Pennsylvania joined about two dozen other states that have similar measures, sometimes referred to as a "Make My Day" law.

GOP Representative Daryl Metcalfe, who chairs the House State Government Committee in Pennsylvania, called enactment of the castle doctrine "a significant victory" for the Tea Party. "Above all, what the majority of Tea Party members consider a victory is any and all legislation that guarantees more liberty and less government."

TO COOPERATE OR NOT

Tea Party activists vary widely on a key tactical question: How much to cooperate with GOP legislative leaders, as opposed to being an independent thorn in their side.

In Kansas, collaboration prevailed.

"The state took a serious right turn in 2011, but the Tea Party proper wasn't at the center of this," says Burdett Loomis, a political scientist at the University of Kansas. "The new conservative legislators, who were most comfortable with many Tea Party preferences—smaller government, anti-immigration policies and so on—provided the votes and the caucus power for the consideration of and passage of a Tea Party–like agenda."

Elsewhere, though, Tea Party–aligned legislators effectively drove a wedge between hard-line Republicans and more pragmatic ones, which in many cases included legislative leaders.

In Arkansas, Tea Party–backed legislators used their numerical leverage to extract some concessions on tax and spending issues, since lawmakers need a three-quarters majority on key votes. But on other issues, "when push came to shove, 'institutionalist' Republicans tended to peel off," says Jay Barth, a political scientist at Hendrix College in Conway, Ark. "The more mainstream Republicans generally refused to go along with anti-immigration legislation and other Tea Party bills."

And even in New Mexico, where the Democrats control both chambers, legislators aligned with the Tea Party torpedoed a bipartisan effort to install a more moderate Democrat as House speaker. Political observers interpreted this as a desire by Tea Party activists to aid their cause by keeping partisan differences sharp.

Montana Representative Krayton Kerns, a Republican, says he and his Tea Party–backed colleagues didn't chalk up many victories this year, despite having a GOP-controlled chamber, since key posts were held by more establishment types. "There is no significant difference between moderate Republicans and Marxist Democrats," he says, and as a result, "constitutional conservatives" had little effect on the session.

In Louisiana, one of the biggest impacts of the Tea Party has been conservative, white Democrats . . . switching to the GOP fold. "These party changes are coming fast and furious and were a major contributor in the ascendancy of Republicans in both houses of the Louisiana Legislature for the first time since Reconstruction," says Pearson Cross, a political scientist at the University of Louisiana at Lafayette.

Still, Cross adds: "It's hard to separate Tea Party legislative victories from the normal operation of a Legislature in a state that was conservative and is becoming more so with each passing year and election."

POSSIBILITY OF A BACKLASH

Not all is lost for the Democrats, of course. They are hoping for a voter backlash against Tea Party–driven, Republican-enacted policies, particularly in swing states such as Maine, New Hampshire, Ohio and Wisconsin.

A backlash is even possible in a state that's leaned very conservative in recent years—Arizona. There, Senate President Russell Pearce, a leading Tea Party figure, faces a serious threat from a recall election. That comes after his chamber pursued an aggressively conservative agenda, including heightened immigration restrictions as well as a bill—ultimately vetoed by Republican Governor Jan Brewer—that would have required presidential candidates to prove their U.S. citizenship to appear on state ballots.

"It appears there is a revolt in the business community that will result in well-funded efforts to elect more moderate Republicans," says Earl de Berge, research director at the Behavior Research Center, a polling outfit in the state.

And despite notable national gains for Republicans and their Tea Party allies, there's strong evidence that the movement's muscle is geographically inconsistent.

In Hawaii, the Tea Party is "almost a nonentity," says Richard Castberg, a University of Hawaii at Hilo political scientist. "Some letters to the editor, but no presence in the Legislature or viable candidates for office." Much the same prevails in California, where "the Tea Party is a tiny, anemic entity," says Garry South, a Democratic strategist.

"It just gets lost in a state this big," he says. "The whole movement is completely out of sync with where a vast majority of Californians are."

Legislatures

State legislatures really only do three basic things: (1) they pass laws, (2) they represent the people, and (3) they oversee public agencies in other branches of government. Those three things, though, represent an incredible workload and a phenomenally complicated juggling act.

The average state legislature deals with at least 1,000 proposed laws in any given year, bills covering everything from potholes to pot, income taxes to the death penalty.[1] People clearly expect a lot from their legislators as the job means being an expert on, well, just about everything.

Representing constituents is, if anything, harder than attending to the (literally) 1,001 bills competing for legislators' attention. Constituents tend to be a tough crowd. For one thing, voters tend to have very low opinions of the work habits, ethics, and general character of those in elected office, and, for another, there are a lot of voters. Constituents outnumber state legislators by tens of thousands—even hundreds of thousands—to one. Ever try pleasing 100,000 people? Don't bother; whatever you do, someone will view your vote, speech, media interview, or expression of support/opposition for a bill, an issue, or a proposal as just one more piece of evidence of what a lazy, unethical, and generally bad character you are.

And if that isn't enough, legislators are expected to keep an eye on pretty much all state agencies. One of these organizations makes a bad mistake or fritters away the taxpayers' dough, and it's not just the bureaucrats who get in trouble; voters want to know who in the legislature was sleeping at the switch while the Department of Dubious Behavior was up to no good.

Given all this, you'd think that being a state legislator is more than enough for one full-time job—except it's not a full-time job, at least not in the sense of getting a full-time paycheck. The National Conference of State Legislatures (NCSL) estimates that in roughly forty states, most legislators cannot make a living on the salaries they get for being in elected office.[2]

The thanks for the hard work and generally low pay is mostly no thanks at all from your boss (i.e., the voting public). It used to be that you could at least count on some measure of job security, but that's not true anymore. Incumbency still has its advantages, but between term limits and the throw-the-bums-out mood that economically stressed voters have been in the past couple of election cycles, legislative job security is not what it used to be. Long hours, low pay, big problems, and small praise kind of make you wonder who'd actually want to be a state legislator.

Yet despite being a pretty tough gig, being in a state legislature has one huge positive: If you want to make a difference (for good or ill), it's the place to be. Because their policy portfolios are so comprehensive and because their constitutional jurisdiction makes them the chief revenue raisers of state government, state legislatures probably affect the daily social, economic, and political life of U.S. citizens more than any other institution outside of family. That's reason enough to pay close attention to current trends in state legislatures.

Two big issues related to such current trends are addressed in this section's readings. The first issue deals with something that the public tends to be pretty skeptical about: legislator ethics. The first essay, by Peggy Kerns, examines ethics laws and their impact on state legislators. She finds that ethics laws are mostly about dealing with the last scandal rather than the next one. Still, ethics laws do seem to have something of impact; they can signal a shift in culture within a legislative chamber. The following essay picks up on the ethics theme but examines how new information technology has raised ethical questions for state legislatures. Everyone has a Facebook page these days, including a lot of state legislators. Those sorts of social media are sometimes used to connect with constituents and update thoughts on proposed bills and public policy. So who should have access to those pages? Should a legislator's Facebook page be considered their private domain, and should they be free to friend who they do or do not want to access their page? Or should it be publically accessible? Who gets to decide who can say what to whom in these sorts of forums? This is a relatively new ethical dilemma for state legislators, and Judy Nadler's essay considers its implications.

The second big issue dealt with in this section's readings is redistricting. The once-a-decade exercise has just been completed in most states, but the bare-knuckle partisan brawling involved has led many people to question the process. In many states, legislators themselves have primary responsibility for redrawing districts, which many see as creating unavoidable conflicts of interest. In response, a number of states are experimenting with using independent commissions in hopes of reducing, if not eliminating, partisan bias in redistricting. Two essays, one by Alan Greenblatt and one by Josh Goodman, conclude that redistricting is an inherently political process and that outsourcing the job to an independent commission cannot change that.

NOTES

1. Kevin B. Smith, Alan Greenblatt, and John Buntin, *Governing States and Localities* (Washington, DC: CQ Press, 2005), 178.

2. National Conference of State Legislatures, "Full- and Part-Time Legislatures," June 2009, www.ncsl.org/legislatures-elections/legislatures/full-and-part-time-legislatures.aspx.

12

Do Ethics Laws Work?

By Peggy Kerns

Ethics laws are more about preventing the behavior that caused the last scandal than stopping the behavior that will cause the next scandal.

When scandals erupt, legislatures pass laws. Usually, the laws have nothing to do with the scandal and would not have prevented it anyway.

Nothing new here. The Watergate scandal of the early 1970s prompted Congress to pass the Ethics in Government Act of 1978.

"Watergate was about burglary, cover-ups, lying and campaign irregularities," wrote G. Calvin Mackenzie in his book "Scandal Proof."

"Little in the bill would have prevented the kinds of activities that composed the Watergate scandal," wrote Mackenzie. "The ethics act sought to restore public confidence in government after Watergate by creating an array of new regulations that bore little relation to the scandal that inspired them."

Carol W. Lewis, a professor of political science at the University of Connecticut, agrees. "Ethics laws are misnamed. These laws forbid you from doing the last thing that someone else did," she says. "They come into play 'post-hoc,' after the fact. They're a list to clean up dirty laundry."

Although Mackenzie believes government operates more ethically than ever, he says the "expansion of ethics regulations and enforcement agencies and personnel has not produced a concomitant increase in public confidence in government integrity."

If ethics laws don't work, why pass them?

"What laws do best is to help change the culture of the legislature," says Alan Rosenthal, professor of public policy at Rutgers University. He cites Florida and Kentucky as two examples of where tougher restrictions on gifts and strong disclosure laws changed the

From *State Legislatures*, July/August 2011.

tone of the legislature and helped reduce the incidence of abuse by legislators.

In the past five years, Southern states—Alabama, Georgia, Louisiana, North Carolina, Tennessee—have been the most active in strengthening and, in some cases, overhauling ethics laws. Even before then, South Carolina initiated a strong gift ban, and Georgia and Mississippi strengthened their financial disclosure laws in response to a low rating by the Center for Public Integrity.

Rosenthal warns about over regulation, however. When laws are excessively restrictive and numerous they tend to lead to violations, he says. "Legislators who do not exercise extreme caution, checking their every move, may inadvertently step over a line they didn't know existed," he says.

In the past 10 years, states have instituted stricter gift laws—limiting or totally banning gifts from lobbyists to lawmakers. These laws have spawned some unintended consequences.

"Certain actions can affect the culture," says Iowa Representative Scott Raecker. Former members have told him how, after a $3 gift ban passed following a scandal in the 1990s, social interactions among members declined.

"The result was the culture of civility diminished," he says. "Relationships that developed and were important in working together were not built in the same way."

> *"Ethics laws provide the public with a benchmark, although the laws are only the floor of how we should conduct ourselves."*
> —Iowa Representative Scott Raecker

Raecker acknowledges ethics laws are important, but they're not the whole answer. The culture of the legislature is tied to the ethics of the chambers and the character of the members, he says. "Ethics laws provide the public with a benchmark, although the laws are only the floor of how we should conduct ourselves."

For this reason, codes of ethics in the Iowa House and Senate each start with a description of the chamber's aspirations. "The preambles show the public that we intend to operate with high levels of ethics and accountability," he says.

Ethicists warn public officials not to rely on laws alone if they want to be ethical. "Ethics is concerned with moral obligations . . . based on moral duties and virtues," says Michael Josephson, founder and president of the Josephson Institute of Ethics. "Laws establish standards of behavior that may or may not correlate with individual conscience. Laws coerce from the outside, ethics control from the inside."

Lewis urges public officials to understand there are two bases for ethical decisions—moral choice and moral judgment.

"Moral choice is about right and wrong. Moral judgment is about conflicting duties and principles," she says. "Codes and laws can address only moral choice. That's their limitation. They don't address the gray areas where someone has to rely on personal will and integrity."

13

Should everyone have access to a state legislator's Facebook page? Social media create a new set of ethical dilemmas for state legislatures.

Blog, Tweet and Post: Proceed with Caution

By Judy Nadler

The casual and lightning-fast nature of social media makes it an easy and inexpensive tool for public officials. Despite the many advantages these new technologies bring, there also are thorny ethical considerations, such as blurring the lines between personal and public information and privacy. How can new communications technologies be used effectively but ethically to engage citizens? Consider these two hypothetical cases, based on real experiences.

FACEBOOK

When Shirley ran for the legislature, her campaign advisers set up a website, Facebook and Twitter accounts, and a blog. The cost of creating and maintaining her web presence was borne by her campaign. The content was devoted to policy statements, endorsements, media clips, a calendar of personal appearances, and photos and videos with the public.

Her greatest exposure came through Facebook. By the end of the campaign, her Facebook page had thousands of "friends" and hundreds of postings about her campaign.

Shirley shut down the campaign website but decided to keep the popular Facebook account, and began to post legislative messages and constituent polls. The task of maintaining her Facebook page

From *State Legislatures*, October/November 2011.

was assigned to a staff member, who worked on it during regular office hours. A "push" was organized to add key lobbyists, government contractors and others as "friends." Several ethical issues arose after the election.

> *The immediate nature of social media places a special obligation on the officeholder to use them with caution.*

- Can a government official use Facebook as a way to discuss public issues?
- If so, can an official limit access to such a Facebook page in any way?
- Do all members of the public have a right to see what is on a publicly maintained Facebook page? What about a completely personal one?
- Can an officeholder "unfriend" certain individuals or remove selected posts on a publicly maintained Facebook page?
- If a Facebook page is completely personal, must the official confine all comments to personal rather than public matters?

Blogs

Lance was an assemblyman representing a high-technology district and was an early adopter of social media. His primary means of communicating with his constituents was his blog. A Twitter account was mostly for fun, and he used it to chat about his family and to share banter with many of his friends and followers.

As chair of the Assembly Budget Committee, Lance found himself in the middle of a fierce lobbying effort from employee unions, social service agencies, and the state school system, among others. In his daily blog posts, he tried to explain the complexity of the issues, discuss the difficult choices facing the state, and encourage input from the public through the comment feature of the blog.

His attempts at civil discourse were shattered when an increasing number of anonymous comments were very critical of his position on the issues, and often misquoted or misrepresented his proposals or voting record. At one point, the negative comments outweighed the positive two to one—and several were nothing more than personal attacks.

The social media experts he consulted suggested a system requiring stricter guidelines—registration requiring a valid name and email address—but he was concerned the extra steps would dissuade the legitimate dialogue he was seeking. A good friend offered to monitor the blog comments and remove all that disagreed with the assemblyman's positions.

This experience, too, raised ethical issues.

- What ethical guidelines should Lance use in maintaining his blog?
- Is the use of social media itself an obstacle for constituents who do not have access to technology?
- Does the anonymity of the comments and tone suggest he should eliminate the blog, or are these posts part of the "rough-and-tumble" world of a legislator?
- What problems might be solved if his friend monitored the blog and made it more positive? What problems might be created?
- Does the public have a right to see all blog and Twitter postings by a legislator?

General Principles

Access is a fundamental ethical principle in government. New media can improve access to and from citizens by expanding the number and variety of channels of communication, but these same media can simultaneously restrict access or favor certain constituencies. The medium will change over time, so we should develop principles that can guide us on whatever platform develops in the future. Open access is an ethical starting point.

The Facebook page in the first example opens the potential for restricting or favoring access for particular groups. If the site is restricted to "friends" only, then it could run afoul of principles of open government. This is particularly of concern if the site is maintained with public funds. It can also be improper if it is promoted only to a narrow group of interests before the legislature.

Access to a purely personal Facebook page can probably be restricted to a few real friends, but the officeholder needs to be very cautious that the "friends" and the talk on that page are indeed personal and not political.

A second critical ethical principle is the public's right to know. An officeholder's blog or Facebook site are particularly vulnerable to the extreme rhetoric often seen at public meetings and rallies, only with greater anonymity and distance.

Any officeholder would be wise to establish both a registration process to tone down the most extreme rhetoric and a set of clear guidelines about the kind of inflammatory language that is banned from the site. The credibility of the site as a vehicle for public dialogue would suffer if all critical comments about the office holder were excised. The public's right to know probably requires that a determined reporter or citizen be permitted to view even the most vile, profane and racist comments if they wish to do so—perhaps by visiting the legislator's office in person.

A third principle is the obligation to choose one's own words prudently. The immediate nature of social media places a special obligation on the officeholder to use them with caution. Great damage can be done to others, often inadvertently, by a comment posted with little thought and based on early and possibly erroneous information.

Old-fashioned vetting and review by a legislator's staff may be missing if the officeholder tweets or blogs directly. And an officeholder's "tweet" is much more likely to be passed on or quoted in other media.

14

Can Redistricting Ever Be Fair?

By Alan Greenblatt

Independent commissions were supposed to make redistricting less partisan. Democrats and Republicans are both upset over the maps they are producing, so maybe the commissions are doing something right.

Redistricting always creates drama. Every 10 years some number of legislators and congressmen find the new redistricting map draws them out of a job or puts them in a much more precarious position. One party or the other finds itself handicapped by the shape of the new districts. Naturally, politicians raise a fuss. "There are always going to be sore losers with redistricting," says Justin Levitt, a professor at Loyola Law School in Los Angeles. "Redistricting is, in many ways, the thing that legislators take most personally."

When given the chance, legislators try to spare their own feelings—to protect their bailiwicks. The ability of politicians to trade favors and votes is never more in evidence than during redistricting season. Leaders of the two parties can enter into a nonaggression pact, protecting as many of the incumbents on both sides as possible. That happened 10 years ago, when the brother of a Democratic congressman in California charged incumbents $20,000 apiece for his services in drawing districts that made re-election an entirely safe bet. The result was that when the new maps were put to the test in 2002, not a single seat changed party hands in the state Senate, Assembly or congressional delegation.

All told, over the course of 765 congressional and legislative elections held in the state during the past decade, only five seats ever changed party hands. "California's whole system of redistricting had always been at one end of the spectrum," says Tim Storey, a redistricting expert with the National Conference of State Legislatures. "It had clearly been a state that had given full protection to incumbents. They set themselves up for major reform."

From *Governing*, November 2011.

California was not the only state at the far end of the spectrum. Florida had a problem as well. Statewide elections are generally competitive, including presidential contests, but Florida had been sliced into districts that were so safe for one party or the other that few candidates bothered taking on incumbents. In 2004, only a handful of state legislators faced major party opposition at all. Not a single incumbent was defeated. Only six challengers finished within 10 points of the incumbent.

Across the country, several states have dabbled with ways to bring less bias to redistricting—by setting up panels to provide a first draft or by asking for citizen input. The issue of redistricting and how to do it fairly is a never-ending one. But in Florida and California, the sense that politicians were able to choose their own sets of voters, rather than the other way around, convinced many people in those states that the redistricting laws had to change.

Last year, Floridians approved a law meant to bar legislators from drawing maps with the intention of favoring one party or the other. In true bipartisan fashion, the law was challenged by two members of Congress, one Democrat and one Republican, but in September a federal court upheld it. It's not clear how a mandate for not just compact but also politically competitive maps will be carried out in practice: The Florida Legislature has yet to release its product.

In California, voters in 2008 established a 14-member commission to draw legislative maps. Two years later, it was granted the additional responsibility of creating congressional districts. But that responsibility came with specific orders. The commission was told to ignore incumbent protection—and even legislators' home addresses—while creating districts that are compact and keep intact when possible what are known as "communities of interest" and political jurisdictions such as whole cities.

Although outside observers say the commission did its job fairly well, especially given the convoluted rules involved in setting up the commission in a short amount of time, not everyone is happy. In fact, Republicans are livid. The GOP is convinced the new map puts them at a disadvantage both for U.S. House seats and, in particular, in the state Senate. Hispanics don't like the maps much either. Groups such as the Mexican American Legal Defense and Educational Fund are eyeing the Voting Rights Act and considering suing over the issue of inadequate Latino representation.

But it's Republicans who are making the loudest noise. Democrats dominate California politics, and Republicans warn that the Senate map will shut them out of power entirely. Tax increases require a two-thirds majority in both chambers in California. The GOP has only two seats to spare in the Senate—both of which Republicans believe they will lose as a result of redrawn districts. "It pretty much guarantees that Republicans will lose the one-third voting bloc when it comes to tax increases and fee increases," says Mimi Walters, a Republican who represents parts of Orange and San Diego counties in the state Senate. "We will be in a super-minority position if in fact we don't redraw the lines."

Walters is spending a good deal of her time these days traveling up and down the state in search of funds to help finance a ballot measure to toss out the commission's map and have courts appoint a special master to do the job over. The California Republican Party is sponsoring the effort, which is allowed by the initiative that created the commission.

California Republicans are also going down a more tried and true avenue of complaint—namely, by filing a lawsuit. The commission violated its own rules, they say, with indications of partisan bias among some of the commissioners and the consulting firm it hired to do the actual line drawing. The commission also failed to keep some communities of interest intact, says Tom Del Beccaro, who chairs the California GOP. "They extinguished Republican seats not based on demographics or the guidelines, but from a desire to create a certain outcome," he says. "They didn't follow the rules and the process was corrupted."

California is not the only state besieged by such complaints. In Arizona, which is now in the midst of its second redistricting cycle using a commission created by ballot measure, Republicans argue that the supposedly independent nature of the commission has been compromised by partisan leanings. Its mapmaking consultant had ties to President Obama's 2008 campaign, while the husband of its chair, who is a registered independent, worked for a failed Democratic legislative candidate. "To me, this commission and its work is tainted," state Sen. Al Melvin, a Tucson Republican, complained at a hearing. Lawsuits seem likely there also.

Is it possible to delete partisanship from the redistricting process? The designers of California's commission tried hard to make it happen. Commissioners and their immediate family members can't have run as a candidate within the past 10 years or served on party committees. They're also not supposed to have worked as lobbyists or given sizable campaign contributions. Thousands of applicants were narrowed down by the state auditor to a pool of 60: 20 Republicans, 20 Democrats and 20 independents. Legislative leaders from both parties were able to strike a few individuals each from that list, with the remainder of the names going into a bingo-style spinner. Eight were picked out randomly. They, in turn, chose six more of their colleagues, resulting in a commission made up of five Democrats, five Republicans and four who were neither.

Nevertheless, Republican complaints now turn on the notion that Democratic operatives managed to sneak onto the commission and trick most of the GOP members for their own purposes. "The idea of the commission is good," says Del Beccaro. "But in practice sometimes it gets abused."

Not everyone sees it that way. For one thing, the maps won near-unanimous support from commissioners, with the exception of one Republican who opposed all of them and one other who voted against the new congressional map. Vincent Barabba, the Republican who chaired the commission, says there was "no basis" for accusations that decisions were made for partisan reasons. As Levitt, the Loyola law professor, sees it, all the evidence suggests the opposite. "If the consultants in California were perceived to be Democratic-leaning," he says, "I don't believe the Republican commissioners would be repeatedly hoodwinked in a way that would be possible to steamroll them."

The California commission's work offers more proof, if any were necessary, that it's impossible to remove politics from redistricting. "Whether you think they did a good job or not depends on whether your ox was gored, but that's true of redistricting in general," says Nathaniel Persily, a redistricting consultant at Columbia Law School.

Still, Democrats say that the GOP complaints amount to nothing more than sour grapes. The state is firmly Democratic, providing one of the nation's few bright spots for the party after last year's Republican sweep. It's difficult to imagine that Republicans would

have fared much better under the old rules, with a process controlled by a solidly Democratic Legislature and governor. Del Beccaro dismisses that argument, saying that it's not important to ask whether Republicans "could have fared worse under a more flawed method," but to look at the abuses he says were perpetrated by the commission.

It's certainly the case that the same sort of charges Del Beccaro has lodged—that particular candidates were favored in the drawing of districts, that there were conflicts of interest among those doing the drawing, and that counties and other communities were cut up and glued with other areas in odd pairings—have also been raised repeatedly when legislators themselves draw the maps. Similar complaints—and worse—have been brought up in states where one party controls the whole process this cycle, such as the Democrats in Illinois and Republicans in Texas.

Already, legislative action has been blocked and the courts have taken over the job in Colorado and Minnesota. "The districts are plainly and in some cases baldly and expressly designed to help particular candidates and hurt others," Levitt says. "They're drawn not only permitting self-interest but in some respects almost entirely because of self-interest."

It's hard to imagine that California's commission—or anyone else—could have drawn districts there that didn't, for the most part, favor one party or the other. Iowa has long been held up as the model by people who have sought to overhaul the redistricting process. Its nonpartisan legislative staff is charged with drawing lines that don't take incumbent addresses into consideration. Over the years, its maps have put the Legislature in play and left Iowa with a high number of competitive congressional races, considering the modest size of the state's delegation.

But Iowa is Iowa. It's square and homogeneous and no matter how you slice it, you have Iowa. California is different, with the greatest amount of racial diversity of any state and a topography of dramatic variability, from congested coastal cities to large stretches of unpopulated desert, major agricultural areas and mountains.

What might be called its natural political map, moreover, makes it difficult to create many competitive seats. The population centers that hug the coast are among the most Democratic parts of the entire country, while

Republicans tend to be found in more sparsely populated counties inland. In order to make Nancy Pelosi's San Francisco congressional district competitive, Persily jokes, you might have to stretch it out all the way to Nevada. Or possibly Utah. "The coast is so Democratic and the interior so Republican," he says, "my feeling is that in California, if you're not going to pay attention to incumbency and you start drawing districts from north to south, there's only so much partisan impact redistricting is going to have."

A similar story can be told in most parts of the country. Probably two-thirds of the congressional districts nationwide are going to be safe for one party or the other, regardless of who draws the line. Geographic polarization is happening all over the country, with Democrats and Republicans living in separate areas— not so much because they check voter precinct data when they're deciding where to live, but because they pick up on cultural clues that suggest areas where they'd be most comfortable. Political affiliation seems to follow cultural preferences. "People appear to be moving to places where they find those who look, think, act—and vote—like they do," says Bill Bishop, author of The Big Sort, a book tracing this phenomenon. "Over time, this makes communities more Republican or Democratic, and this creates increasing polarization over time."

If Bishop is right—and most political scientists seem to agree with him—it's going to be impossible to draw most congressional and legislative districts in ways that are competitive. Redistricting exacerbates geographical polarization, but it doesn't create it.

Redistricting is, and always has been, used to gain maximum advantage from the demographics at hand. If only one-third of congressional districts could be competitive under optimum circumstances, perhaps less than 15 percent could be counted on to be consistently competitive in recent years, despite the large amount of partisan turnover lately. (The U.S. House changed partisan hands twice in the last three elections.)

There aren't going to be many more states where redistricting is taken out of the hands of legislators entirely. Given legislative self-interest, moving to an independent commission system pretty much has to be done by ballot measure, and there aren't that many initiative states to begin with. Selling voters on the need to change something relatively arcane like redistricting has been difficult for so-called reformers. They couldn't make the case in Ohio, and California required repeated tries. The current controversies in California and Arizona, whether overblown or not, won't make it any easier. It's worth remembering that the ballot initiatives in those two states were pushed primarily by political parties who ended up unhappy with the commissions' final products.

But independent maps are being drawn in an increasing number of states. States such as Virginia are setting up advisory commissions that lack real authority but nonetheless produce maps that can serve as guidelines. Minnesota's Supreme Court, which took the reins of the redistricting process this year, said recently that it would take into account maps drawn by the public as part of its deliberations.

It might be impossible to draw political maps that don't help one party at the expense of the other. Something other than the usual goal of ensuring job security for incumbents might become paramount, at least in some places. "Someone from the public can draw a map that can illuminate to the courts what opportunities there are for improving maps," says Michael McDonald, a political scientist at George Mason University, who has promoted public participation in the redistricting process. "It could mean greater restrictions on gerrymandering, especially in states with constitutional requirements that must be met. Having a map that demonstrates a better way to achieve those requirements puts pressure on the legislature to conform to those requirements."

15

Why Redistricting Commissions Aren't Immune from Politics

By Josh Goodman

Independent commissions can bring partisan balance to the redistricting process. Partisan balance, though, is not enough to secure bipartisan agreement.

Mario Carrera was the only independent to serve on the Colorado Reapportionment Commission. Republicans accused Carrera of siding with Democrats in redistricting. Carrera says a good purpose was met by having a commission draw political maps rather than legislators.

Until recently, not many people in Colorado had ever heard of Mario Carrera. An executive at Entravision, which owns a number of Spanish-language TV and radio stations, Carrera's world existed off-camera, far from the drama of politics playing out on the news on his stations.

That changed last May when Carerra was appointed to serve as the lone independent on the state commission charged with handling state legislative redistricting in Colorado. By the end of the year, the man who came to be known as "Super Mario" was the most controversial person in Colorado politics. Upset with how the commission's political maps turned out, the Republican speaker of the state House of Representatives called Carerra a "failure." The conservative group Compass Colorado went a step further when it called on Entravision to fire Carrera from his day job.

The anger came from the fact that Carrera had sided with the commission's five Democrats—and against its five Republicans—on a new political map for Colorado. One GOP member on the commission said that Carrera hadn't been independent at all but rather a "wolf in sheep's clothing," a view that Republicans saw as confirmed when word circulated that he had attended a fundraiser for President Obama while on the commission. For his

From *Stateline.org*, January 2012.

part, Carrera pointed out that the chairman of the Colorado Republican Party had recommended his appointment.

The irony of all this is that Carrera was appointed specifically to try and take some of the politics out of redistricting. Colorado set up an independent commission back in 1974. The idea was to take the job of drawing political boundaries out of the self-interested hands of state legislators, a concept whose appeal has been growing. More than a dozen states now use some variation of an independent commission, with California the latest to give it a try.

In Colorado, legislative leaders, the governor and the chief justice of the state supreme court all get to make appointments. In past decades, one party always ended up with more members. This time, though, Governor John Hickenlooper, a Democrat, and Chief Justice Michael Bender, a Democratic appointee, acted to ensure neither party had a majority.

But partisan balance doesn't necessarily create partisan comity. Bob Loevy, a Republican who served on the commission with Carrera, has published an online book on the experience called *Confessions of a Reapportionment Commissioner.* "The commission essentially, all through its work, says, 'Do we want to take the Republican or the Democratic plan,'" Loevy told Stateline. "What looks like a great reform in 1974, it's all just a cover for the political parties."

Colorado isn't the only state in the latest round of redistricting where an independent commission intended to tamp down partisanship wound up sparking partisan fireworks anyway. Commission processes in Arizona, California and Idaho were also contentious and litigious. The lesson from these states seems to be that even when independent commissions take partisans out of redistricting, they can't take out the partisanship.

However, that doesn't necessarily mean that independent redistricting commissions have failed. To the contrary, many of the people who have served on independent commissions argue that, in some cases, it may be evidence that they have succeeded in crafting plans that didn't serve elected officials' self-interest. "Everyone is so entrenched in their own agenda and party," Carrera says. "I do believe that there is a purpose that was served by separating this commission from the legislature."

VARYING STRUCTURES

Commissions are in charge of redrawing maps for legislative districts, congressional districts or both in 13 states: Alaska, Arizona, Arkansas, California, Colorado, Hawaii, Idaho, Ohio, Missouri, Montana, New Jersey, Pennsylvania and Washington. Some of these states go to greater lengths than others to achieve independence. Some of the commissions forbid elected officials from serving, while others include them by law. Some prevent party-line votes, while others are regularly dominated by one party or the other. Still, each of these commissions was created for a similar purpose: to take redistricting out of the hands of state legislators who have a personal stake in the outcome.

No state has created a more elaborate process to do that than California, where a 2008 ballot initiative created the California Citizens Redistricting Commission. Among other things, the law rejects out of hand anyone who in the past 10 years has run for state or federal office; anyone who has been a registered lobbyist; anyone who has worked for a political candidate, campaign or party; and even anyone who has made large political contributions.

Before the California commission ever drew a map, however, Republicans were already accusing the body of being co-opted by Democrats, based on its selection of consultants. Those accusations gained some weight when a ProPublica investigation pointed to places where the commission had adopted district lines promoted by supposed "good government" groups that actually were run by Democratic operatives. Democrats are expected to gain seats under California's new maps. "It wasn't so much that the Democrats tried," says Douglas Johnson, a fellow at the Rose Institute of State and Local Government and one of the consultants the commission passed over. "Of course they tried. The surprise is that it worked."

Democrats and many of the commission's members say those allegations are overblown. The congressional map is currently in court, while the state Senate map may be subject to a voter referendum instigated by Republicans.

Arizona's independent commission also riled opposition. Republicans accused the commission of violating state open meeting laws, procurement laws and the state constitution's standards for drawing of districts. Much of their ire was focused at the commission's lone independent, Colleen Mathis, whose husband had worked on a Democrat's legislative campaign in 2010. Governor Jan Brewer and fellow Republicans briefly succeeded in impeaching Mathis, only to have her reinstated by the Arizona Supreme Court. They also briefly contemplated trying to eliminate the commission entirely.

Then, there's Idaho's Reapportionment Commission, whose membership of three Democrats and Republicans has been rotating through a cast of new characters for months. First, the commission failed to meet a September 6 deadline for drawing state legislative districts. So the state Supreme Court disbanded the group and had a new commission appointed. The second panel did approve a map, only to have the Court reject it for violating the state constitution's standards.

After that, Republicans engaged in a struggle over whether a third effort at drawing maps should require a third set of commission members to do the work. Idaho Republican Party Chairman Norm Semanko and House Speaker Lawerence Denney wanted to remove the people they appointed to the second commission—Denney says his caucus believes they conceded too much to the Democrats—but were rebuffed by the Idaho Supreme Court. Any more delays could become problematic from an elections administration perspective: The filing period for legislative candidates ends March 9, without any districts for them to run in.

Evan Frasure, the Republican co-chair of the first Idaho panel, helped to initiate the commission structure in 1994 when he served in the Idaho legislature. Still, he concedes that taking redistricting out of the hands of the legislature hasn't gone smoothly. "Rather than having 105 legislators duking it out, now you have six people," Frasure says, "but it did not remove the partisan nature of it."

A BETTER RESULT?

Not every state with an independent commission has ended up mired in controversy. In Washington, for example, a commission with two Democrats and two Republicans unanimously approved new legislative and congressional lines. One of the Republican commissioners,

former U.S. Senator Slade Gorton, called Washington's approach, "the best in the country."

Nor is it clear that the states with commissions have been more contentious than anywhere else. Texas, Illinois, Wisconsin and Maryland, all states where legislators themselves control redistricting, have approved plans that the minority party decried as flagrant gerrymanders and all of them ended up in court. It's just that, if the commissions were supposed to take the partisanship out, they haven't done it.

Defenders of commissions argue that their purpose was never to take the partisanship out of the process so much as it was to take some of the partisanship out of the outcome. It's hard to say, though, whether the final product in commission states is really all that different. There's no one set of good-government principles that political maps should follow, let alone an accepted way of proving that those principles have been met. While the maps produced in some commission states seem to suggest partisan meddling, there are also signs that the commissions ended up drawing more competitive districts than legislatures might have if left to their own devices.

In Colorado, for example, Republicans complained that the state legislative maps drew 10 GOP incumbents—including three members of their leadership—into just 5 seats. At the same time, however, the maps also greatly increased the number of seats that both Democrats and Republicans have a chance to win. Even Loevy, a critic of the process, says that Carrera deserved credit for upping the number of competitive seats.

Similarly, in California, the commission process clearly made a difference in terms of competitiveness. Stan Forbes, the independent who chaired the commission, points out that in the past decade, with maps the legislature created, only five times out of 765 elections did a congressional or legislative seat switch hands between the parties. "The 2001 lines were the incumbent protection act and they said so," says Forbes, a bookstore owner. "Everyone was candid that that was what happened."

This time, with the California commission forbidden from even viewing political data, the new congressional map has already shaken things up. Several of the seats are expected to be hotly contested by the parties throughout the decade. Six California members of Congress have announced they won't run again. Four others are in incumbent-on-incumbent races in two districts. With outcomes like those, it's no surprise the maps have prompted an animated debate.

"Anybody that does redistricting in any process, it's always a contentious endeavor," says Kim Brace, a redistricting consultant. "You're dealing with peoples' livelihood. You're making the decisions of does this person live or die, politically."

Governors and Executives

For the past couple of years, it has been a mixed blessing to hold high executive office at the state level. On the downside, state executives continue to struggle with the fallout from the Great Recession; tight budgets mean tough choices. This is especially the case for governors, who often have the unenviable job of putting together budgetary blueprints for legislative consideration. Heads of executive agencies ranging from secretaries of state to attorneys general, though, are not immune. These agencies have been forced to make do with a lot less. Despite the ugly budget situation, there is an upside; state executives are well positioned to make a difference. Regardless of gloomy finances—and sometimes because of gloomy finances—executives are finding ways to influence big-ticket policy items, not just within in their states but nationally.

Making those sorts of differences has not been without controversy. Gov. Scott Walker, R-WI, and Gov. John Kasich, R-OH, executives who rode to power in the red tide election of 2010, spent the first half of 2011 successfully pushing for reforms of the public labor market. They spent the second half dealing with blowback from successful efforts to fundamentally restructure the collective bargaining rights of public unions. Walker was the target of a recall, and Kasich's favored legislation was repealed through a ballot initiative. Yet though the efforts of Walker and Kasich were only partially successful, they triggered a broader national debate on public employee rights and compensation, a topic we will return to in Part VII.

Walker and Kasich were just two of thirty governors who were elected in 2010 and began making big differences in 2011 and 2012. All the new faces in the executive branch and the fact that many of them were reshaping governance in such fundamental ways is at least partially a product of some important differences between state and federal governments. For one thing, states differ from the federal government both in the number and in the nature of their elected executives. All state chief executives win their jobs by a statewide popular ballot, and so do many other state executives (attorneys general, secretaries of state, state auditors, etc.). What this means is a broad cross-section of state executives have made promises to voters and are often eager to put them into action. In contrast, not a single federal executive officer is chosen by a comparable nationwide popular vote (the president is chosen by the Electoral College). No other federal executive—attorney general, secretary of state, whatever—has even a passing relationship with a ballot box. All are appointed by the president and serve at his or her pleasure.

The readings in this section highlight the impact that state executives are having as they pursue often wide-ranging agendas that have national, not just state, implications. The first essay, by Mary Branham, is a Q&A session with Gov. Christine Gregoire, D-WA. Gregoire recognizes that the state governments are facing one of the most challenging environments in generations. Meeting those challenges requires making some hard choices, but if states face rather than duck those choices,

they have the opportunity to make lasting contributions on a broad range of issues.

The second essay, by John Gramlich, is a profile of Gov. Sam Brownback, R-KS. Like Walker and Kasich, Brownback came to office on the crest of the Republican electoral tide in 2010. In many ways, Brownback is pushing a bigger and bolder agenda than his colleagues in Wisconsin and Ohio. It may end up being more successful because Brownback is not just taking on bigger issues; he represents the new face of Republicans in Kansas, which is conservative, committed, and not particularly interested in compromise.

The third essay, also by John Gramlich, takes a look at three more governors who came to office in 2011 after successful campaigns in 2010. Gov. Terry Branstad, R-IA, Gov. Jerry Brown, D-CA, and Gov. John Kitzhaber, D-OR, however, are not gubernatorial rookies like Walker, Kasich, or Brownback. All have previously served as governors. Indeed, they represented more than three decades of gubernatorial experience before returning to executive office in 2011. The big question is whether that experience will help these governors meet the tough challenges faced by their states.

Finally, Alan Greenblatt looks at a non-gubernatorial executive, Secretary of State Kris Kobach, R-KS. Kobach may seem an unlikely leader of a national immigration reform movement, but that is exactly what he is. Thanks to Kobach, ground zero of the national debate on immigration is not Congress in Washington, D.C., but a state executive office in Topeka, Kansas.

Washington Governor: "Set Your Partisanship Behind You, Now It's Time to Govern"

By Mary Branham

16

Gov. Christine Gregoire, D-WA, says tough times require executives willing to put partisanship aside and make tough choices.

From *Capitol Ideas*, July/August 2011.

STATES ARE CONFRONTED WITH DAUNTING CHALLENGES. WHAT CAN STATE LEADERS DO TO CREATE A CLIMATE IN WHICH PEOPLE FOCUS ON SOLUTIONS?

"This year, knowing full well we face unprecedented times, we all set a path (in Washington) of working in a very bipartisan way and not letting politics and partisanship get in our way. We're in a special session. . . . It has been an example, in my opinion, of how you deal with very tough problems in unprecedented times. You set aside everything else, realize you work for the people, work together and get the job done."

WHAT ARE THE MOST IMPORTANT QUALITIES OF A SUCCESSFUL STATE GOVERNMENT IN THE 21ST CENTURY?

" . . . At the end of the day, government has to be absolutely flexible, which as you well know, it is not. (It needs to be) absolutely adaptable; seeing technology as its friend; making sure the lesson learned here is we have sustainable budgets for the long haul and a rainy day fund in case we should run into tough times, with an absolute emphasis on the key to the future, which in my opinion is education. . . . I think all states—it's not unique to us—all states are going to have to fundamentally change, just like every business that's going to survive this recession and, frankly, every family has had to change . . . in order to get out of this recession."

WHY HAS WASHINGTON'S GOVERNMENT MANAGEMENT ACCOUNTABILITY AND PERFORMANCE PROGRAM BEEN SUCCESSFUL?

"I think anybody would say that it's a success. We use data. We have performance measures. We use it as an opportunity to train managers for succession purposes because it gets you at a table looking at real-time data, and asking you to solve the problem. It sets some new standards. We have oral forums. We celebrate our successes and then set higher standards. When things aren't working we go after why not. . . . I don't think it works if you don't have absolute engagement from the top."

WHAT ADVICE WOULD YOU GIVE TO OTHER STATES INTERESTED IN REPLICATING GMAP?

"I warn people if you're going to do it, it's not for the faint. It takes discipline. It takes a laser-like focus. It takes time and it takes continuity. We implemented it in June 2005 and I have not let up one bit. I still go to (the meetings) myself. We celebrate our successes. And when things aren't good, we ask the tough questions and we hold people accountable."

WHAT DOES YOUR HEALTH CARE PLAN LOOK LIKE FOR WASHINGTONIANS?

"Our goal is more affordable health care through higher quality health care. . . . We're implementing the Affordable Care Act. We're one of the first states on the exchanges. We've also said it isn't just about health care reform in the Affordable Care Act, it's about the fact that my state budget is getting eaten up by health care inflation. I can't spend as much money as I could on education because I'm spending it on health care inflation. We brought in the business community. We brought in providers. We brought in insurers. We brought everybody to the table. We set a goal of inflation of no more than 4 percent across the state, with savings projected of $26 billion over 10 years for our state."

HOW IMPORTANT IS INTERNATIONAL TRADE TO WASHINGTON?

"It's our bread and butter. We're the most trade-dependent state in the country. One in three jobs, directly or indirectly, is related to trade in my state. We export about $53 billion a year as of last year. Boeing is a big part of it, no question about it, but it's information technology, it's industrial machinery, it's wood, it's medical products, a big agriculture sector. We're the leading exporter on things like apples and cherries and pears and hops and frozen potatoes. So our total trade import/export was $145 billion in 2010. . . . It's our ticket out of this recession, but it is also our future."

WHAT ATTRACTS BUSINESSES TO WASHINGTON?

"We have wireless technology to software to renewable energy to aerospace. Global health is a new burgeoning field for us. We have all of those things going for us. We have a highly educated workforce; 30 percent of our workforce has at least a bachelor's degree. We've got great research institutions. . . . We're very diverse people, which helps us in trade and all of that. We have a tax structure that's very appealing to business. We have low-cost renewable energy that's important for new sectors like composites. At the end of the day, what always ranks in the top tier of companies that are here or want to come here is our quality of life."

HOW DOES THE STATE HELP THE UNIVERSITY OF WASHINGTON CULTIVATE ITS RESEARCH STRENGTH?

"Every time I go on a trade mission, I bring the university with me. We have exchanges of students and faculty. We sign agreements. We meet alums in every country we go to at large receptions, typically at the ambassador's home. I created the life sciences discovery fund. It's a partnership between our two research institutions, University of Washington and Washington State University, and the private sector. We have a star researcher program where we try to attract and retain innovative faculty; and we have a new emphasis on commercialization of the research. UW is ranked the 16th best research institution in the world. It is (the) largest public university in terms of grants. It's an economic engine in my state."

WHAT HAVE YOU LEARNED THAT MIGHT BE HELPFUL FOR THE 29 NEW GOVERNORS ACROSS THE COUNTRY?

"The first thing I said when they came in was, 'Set your partisanship behind you, now it's time to govern.' . . . Nobody knows what it's like to be governor other than another governor. We share, we trade ideas, we work together. . . . (NGA) had an orientation retreat after they were elected, before they were sworn in. We really shared with them (that) this is probably the most difficult time to be governor since the Depression.

Whatever decision they make, however they go about their business: keep in touch, keep in tune, listen, educate, be a partner with the public that they serve. So at the end, the public understands they've got their best interest at heart."

WHAT ARE YOUR GOALS FOR THE NEXT FEW YEARS?

"As a governor, you set your goals and then circumstances take over, so my number one priority now is get us through the recession and that means I've got to put people back to work. I've got to make it affordable for (the) state and families and businesses to provide health care and I've got to make sure we've got an eye on the future, which means we have to have a highly skilled highly educated workforce, so education has got to be paramount. They're all connected."

17

In Kansas, Governor Sam Brownback Drives a Rightward Shift

By John Gramlich

Kansas's new governor leads a charge to the right that promises to reshape public policies and change the political landscape.

TOPEKA, Kansas—For 14 years, Sam Brownback represented Kansas in the United States Senate, a chamber known for its slow and plodding pace. Now governor, Brownback is in no mood to wait.

The Republican, entering the second year of his term, is pushing what may be the boldest agenda of any governor in the nation. While Republican leaders in other states pursue narrower agendas or steer toward the political middle in a presidential election year, Brownback effectively is betting that Kansans want to see much more, not less, of the conservative vision he started building last year.

The governor's to-do list amounts to a blueprint for fiscally and socially conservative state government. He wants lawmakers to slash and eventually eliminate the personal income tax while getting rid of 23 tax credit programs, including the Earned Income Tax Credit for the working poor. He wants to cap state spending growth at 2 percent a year, a rate that could force deep budget cuts if it doesn't keep up with inflation or a growing demand for state services. He is planning to overhaul a school financing formula that has been in place for two decades, favoring an approach that could result in less state money for large, poor districts.

Multi-billion dollar entitlement programs also are in the governor's sights. Brownback wants to convert the state pension system from a defined-benefit to a defined-contribution model, asking state workers to contribute more of their salaries to their retirement. On Medicaid, Brownback wants to place every one of the program's roughly 330,000 enrollees into a private, managed-care system,

From *Stateline.org*, January 2012.

which he says will save hundreds of millions of dollars over the coming years.

Each of the proposals carries significant political risks for Brownback and, if approved, would represent a considerable legislative achievement on its own. But the governor says he will be disappointed if he does not get all of them on his desk by the time the legislature wraps up its session in May. "They all lean up against each other," Brownback told *Stateline* in an interview in his Capitol office last week. "I'm not sure which of those pieces you can pull out."

Brownback's agenda, meanwhile, sets up a key political showdown with moderates in his own party. Republicans have an overwhelming 92-to-33 majority in the state House of Representatives, and their caucus is dominated by Tea Party–backed conservatives. But a coalition of moderate Republicans and Democrats controls the 40-member state Senate, essentially standing between Brownback and his biggest policy goals. Observers inside and outside the statehouse believe Brownback's sweeping agenda is intended to draw a bright line between the two factions of Kansas Republicans ahead of GOP primary elections in August, when a shift of just a few Senate seats could tilt the balance of power in his favor.

"I think he may want to create a bunch of tough votes for moderate Republicans," says Burdett Loomis, a political science professor at the University of Kansas and former consultant for Democratic Governor Kathleen Sebelius. "Certainly, the Brownback administration would be happy to get rid of six or eight of them."

MODERATES FACE RECKONING

Once known for the kind of moderate Republicanism embodied by Bob Dole, Kansas swung sharply to the right during the last election cycle, so much so that many here wonder whether Dole could win a statewide election anymore.

Brownback, a Tea Party favorite who sailed into office with 63 percent of the vote, represents the new face of Kansas Republicans. He spent his first year in office slashing the budget, abolishing whole agencies and even creating an Office of the Repealer, a new administrative post tasked with identifying and

> **The Brownback agenda**
>
> **Budget:** Cap state spending growth at 2 percent a year.
>
> **Taxes:** Reduce personal income tax rates and eliminate 23 tax credit programs.
>
> **Schools:** Revamp financing formula for K–12 education.
>
> **Pensions:** Change state system from defined-benefit to defined-contribution.
>
> **Medicaid:** Convert health care program into managed-care model.

eliminating government regulations. A Catholic who is outspoken about his faith, he also signed some of the nation's toughest anti-abortion bills into law and sought to cut off funding for Planned Parenthood. In one of his most controversial moves, he made Kansas the only state to eliminate all funding for the arts, arguing it was not a core function of government and that private funds could be used instead.

The way Brownback sees it, "I'm the first conservative governor in probably 50 years in Kansas," even though the state has elected six Republicans during that span.

This year, all legislative seats are up for election, with the 40 members of the state Senate facing the voters for the first time since the Tea Party became a powerful force at the polls. At least nine moderate Republican senators already are facing primary challenges from the right, and at least five of them will square off against current House members. Many members of the House are not shy about their disdain for the Senate, where several high-profile conservative bills, including a phasing out of the personal income tax, stalled last year.

The Senate is run by "liberal Republicans and Democrats," says state Representative Larry Powell, a conservative who hopes to unseat moderate Senate President Stephen Morris in a primary.

The confrontational, House-versus-Senate dynamic has been palpable in the halls of the statehouse in the early days of this year's legislative session. Earlier this month, in a move that some interpreted as opposition research gathering, a conservative state representative was caught secretly tape-recording one of the Senate moderates who is facing a primary challenge in the summer.

Brownback insists he will not get involved in the GOP primary process. But organizations with close ties to his administration have made clear that they intend to target moderates by funneling money and resources into primaries that are normally low-turnout affairs. The organizations include the Kansas Chamber of Commerce and Americans for Prosperity, a political action committee affiliated with Koch Industries, a Wichita-based conglomerate that has funded conservative causes around the country.

"I know that's a goal of a number of these conservative groups," says Morris, the Senate president and a 20-year veteran of the chamber. "They want to purge the party of anyone that's considered reasonable."

TAX CUTS AS "CENTERPIECE"

Before any primary votes are cast, however, lawmakers will weigh in on the governor's proposals, beginning with the tax plan that he views as the centerpiece of his agenda and one that is necessary to help him accomplish his other goals.

Like most governors, Brownback says his top priority is creating jobs, and he firmly believes that tax cuts are the way to grow the economy. While Kansas is projecting a surplus and has an unemployment rate of 6.5 percent, two points below the national average, Brownback believes the state must do all it can to protect itself from sharp cutbacks in the federal budget, which he thinks are imminent. Kansas already felt the pain of proposed federal cutbacks earlier this month, when Boeing announced it would eliminate 2,100 jobs at an assembly plant in Wichita as a result of expected cuts in the defense budget.

"The federal bubble is bursting," Brownback says.

To prepare, the governor is pushing what he calls a "fairer, flatter and simpler" plan that slashes the personal income tax from 6.45 percent to 4.9 percent for income above $15,000 a year, and from 3.5 percent to 3 percent for income below $15,000. The proposal also would eliminate income taxes on tens of thousands of small businesses.

The governor and his economic team, including the former Reagan economist Arthur Laffer, argue that the lower income tax rates will immediately bring more

people and companies to Kansas, leading to growth that can offset lost revenue and help the state pay for other changes in pensions, school funding and Medicaid.

Steve Anderson, Brownback's budget director, regularly cites federal data showing that Kansans are moving to other states where personal income taxes are lower, while those who move to Kansas tend to come from states with higher income taxes. To Anderson, and to Brownback, the correlation is clear: People move where taxes are lower.

Others, however, say it is unlikely that many more people will move to Kansas searching for lower income taxes. Critics are also attacking the plan for its effects on low-wage earners. While Brownback talks about ending a tax system that "picks winners and losers," his own Department of Revenue projected earlier this month that the poorest would collectively pay $90 million more under his proposal while the wealthy would see big savings. That is because the plan also keeps in place a 1-cent sales tax hike passed two years ago, and does away with tax credit programs that help the working poor. Democrats have zeroed in on the plan and even Brownback's allies in the state House are proposing alternatives.

"It's Robin Hood in reverse," Senate Minority Leader Anthony Hensley, a Democrat, said of Brownback's tax plan, according to The Associated Press. "This is stealing from the poor to give to the rich."

MORE FIGHTS AHEAD

How Brownback's tax plan and other policy proposals fare is likely to hinge on the moderate Republicans in the state Senate, some of whom have already expressed reservations about the other items on the governor's list.

Morris, the Senate president, says he is wary of approving a "one size fits all" approach to school funding, suggesting that the debate over a new K–12 financing formula could be every bit as contentious as the fight over taxes. Meanwhile, Morris says he has difficulty adding up the numbers on Brownback's proposed 2-percent cap on annual spending growth.

Increases in pension and Medicaid costs alone "could very well equal 4 or 5 percent every year in (spending) increases, which means that if you have a 2-percent cap, you're going to have to go back and keep cutting other programs," Morris says. "So I'm not sure how that would work."

But Brownback is already well on his way to reshaping the state's Medicaid system. The governor has broad leeway to make administrative changes on his own, and many lawmakers say the managed-care model is a near-certainty. The state recently put out a request-for-proposal to see which companies will run the new system.

"The honest truth is that the legislature cannot stop this process," state Senator Vicki Schmidt, a moderate Republican, told a town hall meeting at a public library in Topeka last week. "The only way the legislature can stop this process is to not fund it, and if we were to not fund the contract, we would not have a Medicaid program, and that is not an answer."

Brownback himself acknowledges that his agenda this year is "very aggressive," but he does not see any of his proposals as particularly surprising. "I've heard of most of this stuff (in other states)," he says.

Indeed, other Republican-led states have experimented with many of the same changes Brownback is pushing: Florida, for instance, converted its Medicaid program into a managed care system, Michigan passed a sweeping tax cut and plenty of states cut back pension benefits for public workers last year. Brownback simply wants to make all of those changes simultaneously.

18

After Years Away, Comeback Governors Try to Rekindle Their Power

By John Gramlich

Three recently elected governors are hoping experience helps them deal with the challenges their states face. California, Iowa, and Oregon are being led by governors who are less fresh faces than a blast from the past.

The 2010 elections brought a sea of fresh faces to governor's offices around the country, from Democrat Dan Malloy, who is pushing broad liberal changes in Connecticut, to Republican Nikki Haley, the South Carolina conservative who, at 39, is the youngest state chief executive in the nation.

But in three states, 2010 marked a return to the days of old.

California, Iowa and Oregon all elected former governors who, between them, had 32 years of gubernatorial experience under their belts even before they settled in for fresh four-year terms in January. With an average age of 67 and most of their political lives behind them, the trio—Jerry Brown in California, Terry Branstad in Iowa and John Kitzhaber in Oregon—represents insider experience and familiarity in a year more commonly associated with barn-storming newcomers like Malloy, Haley and the tea party.

Brown, a Democrat who was known as "Governor Moonbeam" because of his lofty and sometimes eccentric policy goals as a two-term California governor in the 1970s and 1980s, is also a former mayor of Oakland, California secretary of state and attorney general, and three-time candidate for president. Branstad, a Republican, served 16 consecutive years in Iowa's top office, making him one of the longest-serving governors in U.S. history. And Kitzhaber, a former emergency room doctor and two-term Democratic governor, is best-known for promoting a nationally recognized health insurance overhaul in Oregon before reemerging as a gubernatorial candidate in the thick of the national health care debate in 2010. All three upended the conventional wisdom that voters last year were in no mood for insiders. (In two other states, Georgia and Maryland, former governors lost their bids to return to office.)

From *Stateline.org*, August 2011.

But while Brown, Branstad and Kitzhaber have the advantage of experience and name recognition, their encore appearances on the gubernatorial stage show that government insiders aren't automatically better at turning campaign promises into policy. All three men, absent from gubernatorial office for at least eight years, are finding that the dynamics around them are substantially different now. Each of them has had to adapt, with varying degrees of success so far.

"THE NEW REALITY"

Their new challenges range from the cerebral to the mundane. Kitzhaber has picked up right where he left off, striving to find ways to make health insurance cheaper. In Iowa, Branstad notes that one of the biggest adjustments has been to the everyday practicalities of governing in the 21st century. "Technology is so much different," he pointed out in a telephone interview with *Stateline*. "Every cell phone's a camera."

But it is California that has probably seen the most significant changes in the nearly three decades since Brown last held the job. When he first took office in 1975, Brown was 36 years old, the state enjoyed budget surpluses and the party in power could accomplish its legislative goals without requiring a supermajority. Now 73 and the oldest governor in California history, Brown runs a state where finances are in shambles and where, because of structural changes passed at the ballot box, Democrats cannot pass the budget they want, even though they hold commanding majorities in both legislative chambers. Through Proposition 13, a ballot measure approved during Brown's first term in 1978, tax increases require a two-thirds majority to be enacted legislatively, and Democrats have been unable to push through their preferred budget because no Republicans have agreed to raise taxes.

Making matters worse is the fact that partisanship has run rampant in recent years, making compromise, particularly over taxes, an unlikely prospect. "Sacramento's always been a highly partisan place, but none of the old timers—and I'm an old timer—remember it being so harsh, so bitter, so divisive, so stalemated," says Jaime Regalado, a political science professor at California State University at Los Angeles. "This is the new reality that Governor Brown stepped back into."

Branstad and Kitzhaber, too, must negotiate directly with the minority party to pass legislation, a fact that makes governing trickier for any chief executive.

In Iowa, Democrats control the state Senate, which is nothing new for Branstad, who dealt with a Democratic legislature for most of his previous 16 years in office. What has complicated the dynamic is the emergence of the tea party, which did not exist when Branstad was last in office and has now become a powerful player in the state legislature. "Because the extreme conservative wing of the Republican Party is in control of the House, (Branstad) has to toe a pretty conservative line," says Mack Shelley, an Iowa State University political science professor.

In Oregon's case, there is an even 30-to-30 split in the state House of Representatives, giving Republicans a seat at the table after being politically marginalized for the past few years. For Kitzhaber, however, it is nothing new for Republicans to have power; instead, what is different for him is that they have relatively little.

In his previous two terms, Kitzhaber dealt exclusively with a Republican-led legislature, clashing so often with GOP leaders that he took on the nickname "Dr. No" for his record number of vetoes, and he famously called his state "ungovernable." Even the official biography of Kitzhaber on the Oregon State Archives website notes his "chronically bad working relationship" with GOP lawmakers. This time, Kitzhaber is dealing with a smaller opposition party and one that Democrats say is less confrontational than the Oregon GOP of the 1990s. The result was a surprisingly harmonious legislative session.

DIFFERENT OUTCOMES

In that 2011 session, Kitzhaber won more power over K–12 schools than any governor in Oregon history and secured passage of a new law requiring state employees to contribute part of their paychecks toward health insurance. In both cases, he relied on Republican votes to pursue measures that alienated unions, a core Democratic constituency and one that was essential to his own election in November. The man once known as "Dr. No" issued just a single veto in 2011, compared with the 69 he delivered in 1999.

There are several interpretations of Oregon's peaceful session. For one thing, the governor did not pursue higher taxes—which, in Oregon, as in many other places, are anathema to the GOP and often lead to government stalemates. For another, Republicans did not have outright power in either chamber as they did during the 1990s, meaning that any legislation that reached the governor's desk would, by its nature, have to be bipartisan.

Bill Wyatt, who served as Kitzhaber's chief of staff during his first two terms in office, says the governor used the split House to his advantage this year by pursuing moderate policies that could attract votes on both sides of the aisle. "When we woke up one or two mornings after the election and it was apparent that there would be a split in the House, he was the first one to say that this could be a tremendous opportunity," Wyatt says. "That was the wisdom of 25 years of experience."

Bill Sizemore, a well-known anti-tax advocate who lost to Kitzhaber in the 1998 gubernatorial election, credits Kitzhaber for reaching out to Republicans, but believes that the session would not have been so harmonious if the GOP had more power. "I think if we had a Republican-controlled legislature this time," Sizemore says, "he'd be 'Dr. No' all over again."

In California, Brown has found no bipartisan success. Setting a frantic pace for his third term in office, the governor pledged to have his first budget done within 60 days of his inauguration. But it wasn't until the last day of the fiscal year—two weeks after the state's constitutional budget deadline of June 15—that a budget finally was signed, and it was one that did not attract a single Republican vote. In addition, the budget assumed $4 billion in unforecast revenues over the coming year, stretching Brown's own pledge upon returning to office that he would not sign a budget that relied on "gimmicks."

Regalado, the Cal State political science professor, says Brown's difficulties with the legislature this year are not from a lack of trying to cooperate. Brown has spent countless hours meeting behind closed doors with lawmakers from the opposite party, and devoted months to wooing just four Republicans to agree to his original budget so it could pass. He never got them. The philosophical gap between California's two political parties has simply grown too wide, experts say.

Of the three returning governors, it may be Branstad who has turned out to be the most surprising to members of his own party and the opposition alike, taking a tough-minded approach that has steered in a more conservative direction than many lawmakers expected. Iowa's legislative session this year was the third-longest in state history as the result of a sharp divide between the Republican-led House and the Democratic-controlled Senate, and Branstad prioritized several pieces of legislation—including two-year budgets to replace the existing single-year versions—on which he showed little inclination to compromise. On several occasions, he warned Democrats that "a new sheriff" was in town.

"I think there was a real clear mandate from the people," he told *Stateline*.

In the end, he won about 85 percent of the funding for a two-year state budget and an overhaul of the state's economic development efforts, though he was not able to reduce property taxes and eliminate Iowa's universal preschool program, as he promised to do. What stands out to lawmakers on both sides of the aisle, however, is Branstad's more assertive approach to the legislature. Where Democrats see intractability and partisanship, many Republicans see a governor who has become a tougher conservative since he last held the job.

"I expected someone who would do quid pro quos," says Iowa House Speaker Kraig Paulsen, a Republican. "What I experienced was someone who had a laser focus on a smaller number of items and was really, really committed and worked those issues hard."

19

Kris Kobach Tackles Illegal Immigration

By Alan Greenblatt

The national debate on immigration reform is not being driven by lawmakers in Washington, DC. It is being driven by the Kansas secretary of state.

From *Governing*, March 2012.

Not many politicians still mount deer heads on the walls of their offices, but Kris Kobach isn't afraid of going after big game. Despite the relative modesty of his position—Kobach was elected Kansas secretary of state back in 2010—he is smack at the center of two of the most controversial issues states are facing today.

Shortly after taking office last year, Kobach convinced the Kansas Legislature to pass what is arguably the nation's strictest voter fraud law. But Kobach is known most widely for his efforts to turn illegal immigration into a front-burner issue at the state and local levels. "I don't know of anybody else driving the [illegal immigration] issue nationally as much as he is doing," says Kansas state Sen. Steve Abrams, a Republican.

Kobach helped draft the 2010 Arizona law that, among other things, requires state and local law enforcement officials to check the immigration status of individuals they have stopped and have "reasonable suspicion" to believe are in the country illegally. That law has since been imitated by several other states—thanks, in part, to Kobach's own doing. It may spread further if the U.S. Supreme Court upholds it this spring.

Kobach already enjoyed a victory before the Supreme Court last year with another Arizona law he helped write. That one requires businesses to use the federal E-Verify system to check the immigration status of employees. Kobach's success in drafting and defending laws meant to curb illegal immigration—not just in Arizona, but also in Alabama and other states and localities from Pennsylvania to Texas—has turned him into a leading figure of derision for some

Hispanic groups and liberal immigration advocates. After Kobach endorsed Mitt Romney for president in January, the leader of a group of Hispanic Republicans said that Romney had committed "political suicide" by accepting the embrace of such a controversial figure. "I did not anticipate when I first started working on this issue," he says, "that someday I would be seen as a hero by some and a horrible villain by others on a national scale."

For a relatively obscure figure like Kobach to have become a big political target shows that his opponents on the immigration issue view him not just as deeply misguided but also as a real threat. As much as anyone, Kobach has come up with the legal and political strategies that have helped make a traditionally federal concern into an area where states are, by any measure, far more active. Kobach may be the rare figure who has enough depth of understanding of complex issues to write 150-page appellate briefs, while also possessing the political skill to boil them down into digestible sound bites.

"Kris provided the understanding of complex legal issues that could take the sophistication of our approach to a whole new level," says Michael Hethmon, general counsel of the Immigration Reform Law Institute, a D.C.-based advocacy group where Kobach continues to serve as counsel despite his position.

His opponents say the ideas he expresses are dangerous and even inhumane—seeking to prompt illegal immigrants to "self-deport" by making their lives in the states so miserable and tenuous that they'll decide to leave. But even they grudgingly recognize Kobach has been an innovator in creating a role for states and localities to step in to once the feds failed to act on immigration. "He is one of the most important voices in the immigration debate, one of the key people who drove the debate to the states," says Tamar Jacoby, president of ImmigrationWorks USA, a business-backed group that sees immigrants as making important economic contributions. "I disagree with him 100 percent, but he's a very important and influential voice."

Kobach's background sounds like a parody of an inflated resumé: Eagle Scout, valedictorian, a national rowing champion despite a long battle with diabetes. At Harvard, his prize-winning student thesis—later published as a book—examined the role of the business community under apartheid in South Africa. On a scholarship from the British government, Kobach completed both a master's and a doctorate in political science from Oxford University. Then, after earning his law degree from Yale, he became a constitutional law professor. "Everything has the overachievement character about it," says John Ashcroft, who served as President George W. Bush's first attorney general and was once Kobach's boss. "I don't know of a surpassing resumé anywhere in public service than that of his, period."

Kobach caught the political bug early, as a self-described "debate geek" taking part in Kansas' active culture of political argument. Four years out of law school, he was elected to the Overland Park City Council, but his colleagues thought he'd soon have his eye on the next opportunity. "I didn't think he was going to stay on the City Council long," says Kansas state Sen. Tim Owens, a Republican. "I was there for 24 years. He was there for two."

In fact, Kobach grabbed one of the ultimate gold stars for overachievers—a White House fellowship. As it happened, it landed him in the Justice Department. He started in September 2001—a week before the terrorist attacks that, along with so much else, changed the department's entire approach to immigration and border strategy. Kobach quickly rose to become Ashcroft's chief adviser on these issues. Among the policies Kobach helped devise was the creation of the National Security Entry-Exit Registration System, or NSEERS—a controversial program that limited access to the country by individuals, primarily from certain Middle Eastern and North African countries, and required that they be fingerprinted, photographed and interrogated.

"America was no longer a setting in which we could enjoy the insulation of oceans to somehow provide a major component of our security," says Ashcroft. "Kris certainly became the point person in this respect and helped develop some strategies that were very effective."

The experience instructed Kobach in the ways in which local and state law enforcement officials often collaborated with their federal counterparts—and the ways in which they failed to do so. Several of the 9/11 hijackers—including several of the pilots—had previously been in local police custody when they were not in compliance with immigration law, yet they were let go. That, he describes as "a missed opportunity of tragic dimensions."

He wrote about this in a law review article. But as a practical matter, it became his mission to tie state and local law agencies more closely to federal immigration enforcement. Ideas such as requiring the use of E-Verify or creating penalties for landlords who rent to illegal immigrants came later, but the kernel of the idea for SB 1070, the Arizona law now under review by the Supreme Court, came to him while he was still at Justice. And, while he was working for Ashcroft, he came into contact with the Immigration Reform Law Institute, which provided the main base for his legal efforts.

It's fair to say that all of Kobach's ideas about how to discourage illegal immigration have proven to be controversial. Not all of them have passed legal muster. Some local officials whom he's advised regret falling under his sway, saying that he's saddled them with little more than headaches and legal bills. Kobach continues to act as the attorney for several of the jurisdictions whose laws he helped write.

Carol Dingman, former mayor pro tem of Farmers Branch, Texas, which is one of those cities that has had to spend millions to defend a Kobach-drafted immigration ordinance, wrote a letter to a newspaper complaining about him. "Our mayor said he was an expert in immigration law who would help the city on a pro bono (free) basis," she wrote. "Mr. Kobach was paid $100,000. So much for pro bono."

But Kobach has managed to position himself at the center of state and local immigration policies that are being pushed into spaces left open by federal law. It's not a role he's surrendered as secretary of state. "When he worked for Bush, he wrote the opinion that states can detain illegals, and now when he goes around the country, that's the opinion he cites," says Kansas state Rep. Ann Mah, a Democrat and Kobach critic. "In my mind, he's not looking for an immigration solution; he's looking for a job. Cities and states are spending millions defending his laws."

Even as his legal star was rising, Kobach found his climb up the political ladder to be a bit more slippery. He lost a race for Congress in 2004, his opponent having been successful at portraying him as too much of a right-wing ideologue to suit what was then the state's only Democratic district.

He became chairman of the state Republican Party in 2007, where he courted controversy by setting up a Loyalty Committee designed to ferret out and punish local party officials who had helped Democrats. (Kobach later conceded privately that the name was a mistake.) Just days after he announced his bid for secretary of state in 2009, the Federal Election Commission released an audit that found widespread instances of financial mismanagement during his tenure as state party chair. Kobach was quick to put the blame on the party's executive director, saying he'd been guilty of nothing other than a "very bad hiring decision."

All this didn't seem to hurt Kobach during his first statewide race. He overcame serious opposition in the GOP primary and easily defeated Chris Biggs, who had been appointed as the Democratic incumbent. Kobach fashioned himself as the "defender of cities and states that fight illegal immigration." He made voter ID requirements the central focus of his campaign, despite the fact that Biggs and his predecessors said that voter fraud was not a significant problem in the state. "My opponent was very successful in making the race about immigration, which of course is not anywhere near the responsibility of the secretary of state," Biggs says. "He managed to tie the immigration issue to the secretary of state race with a big bow around it."

Kobach is fond of pointing out that voter fraud is enmeshed in Kansas history, back to the 1850s when Missourians stuffed the ballot box to elect a pro-slavery territorial legislature. But even the figures he cites don't point to any such concerted efforts in contemporary times. The figure of 41 incidents of improper voter or registration activity—not actual voting—for 2010 is mainly made up of honest mistakes, says Mah, the Democratic state representative. Instead of examples of impersonation, illegal immigrants or dead people voting, the list is made up more of snowbirds seeking to vote in two states or felons who turned out to be ineligible. There wasn't any evidence that Kansas was seeing large numbers of illegal aliens voting, or that there was a conspiracy on the part of any party or group to affect the outcomes of elections, Biggs says.

During the campaign, Kobach complained that a Wichita man named Alfred K. Brewer had voted in the August 2010 primary, despite having died in 1996. It turned out the vote had been cast by his namesake son. "I don't think this is heaven, not when I'm raking leaves," Brewer told *The Wichita Eagle*.

But Kobach was able to use an argument that's been effective in other states. He said that requiring voters to show a photo ID is no burden at a time when they have to do the same to board an airplane, enter a federal building or even, as he puts it, to "buy the kind of Sudafed that works." He notes that in the first election to be held since the law was enacted—a tax issue in Cimarron, a small town near Dodge City—every voter managed to produce a photo ID, with the exception of one woman who didn't bring hers to the polls in protest against the new law.

Kobach says he "bent over backward" to guard against any conceivable scenarios that might prevent a citizen from being able to register and vote. Still—and again, as in other states—critics of the new law say it will discourage voting among people who lack photo IDs and, in some cases, the birth certificates that may be necessary to get them. (The Kansas law requires that people offer proof of citizenship when they register.) They argue the bill Kobach helped pushed through—not at all unique among states, but tougher than the general run of recent voter ID laws—corrects a nonexistent problem and instead will serve mainly to depress and even suppress voting, most notably among the very old, very young, women and persons of color. In other words, demographic groups that by and large would be expected to support Democrats. "He's doing a better job as secretary of state than he did when he was the Republican state chair," says Mah.

Some Kansas legislators say Kobach can be sloppy with the facts—that despite his glittering academic credentials and his confident, rapid-fire way of speaking, he doesn't always follow through or have his figures correct. As he goes about an average day—addressing legislators as "you guys" during a committee hearing, or speaking to leadership training groups visiting the Capitol—Kobach sometimes does manage to mix up numbers and dates.

Mah speaks of Kobach almost as though he were a virus—a political force that must be stopped in Kansas before he spreads to other states. Just as happened with his immigration language, Mah worries that his especially rigorous approach to voting and registration requirements will influence lawmakers elsewhere. The notion that he's a kind of Johnny Appleseed of conservative legislation is one that Kobach happily subscribes to. He notes that Alabama's voter ID bill copied the Kansas language on proof of citizenship verbatim. "I think Kansas deserves some credit for crafting a model that other states can follow," Kobach told the Kansas House Standing Committee on Federal and State Affairs recently. Kobach influenced Alabama legislation even more directly last year, when he helped draft that state's illegal immigration statute.

Some legislators in Kansas complain that because he's still going around and writing laws in other states—and defending other jurisdictions' laws in court—Kobach is doing a disservice to the Kansas constituents who expect him to devote his attention and energy to his state office. The state ethics commission ruled that Kobach can't accept speaking fees, but won't stop him from pursuing legal or political activities elsewhere. State Rep. Melody McCray-Miller, a Democrat, says Kobach's outside pursuits are unethical anyway.

No one in Topeka seems to expect that secretary of state is the last political job that Kobach, who is 45, will strive after. That leads officials, such as McCray-Miller, to complain that Kobach is using the position to raise his personal visibility, giving him a "bully pulpit" much bigger than he commanded as a constitutional law professor. "He is using a state-held position to further a larger agenda that is not benefiting the voters he is supposed to be protecting," she says.

Kobach hasn't succeeded in persuading his home state to stiffen laws regarding illegal immigration. The state's agricultural and meatpacking interests haven't been encouraged by news reports of crops rotting in the field in Alabama after Kobach's law passed there.

Kobach has argued in court against several state laws offering in-state college tuition rates to children of illegal immigrants, but hasn't been able to convince his own Legislature. (Legislation to block in-state tuition passed the House overwhelmingly last year, but died in the Senate.) The Kansas program requires students to have lived in the state at least three years, which is proof enough that its main intent is to offer a brighter future to children who never intended to break the law themselves, says state Rep. Mario Goico, a Republican who was born in Cuba. "This is not an issue of nationality or illegal immigration—it's an issue of a child getting an education," Goico says. "When you were 14 or 15, did your parents ask for your opinion to move to another state, let alone to another country?"

Kobach remains hopeful that legislators will see things his way—particularly if fellow conservatives are successful in their campaign to oust the dominant moderate Republicans from control of the state Senate this fall. As for his work in other states, Kobach says there's no conflict with the demands of his day job. He offers up as proof the large amount of legislation he managed to push through during his first year on the job.

Kobach maintains that he's able to do his outside legal and political work on his own time. He says he put the final touches on the Alabama statute one weekend while sitting in a turkey blind.

When the issue was raised by Biggs and his Republican primary opponents, Kobach says he made it clear to voters and the media that he would be "a full-time, effective secretary of state"—but that he would also continue to advise cities and states elsewhere. "I can draft a brief from my home at 10 o'clock at night," he says. "I am going to be using my spare time trying to stop illegal immigration instead of playing golf."

VI

Courts

State judicial systems are surprisingly big operations, at least compared to their federal counterpart. Consider that the entire judicial branch of the federal government is run by the fewer than 1,000 judges who preside over all the so-called Article III courts (named after the source of their constitutional authority): the U.S. Supreme Court, courts of appeal, district courts, and the court of international trade. In comparison, Texas alone requires nearly four times as many judges to run its court system.[1]

The size of state court systems is not really that surprising because they handle the large majority of civil and criminal cases adjudicated in the United States. From a speeding ticket to murder, divorce to slander, whatever the infraction or dispute chances are it will be settled somewhere in a state rather than the federal judicial system. If anything, state court systems are not big enough—they are often backlogged, and in some cases judges are forced to prioritize what cases they actually hear. As you might imagine, these court systems can be quite expensive to run and maintain. It is not just a judge's salary you have to worry about but support staff, building maintenance, records administration, and so on. The bill for justice can get pretty big, pretty fast. Paying that bill has become increasingly difficult over the past few years.

Like every other branch of government, state judicial systems have been feeling a big budget squeeze. How bad? Well, the chief justice of the Georgia State Supreme Court begged pencils for law clerks off a research firm. State budget cuts meant the California Superior Court in the county of San Francisco faced nearly a $14 million deficit for the 2011–2012 fiscal year, forcing layoffs, closing twenty-five courtrooms, and slowing court operations to a crawl. Presiding Judge Katherine Feinstein was blunt about the impact of the fiscal squeeze: "The civil justice system in San Francisco is collapsing," she said. The courts would prioritize cases that by law have to be adjudicated within certain time limits. Beyond that, "justice will neither be swift nor accessible."[2]

It is not just the court systems that are facing the squeeze but entire state criminal justice systems. Whether a prison sentence is just or not is increasingly less of an issue than how much it costs to lock someone up. Depending on the state and the facility, it can cost $50,000 to keep someone behind bars. That's $50,000 not being spent on roads or education, or, well, keeping courtrooms open. The general theme of the readings in this section is how court systems and criminal justice systems are being shaped by the severe budget difficulties states have been dealing with for the past three or four years. This is mostly not a pretty story because justice is not cheap and states increasingly cannot afford it.

The first reading is a report by Daniel Hall, of the National Center for State Courts, that provides an overview of the financial impact of the Great Recession on courts and the strategies developed to deal with that impact. Some of these strategies have helped provide short-term financial relief but have long-term consequences for the health of state court systems.

The next two readings deal with state attempts to reduce the cost of prisons. The first, by Emily Badger, takes a look at privatizing prisons. State governments have increasingly looked to private contractors to run prisons as a cost-saving measure. However, an analysis finds that using for-profit companies has not led to the expected reductions. The second, by John Gramlich, examines California's penal downsizing movement. Prisons in California are shedding inmates as a way to deal with harsh budget realities.

The last reading deals with a couple of underexamined impacts of the new focus on costs in the criminal justice system. Richard Williams explores how the cost of having a death penalty is forcing some states to rethink their stand on capital punishment.

NOTES

1. The Texas court system, from municipal courts to the state Supreme Court, has approximately 3,400 judges: www.courts.state.tx.us/

2. Superior Court of California, "San Franciscans Face Long Lines, 5-Year Case Delays from State Budget Cuts That Force the Court to Lay Off 200 Employees, Close 25 Courtrooms," News Release, July 18, 2011.

20

Reshaping the Face of Justice: The Economic Tsunami Continues

By Daniel J. Hall

Tight budgets are forcing courts to rethink how they do business. How can courts adapt to new fiscal realities while avoiding long-term harm to the services they provide?

From National Center for State Courts, 2011.

The Great Recession continues to leave state courts reeling. Across the country courts are being squeezed by eroding resources coupled with an increasing demand for services. Like compound interest, three years of the recession is having a cumulative impact on courts. Several years of cutting staff, reducing salaries, limiting the hours of operation, and shedding functions have forced many courts to cut services to the point where the hollowing out their organizations—permanently eroding the capacity to deliver services—is no longer a threat but a reality. The end of the recession is not in sight. However, through reengineering many courts are reshaping themselves to fit this new reality. These courts offer a beacon to guide courts from crisis to stability. This article chronicles that journey.

According to the Center on Budget and Policy Priorities, 46 state governments face budget deficits in FY 2011. Eighteen have shortfalls of over 20 percent; 10 states have budgets that are short between 10 percent and 20 percent; and 18 state budgets are between 1 percent and 10 percent short. Only a few state governments do not have a shortfall. Shortfalls projected through the first five years of this recession have reached $626 billion. The last recession, which lasted four years, culminated in a $240 billion shortfall. The next few years are not promising. Over the past four years the stimulus provided to states from the Recovery Act mitigated the shortfall by $164 billion. From here on out there are few funds to cushion the shortfalls.

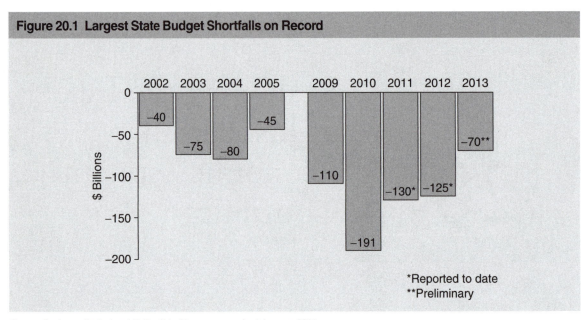

Figure 20.1 Largest State Budget Shortfalls on Record

Source: Center on Budget and Policy Priorities survey, revised January 2011.

Budget cuts are having a cumulative negative effect on courts. State court administrators reported that 29 states had budget decreases for FY 2011. In FY 2010, 35 state courts reported deficits, and in FY 2009, 33 courts reported deficits. While 13 state courts reported small increases in FY 2011 over FY 2010, most of these increases are erased when looking at the cuts that were taken over the two previous years. Most courts have adopted strategies to meet immediate cuts, rather than developed strategies to address the long-term financial malaise. For the third year in a row, strategies have included holding clerical positions vacant, 31 states; holding judicial support positions open, 31 states; freezing salaries, 28 states; holding judicial positions vacant, 25 states; increasing fees and fines, 21 states; requiring staff furloughs with pay reductions, 15 states; reducing the hours of court operations, 14 states; reducing the use of retired judges, 14 states; laying off staff, 13 states; reducing salaries, 8 states; and furloughing judicial officers with a reduction in pay, 8 states (COSCA Budget Survey, NCSC, September 2010).

Three years of implementing these short-term strategies is beginning to hollow-out judicial institutions.

For example, in small-to-medium-sized courts, staff shortages have led to errors that impact defendants by failing to cancel warrants in a timely manner, leading to wrongful arrests. There are fewer judicial support staff (court reporters and law clerks), which forces judges to prioritize the cases and limits the amount of judicial attention. There are more pro se litigants requiring more help and taking more time. Court staff is confronted by more socially challenged people who feel the stress of their own financial situation. Large courts report that domestic-relations temporary orders and parenting-time disputes are delayed. The postponement of these hearings and dispositions has a profound effect on families during difficult emotional and economic times. Processing times for clerical operations, including data entry, records management, financial transactions, and customer service, are increasing. Delays in processing default judgments are becoming apparent in many jurisdictions. Early retirement incentives offered to experienced court staff are creating a "brain drain" throughout courts. As a final example, in Iowa, all courts now operate at 12 percent below staffing standards, causing significant delays in case processing. Even relatively small courts now take up to five days to process an order.

Some courts are having a difficult time keeping pace with the volume of litigation. In Massachusetts, while the clearance rate remains fairly stable, the number of cases pending beyond the time standards increased by almost 6,000 in the first six months of 2010. Backlogs and delays are increasing in Minnesota. Almost one-third of the serious felony dispositions in 2009 (29 percent) occurred beyond the 12-month time standards. Clearance rates for minor criminal cases have fallen below 100 percent for the last five years, resulting in increased numbers of pending cases. It now takes more than a year for a misdemeanor case to be set for trial in many areas of that state. The Utah courts are seeing considerable delay in civil cases. The average age of pending cases is up 84 days over the past two years, approximately 50 percent for many civil cases.

The unprecedented depth and length of the budget crisis pose a real threat to the judiciary. Courts need to take measures to avoid the hollowing out of their institutions. What is needed is an approach that delivers significant operational efficiencies while preserving or improving services. This is called reengineering, restructuring, streamlining, etc. Many courts are undertaking this type of effort. The National Center for State Courts (NCSC) has worked with six states that have significantly reengineered their services—Minnesota, Vermont, New Hampshire, Nebraska, Maine, and Oregon. Four states have done their own reengineering—Arizona, Iowa, Michigan, and Utah. NCSC has begun to work with New Mexico and Kansas. Individual courts, such as Sacramento and Orange County, California, have done significant work also. These pioneers are breaking ground for others to follow.

When looking to reengineer, court leaders should look for ideas that stretch their conception of how courts can operate. Through our work with numerous courts the NCSC has developed a reengineering menu of six items court leaders should consider as they look to restructure their courts.

1. Centralize and regionalize court functions and operations where possible
2. Identify all functions that can be automated and automate them to the maximum

3. Systematically apply case management, which may require overhauling the current system
4. Maximize the number of transactions that can be completed online
5. Reorganize the back office from top to bottom
6. Redistrict and redefine jurisdiction and venue

The table on the following page summarizes the tactics that reengineering courts have undertaken to date. These fall into five categories: centralizing select functions; expanding the use of video conferencing; changing court processes to become more efficient; looking at structural changes; and expanding the electronic environment. Other solutions have looked at leveling the workload throughout the court system, reorganizing the "back office," and pursuing more flexibility in managing court operations. Other options, which have yet to be pursued because they are more difficult, include civil-rules reform, case triage, case review and unbundling, more virtual services, and maximizing online transactions.

In the face of severe and lengthy budget cuts, courts face no other choice than to reshape themselves if they are to remain relevant and vibrant institutions for the 21st century. Courts must not be afraid to ask what litigants and other users want courts to look like. Other industries such as banking give clues as to what customers of the 21st century expect. They want quality service while having a high degree of personal convenience, low transaction costs, reduced complexity, improved access, and high predictability. Courts committed to reshaping themselves offer lessons for others to follow to meet this new future.

Improving court operations may involve overhauling a court's case management system in one of three ways:

Civil Reform—There are two options: (1) a civil track for lightweight processing that offers quicker, cheaper, simpler, and more predictable outcomes by restricting the degree of legal process, and (2) a less expensive process that limits discovery and expedites case events for more complex cases.

Case Triage—Using this approach, courts first determine, according to the issues, what type of processing a case requires: full, classic due process; modified due

Table 20. 1 Reengineering strategies from various states

Centralization	Video Conferencing	Processes	Structure	E-Everything
Electronic payables (fines, fees, restitution, etc.)	Arraignments for incarcerated defendants	Statewide fine schedule for petty misdemeanors	Consolidation of judicial districts	E-file with an electronic document management system
Automated referral to collections	Detention hearings for detained juveniles	Expand the list of misdemeanors and ordinance violations that are payables	Court consolidation— single-tier trial court or single-tier limited-jurisdiction court	Electronic workflow
Traffic citations	Child support hearings	Courtroom docket entry into the case management system to prepare sentencing and other orders with electronic signatures (e.g., in court updating)	Review jurisdiction and venue as related to centralized filing of cases and centralized issuance of orders	E-filing • Centralize/regionalize filing centers • Self-help software • Electronic citation by all law enforcement
Call centers	Additional simple hearings	Digital recording of court proceedings	Expand use of subordinate judicial hearing officers	Electronic signatures on orders, notices, etc.
Jury management • Summons • Qualification questionnaires	Motions in civil cases that do not involve testimony		Consolidation of clerks/managers with expansion of responsibility to multiple locations	Availability of e-case files from every court at one or more call centers
Processing and issuance of default judgment orders	Interpreters			Virtual Web-based information centers providing direct access to records, etc.
Probate reports	Off-site live testimony			
Education				

process; a problem-solving approach; or administrative resolution.

Unbundled Case Review—Some cases may be directed to the most efficient case management queue by staff, rather than judges, based on simple rules and easily identified case characteristics. The key principles are (1) a formal set of processes and (2) an escalation of case review to the next higher level of roles/legal skills only as required.

21

Private Prisons Can't Lock In Savings

By Emily Badger

States turned to the private sector to run prisons more efficiently. While some companies make profits, though, states are not seeing the savings.

From *Miller-McCune*, January 2012.

Back in 1999, private prisons housed 3,828 federal prisoners in America. Now that number is more than 33,000, a more than 800 percent gain. In the state of Arizona, the comparable figure went up 285 percent in a decade, in Idaho—459 percent.

States, and even the federal government, increasingly have looked to private companies to house and manage America's expanding prison population. Three decades ago private lockups were nearly nonexistent in the U.S. Over this period, while the number of prisoners in the U.S. grew by 17 percent, the population inside the walls of fully privatized prisons soared by 80 percent.

Governments have turned to the idea in the face of prison overcrowding, particularly as tougher sentences and the war on drugs creates the need for more beds and cells for people who would not have gone to prison (or stayed so long) several decades ago. The idea also taps into the broader political popularity of privatizing government services, from garbage collection to toll booth operation to fighting wars.

The main argument, though, for privatization—that governments can save money by turning over prisons to the more efficient private sector—has mixed evidence to support it. A new report from the advocacy group The Sentencing Project corrals many of these cost studies into one dubious-looking heap. And, its author suggests, there are some fundamental questions to ask about whether prisons can, and should, be privatized using the same logic that governments do in handing over other services.

"The main difference when you look at it is the commodity it's dealing with," said Cody Mason, a program associate with The

Sentencing Project and author of the new report, "Too good to be true: private prisons in America." "If you're dealing with toll booths, it's for fares to get on the highway. If you're dealing with private prisons, you're dealing with human beings. The entire incentive for these companies is to lobby states and federal governments to put more people in prison. If you privatize garbage, no one is going to be lobbying specifically to get more garbage on the streets."

Many states have turned to private prisons precisely because they're trying to cut down on prison populations and the hefty costs associated with them. (States may not be scaling back their prison ambitions for precisely the reasons The Sentencing Project would like them to, but bad economic times have made strange bedfellows of sentencing reformers and budget hawks.) On the whole, though, there is meager evidence that privatizing prisons makes them cheaper or more efficient.

"There's a huge amount of mixed research either way," Mason said. "If you really break into it, at least what we viewed as the most comprehensive studies largely show that, at best, private prisons can save a little bit of money, and that's not guaranteed at all."

The U.S. General Accounting Office in 1996 looked at several state-funded studies and another that was commissioned by the federal government, all of which reached different conclusions. The GAO, which also criticized the methodology of some of the research, put it this way: "We could not conclude from these studies that privatization of correctional facilities will not save money. However, these studies do not offer substantial evidence that savings have occurred."

Research from 2007 led by Vanderbilt's James Blumfield (and sponsored in part by the Corrections Corporation of America and the Association of Private Correctional and Treatment Organizations) suggested that the competition provided by private prisons reduced costs at both public and private facilities. A 2009 analysis from University of Utah researchers looked at 12 different studies and concluded that privately run prisons "provide no clear benefit or detriment," but only minimal savings at best. Ohio officials, meanwhile, have looked at their data and found cost savings, while the Arizona Department of Corrections has had less success.

Part of the issue may be that prisons just don't have a lot of fat to cut. Private firms may save money on non-unionized workers, lower salaries and less training, and by bypassing some of the red tape of new facility construction. But at some point, Mason fears, that trimming may cut into the quality of services.

"You create this whole industry by privatizing something that government wasn't really having a problem with before," he said. "One problem you could point to is overcrowding. But you create this whole industry, and now it fights to live and expand, which at least in this circumstance goes against a lot of what would be best for these states and the country as whole."

22

California Shrinks its Prisons, but Overcrowding Persists

By John Gramlich

Locking people up in prison is expensive. California is saving money by letting people out.

VACAVILLE, Calif. — Eighteen months ago, the gymnasium at the state prison here was not a gymnasium at all. It was a makeshift dormitory, housing 250 felons in triple bunk beds stretching from one end of the concrete floor to the other.

Correctional officers recall a tense, dangerous environment. Violent offenders, many of them sentenced to decades behind bars for assault, murder and other serious crimes, slept within inches of one another. Tempers rose often, especially during the sweltering summertime months. Fights were common.

Today, the gymnasium at the California State Prison at Solano houses no one. Triple bunking has ended. Instead, this medium-security prison is shedding inmates, with a decline of more than 1,000 offenders over the last year and a half.

The same phenomenon is happening at many of California's 33 state prisons. As the financially battered state enacts huge budget cuts, it has no choice but to downsize its sprawling correctional system, which now consumes 10 percent of the state budget and swallows more taxpayer dollars than higher education—a fact that, if public opinion surveys are accurate, Californians abhor. A single prison bed costs taxpayers $44,500 a year.

The federal courts have dialed up the pressure, putting state officials on notice that severe overcrowding—a fact of life in California prisons for years—is no longer acceptable. Two years ago, a panel of three federal judges found that overcrowding had created unconstitutionally inhumane conditions, ordering the state to reduce its inmate population by more than 40,000—a staggering figure that eclipses the entire prisoner total of all but nine states.

From *Stateline.org*, April 2011.

Now, the U.S. Supreme Court is about to weigh in on the overcrowding problem by deciding whether to uphold, strike down or modify that order. Oral arguments in the case, *Schwarzenegger v. Plata*, made clear that the court's decision could break along familiar ideological lines.

Liberal justices pressed California's lawyer about conditions so bad they once resulted in preventable deaths every week. Conservatives countered that while prison conditions might be deplorable, any order to reduce the population by thousands of inmates—on top of what has already been done—will endanger California residents.

"If this order goes into effect, we will see," Justice Samuel Alito said from the bench during the arguments, suggesting that the public would be safer with these inmates behind bars. "We will see, and the people of California will see."

PATHS TO REDUCE CROWDING

California's prison downsizing efforts began before the Supreme Court's involvement. In 2006, when the state's inmate population reached an all-time high of more than 172,000, then-Governor Arnold Schwarzenegger declared an overcrowding emergency, warning that inmates and guards alike faced "extreme peril."

About 10,000 inmates were promptly shipped to private prisons in Arizona, Mississippi and Oklahoma. More recently, thousands of others had their release dates moved up as state lawmakers, usually known for enhancing criminal penalties, were forced to change course. Through an expansion of so-called "good-time credits," they authorized many inmates to leave prison ahead of schedule while reducing parole supervision for others, hoping to reduce the number sent back for relatively minor technical violations. Today, California's in-state inmate population is down to 152,000.

Governor Jerry Brown, who took office in January, hopes to keep going. Brown wants to shift tens of thousands of low-level state inmates to county jails, even though many of those jails themselves are at capacity. If enacted, Brown's plan could reduce the state prison population by another 38,000 within four years, according to a nonpartisan legislative estimate. It also may force counties to release thousands of offenders from their jails to make room for the state transfers.

In the yards and dormitories at state prisons like Solano, the word has gotten out.

Inmates know the state is under serious budget and court constraints, and many of them are counting on being freed ahead of schedule, says Randy Carter, 47, who has been incarcerated on a first-degree murder conviction in California since he was 19 years old. Carter himself is among those who could be freed. After five unsuccessful parole hearings, he was found "suitable for parole" on March 18 and is awaiting a final decision from the governor.

Al Roensch, a 37-year-old Solano inmate who has been imprisoned for 15 years on an attempted murder conviction, says rumors spread rapidly behind the walls and that inmates frequently repeat a common joke: "We're all going home!"

LIMITS OF CHANGE

As the changes at Solano make clear, California prisons are undergoing a major facelift. Even so, critics point to the sheer magnitude of the problems that remain.

Solano, for example, continues to house about twice as many prisoners as it is designed for. While triple-bunking has ended, double-bunking has not, including in the prison's maximum-security wing, where two female prison guards monitored about 200 offenders on a recent morning.

Statewide, the story is similar. Despite recent downsizing, California prisons are at 175 percent of their design capacity. Health care behind bars remains far from adequate and even the state corrections director concedes that his counterparts in other states view his system as a model of what not to do. Prison guards complain of dangerously understaffed facilities. Meanwhile, a $7.7 billion prison construction plan signed by Schwarzenegger in 2007 has yet to result in a single new prison being built amid squabbles over land use and bond issuance.

In the notoriously divided Legislature, where budget negotiations between Brown and Republicans collapsed last week, it is difficult to find consensus on any policy, let alone one as emotionally and politically charged as prisons. Not a single Republican voted for Brown's plan to shift inmates to the counties. And with funding for the plan now uncertain, there is discussion of leaning more heavily on spending reductions to balance the budget—cuts that could speed prisoner releases and decimate what remains of inmate rehabilitation programs.

Meanwhile, fears about a spike in crime are common. Law enforcement officials warn that more releases—whether they are ordered by the Legislature or by the Supreme Court—will have predictable long-term consequences on crime, given that parolees in California are far more likely than in other states to run into trouble again.

"I'm not Nostradamus, but we have a 70 percent recidivism rate. That is a fact," says Sacramento County Sheriff Scott Jones. "If you release 40,000 inmates, 28,000 of those will reoffend."

MANY MASTERS

To study the California prison system is to wander through a maze of lawsuits, court rulings, voter initiatives, state statutes and powerful federal overseers with titles like "receiver," "special master" and "court representative." Often lost on casual observers is that vast swaths of the system are not under the state's control at all. So many players are involved in different aspects of the state's correctional policies that it is difficult—some say impossible—to keep the prison system moving in one coherent direction.

The federal courts already run health care behind the prison walls, a mammoth undertaking that has placed thousands of employees and hundreds of millions of state dollars at the discretion of one man, J. Clark Kelso, a longtime California state administrator who is now the federal receiver in charge of improving medical care. Dental and mental health care in the prisons are handled by the state Department of Corrections and Rehabilitation, with federal supervision ordered by the courts. Disability services also are under the watchful eye of a federal monitor.

Corrections policy, meanwhile, is made not only in courtrooms and in the halls of the state Legislature but also at the ballot box. Through ballot initiatives, California voters have ordered a range of criminal justice changes over the years, ranging from "three strikes" sentencing legislation to laws cracking down on sex offenders.

In the Legislature itself, partisan bickering isn't the only dynamic at work. The politically powerful prison guards' union, the California Correctional Peace Officers

Association, has tended to oppose policies that could result in any decline in the prisoner population, thus ensuring steady employment for its members.

Union leaders insist that is no longer the case. President Mike Jimenez and others speak of a "new CCPOA," one that has embraced inmate rehabilitation, such as job training and substance abuse treatment, as a way to close the revolving prison door. At the same time, however, the union underwrites crime victims' groups that regularly press for tougher sentences.

The union is not shy about the influence it wields. In a video it released shortly after last November's election, the union boasted that 104 of 107 candidates it had endorsed—including Jerry Brown—had won. "We had a lot of victories," Craig Brown, the union's chief lobbyist in Sacramento, says in the video. "We should get a much better reception in the governor's office going forward, and a much better reception in the Legislature."

Some lawmakers openly acknowledge the debt they owe the union. "Without CCPOA, I wouldn't even have been close," Juan Vargas, a newly elected Democratic state senator, says in the video. "CCPOA made the difference. They literally won this campaign for me, and I'm very, very grateful for that."

AN UNCERTAIN FUTURE

Is lasting change possible in California's prisons?

There are plenty of reasons to be skeptical. For example, in 2004, Schwarzenegger renamed the state's prison agency the "Department of Corrections and Rehabilitation" in order to stress the importance of treatment programs in shrinking the inmate population. His administration later cut funding for prison rehabilitation programs by about 40 percent.

In some areas, there has been clear progress. Kelso, the federal health care receiver, has won many plaudits. His office has improved medical staffing at the prisons by hiring hundreds of doctors, nurses and other clinicians. The receiver claimed savings of more than $400 million last year by reducing unnecessary medical referrals for inmates and taking other steps. Preventable inmate deaths, while still occurring at a rate of several dozen a year, are down 30 percent.

Similarly, the state's transfer of about 10,000 inmates to out-of-state prisons has helped reduce crowding, even if it hasn't resulted in huge savings for taxpayers. Less crowded conditions at prisons like Solano have unquestionably made the environment safer for correctional officers and inmates alike. "I think we've improved in all areas," says Matthew Cate, the corrections secretary who was appointed by Schwarzenegger and kept on by Brown.

Despite the progress, any talk of righting the ship of California corrections appears premature. While many other states have taken bipartisan steps to address ballooning prison populations, Sacramento shows little sign of consensus on corrections. Republicans regularly accuse majority Democrats of being "soft on crime" and allowing violent offenders to walk free in the name of saving money. Democrats counter that Republicans have no positive ideas of their own and only want to enhance criminal penalties, keeping inmates in unsustainably expensive prison beds.

The chair of the state Senate's Public Safety Committee, Democrat Loni Hancock, puts it bluntly. Despite some improvements in recent years, Hancock says, the California prison system remains "an expensive failure."

23

The Cost of Punishment

By Richard Williams

The death penalty is not just tough justice; it is also tough on state budgets. The cost of having a death penalty is forcing cash-strapped states to rethink their stands on capital punishment.

T he question of whether capital punishment is an acceptable way to administer justice has long perplexed the nation's lawmakers and divided its citizens.

Traditional arguments pit those who believe the death penalty has no place in a civilized society against supporters who see it as an appropriate deterrent and punishment for the most heinous crimes.

Capital punishment's unstable history demonstrates how contentious the debate has been. In 1972, the U.S. Supreme Court suspended the death penalty on the grounds it violated the Eighth Amendment's prohibition against cruel and unusual punishment. The decision voided existing statutes in 40 states. Then in 1976, the court reauthorized capital punishment, enabling states to reenact their death penalty statutes. Thirty-seven did, but three of those—Illinois, New Jersey and New Mexico—have abolished their laws since 2007. With those changes, 16 states currently do not use capital punishment.

A COSTLY CONVICTION

Although the debate continues to be rooted in philosophical arguments, the recent legislative action abolishing the death penalty has been spurred by practical concerns.

New Jersey abolished its death penalty in 2007 in large part because the state had spent $254 million over 21 years administering it without executing a single person.

"It makes more sense fiscally to have inmates be sentenced to life imprisonment without parole than to have them sit on death row and to go through the appeals process," says Senator Christopher

From *State Legislatures*, July/August 2011.

"Kip" Bateman, the bill's sponsor, "New Jersey is going through tough times financially and any decision that is ethical in nature and promotes fiscal responsibility is a win-win for the state."

New Mexico lawmakers followed in 2009, ending capital punishment over similar cost concerns.

"There is no more inefficient law on the books than the death penalty," says Representative Antonio "Moe" Maestas, co-sponsor of the bill to repeal it. "It sounds very callous and shallow to talk about cost, but we spend other people's money, and we have to consider scarce resources."

Maestas believes his perspective is particularly persuasive because it's rooted in pragmatism rather than personal idealism. "The bottom line is, I don't care if the most heinous criminals die. They should. But capital punishment is very expensive for our state, and we have to find the best use of taxpayer dollars and prosecutorial resources. How many other murders and violent crimes cases could be prosecuted with the resources from one death penalty case?"

> "This is strictly about abolitionists being morally opposed to the death penalty. That's fine, but be honest about it."
>
> —Illinois Representative Jim Durkin

WORTH PRESERVING

Many state-initiated analyses—including reports from Michigan, New Mexico and South Dakota—have found administering capital punishment is significantly more expensive than housing prisoners for life without parole.

A study released last month found California has spent more than $4 billion on capital punishment since 1978, executing 13 criminals. That's about $184 million more a year than life sentences would have cost.

Much of the cost results from litigating numerous appeals during the convict's time on death row, where the average inmate spends 13 years prior to execution.

This lengthy process also influenced Bateman's decision to sponsor an abolishment bill. "I spoke to many families who went through trying emotional times during the appeals for death row inmates," he says. "Transferring an inmate from death row to life without parole allows for the aggrieved families to have a sense of

calmness in their life without having to relive the tragic events over and over again."

Many believe, however, the punishment is worth preserving even though it is expensive, if it can be made more manageable.

Illinois suspended capital punishment for 11 years before abolishing it in March 2011. When former Governor George Ryan instituted the moratorium, his intent was to give Illinois time to study and improve its capital punishment procedures.

During the moratorium, the Illinois Capital Punishment Commission and Reform Study Committee made several recommendations for improvement, including requiring the state Supreme Court to review all death sentences, setting minimum standards for DNA evidence, and increasing funding for indigent defense. The committee also recommended a full cost analysis, but it was never conducted.

The moratorium was not lifted and many, including Representative Jim Durkin, believe the reforms were not given an adequate chance. "This was not about frustration over a system that could not be made workable," he says. "This is strictly about abolitionists being morally opposed to the death penalty. That's fine, but be honest about it."

Without the death penalty, Durkin believes, there is no adequate punishment for the most vicious criminals. "A lot of these other arguments will not matter when someone is faced with the murder of a loved one."

ONE CRIME CHANGES MINDS

In Connecticut, the state's capital punishment abolishment debate took place at the same time as the trials for one of the most horrific crimes in the state's history, a home invasion that resulted in the murder of three members of the Petit family.

One of the killers, Steven Hayes, was convicted and sentenced to death earlier this year. Joshua Komisarjevsky, his accused accomplice, is set to go on trial in September. Many fear that making any change to Connecticut's current death penalty will make it unavailable to punish these men.

"If there were ever a case to merit the death penalty, this would be it," says Senator John Kissel. "And if the bill passed, while not retroactive, it could give these men grounds for appeal."

During the General Assembly's 2011 capital penalty debate, the Office of Fiscal Analysis reported Connecticut spends $3.3 million a year on death row cases and has performed only one execution since reinstating capital punishment in 1977. Lawmakers also heard from James Tillman, who spent 16 years in prison before DNA testing exonerated him. Some worry similar tests may one day prove the state has performed wrongful executions.

"A government that cannot guarantee the absolute accuracy of its proceedings should not take to itself the power of taking a human life," said Senator Martin Looney, referring to the Tillman case.

"Once someone is killed they are dead forever," says Senator Edith Prague, a long-time supporter of the death penalty. "Between the cost of capital punishment and the recent exonerations of innocent people, I have decided to generally support repeal."

> *"A government that cannot guarantee the absolute accuracy of its proceedings should not take to itself the power of taking a human life."*
> —Connecticut Senator Martin Looney

But Prague ultimately changed her mind and cast the deciding vote against repeal after meeting with Dr. William Petit, the sole survivor of the Connecticut home invasion that robbed him of his family.

"If repeal comes up in the future, I will support it," she says. "The difference with this case is that these are the guys who did it. Their identity is not in doubt, and after meeting with Dr. Petit I know this is the right thing to do."

LEGISLATIVE SEE-SAW

With passionate proponents on each side, the death penalty will likely be on a repeal/reinstate see-saw indefinitely. This year, lawmakers in New Jersey and New Mexico have debated legislation to once again reinstate capital punishment. Although it's unlikely either bill will pass in 2011, the issue will be raised again in the future.

"There are certain heinous crimes that rise to the level of warranting the death penalty—killing a child, murdering a police officer, acts of terrorism," says Senator Robert Singer, the bill's sponsor in New Jersey. "Our old law had problems, but problems that can be fixed."

VII

Bureaucracy

Americans have always expressed skepticism about government, but they reserve a particular disdain for bureaucracy. As one scholar of bureaucracy noted, bureaucracy is generally reviled as the following: a sea of waste, a swamp of incompetence, a mountain of unchecked power, an endless plain of mediocrity. Our media and politicians tell us that public bureaucracy is bloated in size, inefficient compared to business, a stifling place to work, indifferent to ordinary citizens, the problem rather than the solution.[1]

Yet despite the pounding from public opinion, public bureaucracies do a lot of good. Collectively, state and local public agencies employ millions who educate children, enforce the law, and provide an astonishing range of other services ranging from public sanitation to public transportation to public recreation. Despite the popular negative image, most professional students of the bureaucracy agree that most of the time agencies do these jobs professionally and effectively.

Broadly speaking, bureaucracy can be thought of as all public agencies and the programs and services they implement and manage. Most of these agencies come under the executive branches of state and local governments and run the gamut from police departments to schools, state health and welfare departments to public universities.

These agencies exist to implement and manage public programs and policies. When a legislature passes a law to, say, set maximum speed limits on state highways, it expresses the will of the state. The law, however, does not catch speeders zipping down the highway. A traffic cop does. To translate the will of the state into concrete action requires some mechanism to enforce that will, such as the state highway patrol monitoring speeders on state highways. Virtually every purposive course of action that state and local governments decide to pursue requires a similar enforcement or management mechanism. Collectively, these are public agencies and the people who work for them—the police, fire, and parks departments; schools; welfare agencies; libraries; and road crews—in short, the bureaucracy.

These days, state and local bureaucracies are not getting attention because of their generally recognized professionalism and competence. The most notable element of the bureaucracy that has made its way onto the public agenda in the past two years is its cost. Schools, police departments, and the like are labor-intensive propositions, and labor is expensive, especially once you count things like health and pension benefits, which traditionally have been pretty generous in the public sector. As states have struggled with budget shortfalls, those pay and benefits packages have increasingly come under scrutiny. The basic argument is that the taxpayers simply can no longer afford business as usual, and the bureaucracy—read teachers, cops, welfare workers—are going to have to get used to a not-so-generous deal.

Okay, fair enough, times are tough and most realize that everyone, bureaucrats included, have to tighten their belts. Yet in some states the scrutiny of public sector pay and power has exploded into something else. Public employees have been held up as public enemy number one, with some lawmakers accusing public employees of living large while taxpayers tighten belts, driving gaping budget deficits with their unjustified and unsustainable compensation packages. This argument has driven a broad effort to reduce the role of public labor unions and raised big questions about the very nature of public employment.

The readings in this chapter take a look at the highly controversial fight over the power, pay, and perks of public sector employees. The first essay, by Steven Walters, is an on-the-ground report of the controversy that erupted in Wisconsin as a result of Gov. Scott Walker's, R-WI, drive to sharply curtail the collective bargaining rights of public employees. Pitched as a budget-reducing tool, it sparked a ferocious backlash that did not shake up simply the bureaucracy but statewide politics as well.

The second essay, by Ben Wieder, takes a broader look at the shift in relationship between state and local employees and their employers. Curtailed collective bargaining rights and reduced health and pension benefit contributions have been pursued by a wide variety of states in the past few years. Fallout from these attempts to curtail power and pay include eroding morale and increased retirements in the public sector. Public sector unions are trying to adapt to these new rules, but they are also fighting them.

The last two readings take a look at the core argument that is justifying the drive to rein in collective bargaining rights and that these rights are directly responsible for producing compensation packages that are busting budgets. An essay by Emily Badger looks at whether states with strong collective bargaining rights are more likely to have budget shortfalls. The answer is complicated; it depends on whose numbers you believe.

The final essay, by Helisse Levine and Eric Scorsone, takes a look at how the Great Recession is reshaping public employment relationships. They argue the changes being pursed in many states—not just collective bargaining but the right to unionize and to collect union dues—are likely to have long-lasting effects on state and government bureaucracies. These are related not just to the cost of government but to the type of people who will be working for them and even the quality of services they provide.

NOTES

1. Charles Goodsell, *The Case for Bureaucracy,* 4th ed. (Washington, DC: CQ Press, 2004), 3.

24

Showdown in Madison

By Steven Walters

Gov. Scott Walker, R-WI, decided to go after public unions. Public unions responded by going after him.

The four-week firestorm in and around Wisconsin's Capitol earlier this year will reshape the state's politics for years to come.

The debate over first-term Republican Governor Scott Walker's call to stop just short of eliminating collective bargaining for most public employees divided Wisconsin, prompted a walkout by all 14 Senate Democrats and sparked recall-election showdowns that will measure the political clout of unions.

From mid-February through mid-March, the Capitol in Madison was swarmed by tens of thousands of chanting, singing, shouting, sign-carrying protesters. Some of them slept in the Capitol for days, turning a first-floor hallway into a food pantry. Handmade signs were taped to miles of marble.

More than 500 police officers, on loan from the largest and smallest communities, worked 18-hour shifts. Lawmakers included a $10 million line item in the fiscal year 2012 budget for Capitol security. When one lawmaker refused to identify himself and go through a metal detector, an officer pushed him to the ground. State troopers were sent to the homes of Democratic senators, trying to catch any who returned from their self-imposed exile in Illinois.

About 90 threats against lawmakers and the governor were serious enough to investigate.

From *State Legislatures*, July/August 2011.

ALL EYES ON THE BADGER STATE

The whole world watched. Reporters from Germany, France, Italy, Canada and Mexico joined American news crews.

By March 10, the drama was at a climax. That day, two Assembly members—Representatives Richard Spanbauer, a Republican, and David Cullen, a Democrat—had to crawl through a first-floor Capitol window just to go to work.

Spanbauer and Cullen climbed into a Democratic senator's office because police had ordered a lockdown of the Capitol—"nobody in, nobody out"—while they dealt with dozens of protesters who had camped overnight in the vestibule outside the Assembly chamber. The demonstrators were finally dragged or escorted from the area.

They were the remnant of thousands who took over the first three floors of the Capitol the night of March 9, forcing police to retreat and protect the Capitol's two top floors.

Alerted by social media—"OMG. Meet me @ the Capitol in 20 minutes!!!"—protesters were incensed that Republican senators had quickly taken up, passed and sent to the Assembly the historic change in collective bargaining laws that Walker had announced he wanted one month earlier. All the Senate Democrats were still holding out in Illinois in an attempt to kill the bill.

The original plan called for Senate Republicans to pass the governor's collective-bargaining bill on Feb. 17, less than a week after he unveiled it. But when all 14 Democrats bolted to Illinois that day, the Assembly had to go first.

After a record 62 hours of debate, with thousands of protesters massing in the Capitol rotunda daily, the Assembly passed it, 51-17, on Feb. 25. The 1:05 a.m. roll call caught so many exhausted, sleepwalking lawmakers by surprise that 28 of them never got a chance to even vote, since the electronic voting machine was kept open for only 17 seconds. Republicans left the chamber in a single-file line, as Democrats shouted "shame" and other insults.

The waiting game in the Senate then started: When would the 14 Senate Democrats return for a showdown

> *"We had just enough members to be able to deny a fiscal quorum."*
>
> —Mark Miller, Wisconsin Senate Minority Leader

vote they knew they would lose? Walker aides talked about possible compromises at a Kenosha McDonald's and other places in both states.

No deal could be struck, however. So, on March 9, Senate Republicans stripped Walker's bill of all non-spending issues, which eliminated the requirement that 20 senators had to be present to vote on it, and quickly passed it, 17-1.

That set up the Assembly's second vote for the collective bargaining changes—a 53-42 vote for it on March 10. Walker signed it in private the next morning, then held a ceremonial signing hours later in front of about 100 reporters.

Although a Dane County judge blocked the bill from becoming law on the grounds that it violated the state's open meeting law, a divided Wisconsin Supreme Court ruled on June 14 that the bill had been legally passed—a ruling that meant the Legislature didn't have to pass it a second time.

CHAOS AND HISTORY

On Feb. 11, when Walker announced details of his "budget-repair bill," neither he nor any of the four partisan leaders of the Capitol knew how much history it would make, or how much chaos it would cause.

Walker wanted to reverse decades of Wisconsin labor laws, laws the governor and the top two Republican leaders—Senate Majority Leader Scott Fitzgerald and his younger brother, Assembly Speaker Jeff Fitzgerald—said had given public workers generous salaries and fringe benefits that cost taxpayers billions of dollars.

Under the new law, collective bargaining by public employees is limited to cost-of-living raises tied to inflation. To minimize the political push-back and avoid any illegal strikes that could cripple emergency services, the governor exempted local firefighters and police officers and State Patrol troopers from the changes.

The law also requires workers to vote annually to recertify public employee unions, makes payment of union dues optional, and requires all public employees to contribute more toward their pensions and health care. Unions had agreed to the higher fringe-benefit contributions—which will cost state workers about $300 million over the next two years—but refused to accept the other changes, saying they end decades of workers' protections.

The new law could cripple public employee unions financially. In one year, $11.2 million in union dues was withheld from the paychecks of executive-branch employees of state government and $2.6 million in union dues were withheld from the paychecks of University of Wisconsin-Madison workers.

The governor defended his changes this way: Local governments need these new "tools" to offset cuts he was proposing in state aid for schools, local governments, and public colleges and universities. Walker said the cuts were needed to fix a two-year, $3.6-billion budget deficit—a deficit that he widened by pushing through the Legislature $81 million in tax breaks for businesses in January.

The governor's plan to take away bargaining powers public employees had for decades touched historical, emotional and political nerves. In 1959, Wisconsin was the first state to let public employees join unions. In addition, Madison is the birthplace of the giant American Federation of State, County and Municipal Employees.

Walker and Republican legislators thought they had picked a fight with only a few public employee unions.

They were wrong.

A CIRCUS OF SORTS

Uniformed firefighters, led by a bagpiper, marched through the Capitol in an emotional show of solidarity. Police unions joined in, too.

Soon, all major private-sector unions, their leaders and the Rev. Jesse Jackson were in Madison, turning the capital city into an international battleground in the fight over workers' rights.

It forced legislative leaders to make career-changing choices.

Senate Minority Leader Mark Miller, for example, convinced all Senate Democrats—including the pregnant Julie Lassa—to flee to Illinois. That left the 19 Republicans frustrated, but unable to take any major action.

The Democrats' flight started with an innocent call to the Senate chief clerk: Since the state Constitution requires a three-fifths quorum in both houses of the

Legislature to pass spending bills, what's that requirement in the 33-member Senate—19 or 20?

The answer: At least 20 senators must be present to pass a spending bill. That meant every Republican and at least one Democrat.

Miller bristled at the GOP push to "railroad through" Walker's changes only days after the governor introduced them. Miller remembered that Texas legislators had once fled that state to block passage of a bill, so he convinced the other 13 Democrats to pack up and meet in Rockford that afternoon. Democrats knew state troopers, who may have been able to escort them back to Madison if they were caught within the state's borders, had no jurisdiction in other states.

"We had just enough members to be able to deny a fiscal quorum," Miller says. That way, they could lengthen the time "the bill was exposed to public scrutiny."

Miller says Democrats made this "once in a generation" decision to flee because "everybody knew what was at stake: We were standing up for the long-established ability of workers to bargain collectively. . . . This was an assault on all workers."

Walker's goal is to destroy public-employee unions so they can't help elect Democrats, Miller says. "It's a political agenda."

The Democrats ended up staying in Illinois more than three weeks, moving often to avoid Tea Party activists who tracked them and followed them to interviews with TV crews. They didn't return to the Capitol until March 12—when they were cheered as heroes.

STANDOFF

Senate Majority Leader Fitzgerald was incredulous that all 14 Senate Democrats had fled Wisconsin.

"I still wasn't taking it seriously," he says. "I thought it was a gimmick, a stunt. I thought they'd be back in a day or two."

Two weeks later, however, another Senate Republican said to him: "Fitz, I don't think they're coming back."

They weren't. Democrats said that since neither Walker nor Senate Republicans would change the bill, despite the unions' willingness to pay more for health care and pensions, they had no reason to return. Democrats also had no end-game strategy, which bothered two of their veterans, Tim Cullen and Bob Jauch.

Senate Republicans tried to force the Democrats back to the Capitol. They got no help from rules or laws, Scott Fitzgerald recalls. "We were winging it."

Republicans halted any direct deposit of Democrats' salaries, trying to force them back to pick up their paychecks from Fitzgerald's office. One Democratic senator signed a power-of-attorney form, which meant an aide could pick up his boss's paycheck.

Republican senators passed resolutions holding the 14 Democrats in "contempt" and fining them $100 a day. No fines were ever paid, however.

Republicans also told any police officer who found a Senate Democrat in the state to escort him or her back to the Capitol.

"You can't really remove somebody from office [for] refusing to do their job," Scott Fitzgerald says.

Late in the afternoon of March 9, Republican leaders had had enough. The Fitzgerald brothers decided to strip spending elements from the bill, call a conference committee on the collective bargaining changes that were left, and pass it through the Senate in a five-minute session that started shortly after 6 p.m.

The 17-1 vote sent the revised bill back to the Assembly. Police had to escort Republican senators, besieged by chanting, shouting protesters, from the Capitol.

Within minutes, thousands of protesters stormed the Capitol. "There's a real level of intimidation" that senators felt when protesters blocked them from using their offices for three weeks, Scott Fitzgerald says. If lawmakers can't "think freely, that changes the process," he adds. "That should never happen."

As the protests built and Democrats refused to leave Illinois, it unified Senate Republicans, Fitzgerald says. "They were 'tightening' us. . . . I don't regret any decisions we made."

> ### "I still wasn't taking it seriously. I thought it was a gimmick, a stunt. I thought they'd be back in a day or two."
> —Scott Fitzgerald, Wisconsin Senate Majority Leader

> ### "I was nervous. I had the votes. But I was afraid [the weekend] could sway it the other way. It did the exact opposite."
> —Jeff Fitzgerald, Wisconsin Assembly Speaker

THE ASSEMBLY WAS READY

When the bill first came to the Assembly in February, Speaker Jeff Fitzgerald was ready. After all, 25 of the 57 Assembly Republicans were first-term conservatives. They came to Madison to dismantle spending and programs built up during the eight-year term of former Democratic Governor Jim Doyle.

The 99-member Assembly was prepared to start debating Walker's bill when police called Speaker Fitzgerald. "We can no longer provide security for your members," the officers warned.

Fitzgerald had no choice but to send Assembly members home for the weekend, not knowing if angry voters back home would derail support for Walker's bill.

"I was nervous. I had the votes," Fitzgerald says. "But I was afraid [the weekend] could sway it the other way. It did the exact opposite."

He was even worried about how he would be treated at his son's Saturday basketball game, but was surprised at the number of neighbors who encouraged him.

When Assembly Republicans returned to the Capitol the next week, Fitzgerald says they were more unified than ever. "That silent majority is out there," he says.

The first-term speaker said his fellow Republicans sympathized with their leader. "The protesters bonded me with my caucus. It was very rewarding for me."

That bonding led to the initial 51-17 vote in February following the marathon debate. When the stripped down bill came back to the Assembly from the Senate, the debate on March 10 lasted only a little over three hours and passed by a 53-42 vote.

DEMOCRATS LEFT BEHIND

With Senate Democrats in Illinois, Assembly Minority Leader Peter Barca became the top Democrat in the Capitol. He had to keep his 38 Democrats unified, fight to reopen public access to the Capitol, hold press conferences and be in the center of daily—sometimes hourly—rallies.

Assembly Democrats had to "lead the fight," Barca says. "It was a lot of pressure."

Barca had served in Congress during the national brouhaha over President Clinton's attempt to rework the nation's health-care system. But the tumult in Wisconsin's Capitol was the most jarring, emotional and explosive thing he had ever experienced, he says.

"The magnitude of the [unions'] solidarity was extremely impressive," Barca says. "It was remarkable."

Barca was surprised the governor, who had served in the Assembly for eight years, pushed such a controversial anti-union agenda only days after taking office. It

> *"We felt, from day one, that we were on the right side of history."*
> —Peter Barca, Wisconsin Assembly Minority Leader

awakened a "sleeping giant," the Assembly Democrat says.

Barca and Miller predict the collective bargaining firestorm will eventually lead to Democrats regaining control of the Legislature.

Control of the Senate could switch this summer if Democrats win three of nine recall elections that target six Republican senators. But three Democratic senators also face recall elections, although all nine targeted senators have filed court appeals challenging the decision to call recall elections. Union leaders have told their members to focus on winning enough of the recall elections to flip Senate control to Democrats.

"We felt, from day one," Barca says, "that we were on the right side of history."

Unions Adapt to New Rules, Even as They Fight to Reverse Them

By Ben Wieder

States are trying to limit the right to unionize, to collectively bargain, and to collect union dues. Unions are not just trying to adapt to this new world of public employment; they are sometimes successfully fighting to change it.

It took nearly a year for Dale Kleinert to negotiate his first teachers' contract. When Kleinert started his job as schools superintendent in Moscow, Idaho, the talks were already underway. Then, discussions reached an impasse. There were disagreements over pay and health care costs, and the pace slowed further when first an outside mediator and later a fact-finder didn't render a decision. It wasn't until May of 2011 that Kleinert and his union counterparts finally reached an agreement.

Just before then, while Kleinert and the teachers were still stuck, Republican lawmakers in Boise were finishing work on plans to take away much of the leverage that Idaho teachers had long enjoyed in these kinds of negotiations. So for Kleinert's next round of talks with Moscow's teachers, which began pretty much right after the previous ones wrapped up, the rules were very different.

This time, teachers were limited to bargaining over salary and benefits only. So a range of workplace issues, from class sizes to curriculum were off the table. Negotiations had to happen in public meetings rather than backrooms. Most important, there was now a June deadline on negotiations, so there was no room for foot-dragging on either side. Kleinert and the union struck a deal in just a month.

Arguably, Moscow's teachers made out alright in this latest agreement. They got a 1-percent pay raise at a time when tens of thousands of teachers around the country have been laid off and many more have seen their pay frozen. "That's not very much," says Kari Golightly, co-president of the Moscow Education Association, "but it's something." The school district agreed to pay more health care costs for teachers,

From *Stateline.org*, January 2012.

too, and give them a large chunk of any unanticipated revenue received by the district during the session.

Still, Idaho teachers are upset about how labor issues went down last year at the legislature. They feel that lawmakers, Republican Governor C. L. "Butch" Otter and state superintendent Tom Luna didn't consult with them, not only on the bargaining question, but also on the introduction of performance pay, the elimination of tenure, and a new requirement that high schools offer online classes. Hundreds of teachers protested at the Capitol when these changes passed last year—protests that fueled off of other labor rallies in Wisconsin, Ohio and other states. Now, Idaho teachers are hoping to springboard off labor's November win in Ohio—where voters repealed a controversial bargaining law—with a repeal vote of their own in 2012.

As public-sector unions across the country leave a tumultuous 2011 behind, the situation in Idaho is not unique. On one hand, labor is learning to live by a new set of rules governing collective bargaining and other matters, the product of new laws in nearly a dozen states. On the other hand, labor is fighting back in a number of states, hoping to reverse some of what was lost and in some cases to exact revenge on political opponents.

Most notably, unions are pushing to recall Wisconsin Governor Scott Walker, the Republican who pushed the state's new law restricting collective bargaining. If they succeed in getting a recall on the ballot, Walker, who was elected in the Republican wave of 2010, will have to face voters as early as this June. "There's an energy and a momentum generated about both the Ohio and Wisconsin fights," says Naomi Walker, director of state government relations for the AFL-CIO. "These attacks inspire a level of activism that we haven't seen before."

ELECTION ACTION

Labor's electoral strategy has had mixed success so far. Last year, national and local unions spent millions of dollars trying to recall enough Republican senators in Wisconsin to flip the GOP-controlled chamber into Democratic hands. They failed in that quest. But in Michigan, the teachers succeeded in a campaign to recall Paul Scott, the Republican chairman of the House Education Committee. And in Ohio, the campaign to repeal Senate Bill 5 won 60 percent of the vote.

In Wisconsin and Ohio, the recall and repeal efforts seem to be heading off more anti-union bills, at least in the short term. The possibility of Walker's recall in Wisconsin has lawmakers there thinking twice about pushing new legislation, says Brett Healy, executive director of the MacIver Institute, a conservative Wisconsin think tank that supports Walker's changes. Healy thinks that concern about the recall will limit activity during the 2012 session. "Everyone's nervous," Healy says. "Politicians are naturally worried about the next election." In Ohio, Republican Governor John Kasich, bruised by the repeal of SB 5, doesn't have any plans to reintroduce it this year. "We heard the voters loud and clear in November," says Kasich spokesman Rob Nichols.

In Michigan, however, the recall of state Representative Scott hasn't had the same chilling effect, according to Phil Pavlov, chair of the Senate Education Committee. Scott had earned the ire of the Michigan Education Association after successfully championing a package of bills that changed tenure laws and eliminated the policy of basing staffing decisions on seniority. One month after Scott's ouster, Pavlov, a Republican, pushed through a bill that lifted the cap on the number of charter schools allowed in the state, despite the opposition of the MEA. "The fact that Paul Scott was recalled certainly hasn't changed the agenda," he says.

In Idaho, the three bills responsible for education changes are all on the ballot for voter consideration in November. Both unions and supporters of the education overhaul say they anticipate national attention to build, and outside money to flow in, as the election nears. Whether it will be the next Ohio—and whether weakened unions can financially afford another big fight—remains to be seen.

Melissa McGrath, a spokeswoman for Idaho's Department of Education, says there's a crucial difference between Idaho and Ohio: In Idaho, voters will have a full year to assess the education changes before deciding whether or not to keep them. "By November 2012," she says, "the voters in Idaho will have seen the positive impact that these reforms are having on their education system."

Penni Cyr, president of the Idaho Education Association, disagrees. She says there is widespread dissatisfaction with the approach Idaho has taken, and

Where the Labor Battles Were

Last year saw an unprecedented number of moves by states to limit the power of public employee unions. The battle isn't over: In 2012, Idaho will vote on whether to repeal the changes.

State	What Passed	Status
Idaho	Restricts collective bargaining for teachers to salary and benefits	3 laws signed into law, but repealing them is on the Nov. ballot
Indiana	Restricts collective bargaining for teachers to salary and benefits	Signed into law
Massachusetts	In some instances, allows local governments to put workers on state health plan, rather than typically more generous local health plan	Signed into law
Michigan	Limits scope of collective bargaining for teachers, allows emergency fiscal manager to reject collective bargaining agreement	Signed into law
Minnesota	Eliminates collective bargaining on teacher salary issues, also restricts rights of teachers to strike	Vetoed
Nebraska	Narrows role of labor commission to set "prevailing wages" in labor disputes, gives local governments more power in negotiations	Signed into law
New Jersey	Increases employee pension and health contributions, takes them off the negotiating table for four years	Signed into law
Ohio	Eliminates collective bargaining over salary, bans strikes and prohibits unions from deducting dues from workers' paychecks	Repealed by voters
Oklahoma	Repeals law requiring cities above 35,000 to perform collective bargaining with non-uniformed public employees	Signed into law
Tennessee	Replaces collective bargaining for teachers with "collaborative conferencing"	Signed into law
Wisconsin	Removes most collective bargaining rights for all public employees and requires unions to seek annual recertification	Signed into law

Source: *Stateline* research.

broad support for repealing the three laws in the package. "We received almost 75,000 signatures on each of those," she says, far more than the number required to put the measure on the ballot. "I think Idahoans have spoken by their signatures."

ADAPTING TO THE NEW RULES

As the election dramas unfold in Wisconsin and Idaho, public-sector unions are navigating new realities at the bargaining table. For one thing, membership is down for some unions. The National Education Association lost nearly 120,000 members across the country last year, a 3.6 percent decline, according to the annual report filed with the U.S. Department of Labor. In Wisconsin, low morale in the wake of last year's legislative battles contributed to a 33.6 percent increase in retirements among public employees.

The Tennessee Education Association is also seeing a dip in membership as it adjusts to a new role following legislative changes. "We're in a transition phase now," says Gera Summerford, president of the state's largest teachers union. "We'll continue to do the best we can under the new laws to ensure that teachers are treated fairly."

Those new laws replace "collective bargaining" with a new practice called "collaborative conferencing." Under the new process, local negotiations can involve a group of seven to 11 teachers meeting with an equal number of representatives from the board of education to reach a "memorandum of understanding" about wages, benefits and working conditions, among other things. The memorandum then goes to the board for approval. The law gives more power to local boards and also allows people other than union officials to negotiate on behalf of teachers.

"Under collective bargaining, there was only one group of teachers that represented all teachers," says Lee Harrell, director of government and labor relations at the Tennessee School Boards Association. "This opens the door for there to be multiple parties."

In Tennessee, teachers were among the only public workers who still retained collective bargaining rights before the law passed. Harrell says that explains why Tennessee's change didn't get as much outcry as the overhauls in Ohio and Wisconsin did.

In Wisconsin, by contrast, the new law has dramatically changed the rules in what previously had been a very labor-friendly state. More than 90 percent of state employees who previously participated in collective bargaining opted out this year, according to Peter Davis, general counsel for the state's employment relations commission. The new law requires unions to "recertify" every year for participation in collective bargaining, a process that requires a costly annual voting process.

AFSCME's Council 24, which represents more than 20,000 state employees, is one of the unions that has decided to let its collective bargaining status lapse under the new rules. The union is shifting its focus toward providing more legal counsel for its members and representing them in the grievance and arbitration processes, says Martin Beil, the Council's executive director. "We felt our resources were better spent there than to be in permanent recertification mode," he says. And though the union isn't involved in official negotiations with the state anymore, Beil says that some union representatives are still maintaining informal relationships with managers to create departmental rules and handbooks.

In Indiana, another state where labor battles boiled over last year, Tony Bennett, the state superintendent of public instruction, has been speaking of the need to "mend fences" with teachers. But Brenda Pike, executive director of the Indiana State Teachers Association, says Bennett's conciliatory tone hasn't changed teachers' opinions about him: "I don't believe our people could dislike him more," she says. At the local level, however, Pike says talks with school administrators are occurring in good faith. "While a lot of our folks are unhappy with the situation," she says, "there's still a lot of bargaining going on."

In Indiana, the collective bargaining changes were part of a broader legislative package that also introduced the country's most sweeping school voucher plan and an expansion of charter schools. In many school districts, that created a funny political dynamic between management and labor. While school administrators and teachers generally fell on opposite sides of the collective bargaining issue, they found common cause around opposing many of the other plans.

In Moscow, Idaho's contentious legislation seems to have actually improved relations between the local union and school administration. "It kind of drew us together, actually," says Dawn Fazio, who chairs the school board. Golightly, the local union co-president, says that board members clapped along with labor leaders when they were told during negotiations that the three referendums had gotten thousands more signatures than necessary.

Superintendent Kleinert says that the small raise and benefits were a way for the district to make clear to teachers that it supported them. "We wanted to do something for teachers," says Kleinert. "They'd been beaten up pretty badly during the legislative session."

26

Bargaining and Budget Shortfalls: Are They Linked?

By Emily Badger

Are the collective bargaining rights of public unions increasing state budget problems? The answer depends on whom you ask.

W isconsin Gov. Scott Walker's ongoing political show-down is premised on the idea that public-sector unions —and their ability to bargain collectively—are closely tied to the presence and size of the state's budget fiasco.

The more powerful the union, in other words, the more dire the state's money woes. Walker seems to accept this correlation as self-evident. "Collective bargaining is a fiscal issue," repeats a popular refrain by his office throughout the standoff.

But is it really? This should be a testable hypothesis, if a messy one to isolate. Is collective bargaining—or the power of any public union—actually correlated with state deficits?

"It's an extremely difficult question to answer," said Matthew Di Carlo, a senior fellow with the pro-organized-labor Albert Shanker Institute. "You're talking about drawing a causal connection between collective bargaining and state budget troubles, and there are count-less factors mediating that relationship."

States have different tax structures, foreclosure rates and unem-ployment figures and all contribute to income flow and the presence and size of any deficit. It's possible, Di Carlo says, that someone could draw an association between collective bargaining and deficits as well.

"But saying that unions actually caused that situation is a whole different ballgame, and we should be careful about that," he said. "And this applies when making pro-union arguments, too, by the way."

In his own analysis (done before state employees began camp-ing out in the capitol building in Madison), Di Carlo looked at

From *Miller-McCune*, March 2011.

state budget gaps (as a percentage of total budgets) in comparison to the share of public-sector employees represented by unions in each state. He controlled for median income and unemployment, and he separately examined states with collective bargaining and those without.

He acknowledges that the analysis is limited, particularly dealing with a state-level data set of only 50 cases. But his results at least suggest that Walker's certainty is misplaced. Di Carlo found no consistent relationship between budget gaps and unionization. George Washington University political scientist John Sides ran a similar analysis and also couldn't find a definitive correlation.

"I have not seen any evidence, whether in what I did or what anyone else did, that the presence of collective bargaining or the strength of unions is related to the size of states' budget shortfalls," Di Carlo said. "It would seem to me the reasons for state budget shortfalls are rather clear—they are predominantly massive revenue declines due to circumstances created by the financial crisis, especially unemployment and foreclosures. I thought this was pretty clear to everyone else, too."

Nevada, for example, doesn't allow collective bargaining for state government workers but has the largest percentage budget gap in the country (perhaps more telling, Di Carlo suggests: It ranks in the top five in the nation in foreclosure rates). Blaming unions, he said, is a little absurd. Public-sector unions have, after all, been around for years, and today's budget shortfalls are an unprecedented phenomenon.

But Chris Edwards, director of tax policy studies at the libertarian Cato Institute, says others are looking at the wrong statistics.

"Deficits aren't really a good measure of anything," he said. "They don't really mean anything because states have to balance their budgets every year. By July 1 of this year, state deficits will all be at zero. Those deficit measures really have more to do with how accurate states are at doing their budget forecasting."

Edwards has, instead, looked at state-level *debt* as a percentage of gross domestic product, a measure that he says more accurately takes into account the long-term accumulation of all those deficits that get reset each summer. Like Di Carlo, he compared those numbers to the level of unionization among states' public workers.

"Stats show that it's not random," Edwards said. "It's strongly correlated."

Today's state budget problems may be relatively new in scope, he said, but they're the product of fiscal trends as old as the state employee unions themselves.

"There's lot of other factors here," he said, "but [my] suggestion was that over time, over many years, if you have heavily unionized states like California, and it becomes very difficult for policymakers to make needed reforms, states gets further and further into debt."

It's a far leap, though, from correlation to causation, and causation seems to be what Scott Walker is counting on. He must weaken state employee unions, he suggests, so that Wisconsin can manage its budget better in the future. That is, at the very least, an assumption that should be questioned.

27

The Great Recession's Institutional Change in the Public Employment Relationship: Implications for State and Local Governments

Changes in public sector employment will shape a lot more than collective bargaining rights. It will change who works for state and local governments, the type of work they do, and the quality of service they provide.

By Helisse Levine[1] and Eric Scorsone[2]

From *State and Local Government Review*, December 2011.

INTRODUCTION

The aftermath of the 2008–09 recession often dubbed the "Great Recession"[1] has already affected state and local governments and their employees (e.g., Pollin and Thompson 2011; American Public Transportation Association 2011; Jacobs, Lucia and Lester 2010; Vestal 2009). From modified work schedules and furloughs to pension and benefit reforms such as raising the retirement age and increasing employee contributions, public sector employers and employees have had to adapt themselves to new work arrangements. The objective of this article is to explore the ramifications of compensation and benefit changes on the fiscal health of state and local governments.

This article examines the implications of employee benefit and compensation changes on the fiscal health of state and local governments and their employees. In order to do so, it first looks at the evolution of labor relations in the public sector as it pertains to state and local government. In the next section, it reviews significant recent institutional changes in state and local governments in the area of employment and compensation and reviews these. Finally, it concludes with a few thoughts about the potential impact of these changes in the public sector.

EVOLUTION OF THE CURRENT INSTITUTIONAL RULES: PUBLIC SECTOR EMPLOYMENT RELATIONS

Local government fiscal health is the ability of a local government to balance revenues and expenses while providing adequate levels of service to residents. As the housing market has collapsed, it has depressed both property tax income and other government proceeds such as permit and inspection fees. Thus, the Great Recession has squeezed the revenue side of the equation severely for state and local governments. Given that employee compensation typically represents a major portion of the overall cost of state and local government, it is not unexpected that political officials would seek to rethink the employment relationship in order to ensure their fiscal health.

The employment relationship between public sector employees and employers is one that has been fraught with tension for many years. Starting in the 1960s, employees began to gain the right to collectively bargain over wages and working conditions. Legislatures, particularly those in northern states with large union populations, passed collective bargaining laws for public employees. Prior to this time, public employees were considered to have a special duty to the "state" and therefore could not enter into employment contracts. In 1959, almost no state granted an explicit right to unionize or bargain collectively (Freeman 1986, 50). Starting in the 1960s, states began passing laws that allowed state and local government employees to form unions. By the 1980s, almost forty states had some degree of protection for employee unions and collective bargaining. Many states also added arbitration to ensure a settlement mechanism if bargaining failed. This was a massive sea change from the period before the 1960s when public sector unions were nonexistent. By the 1970s, about 40 percent of the public sector workforce was unionized (Freeman 1986, 52). This percentage has stayed constant over the past twenty years despite the massive relative decline in private sector union membership (Blanchflower 2004, 386).

There has been considerable economic research on the effects of public sector unions on government costs. The consensus is that public sector unions do raise the cost of government (Freeman 1986, 42; Blanchflower 2004, 383). They also have an impact on the non-unionized workforce by raising their costs as well. However, the authors believe that much of this research incorrectly treats the public and private sectors alike.

In fact, the rules of the game for the two sectors are somewhat different. Bargaining of any sort between employers and employees is governed by the rights, power, and constraints over both sides given by labor laws along with other procedures and practices. Thus, for private sector employers and employees, the rules of the game are set by institutions outside the game, the state or federal government. The business or labor community can use strategic pressure to lobby their legislators to change these rules. In the case of the public sector, the "rules of the game" are written by the same people who are sitting at the bargaining table. Though public employees effectively lobby government too, the comparative interest of the parties in the outcome is different.

Part of the argument against collective bargaining rights for public employees is that they are also part of the electorate and help choose their own employers. Some see this as an inherent conflict of interest. It allows employees to drive up their own wages and benefits at the expense of other citizens. In economic parlance, public sector unions may be able to shift the demand curve for labor outward—affecting both price and quantity—resulting in higher wages and higher employment. Their ability to shift the demand curve depends at least partly on the institutional framework or rules of the game in place. Therefore, a key question is the extent to which institutional changes such as reducing collective bargaining rights or reforming arbitration processes may result in a transfer of government resources from employees (unions) to employers (governments). From the perspective of state and local government officials, this shift may be critical in sustaining fiscal health.

INSTITUTIONAL CHANGES: COMPENSATION AND BENEFIT CHANGES IN STATE AND LOCAL GOVERNMENTS

Changes in public sector compensation plans have been widespread and quite large in some cases. For example, in July 2008, Utah became the first state to declare a four-day workweek for close to 75 percent of its 24,000 executive-branch employees. Most recently, in New Jersey, workers will be required to pay a greater share of their pension and health benefit costs, cost-of-living benefit increases will be eliminated for all current and future retirees, and the retirement age for new employees will be increased to sixty-five. New Jersey's unfunded liability for other postemployment benefits in health care is $71.4 billion. New Jersey spends $4.4 billion annually on public employees and retiree health care costs, with the cost of health benefits making up 9 percent of the state's budget today.

According to a report released by the New Jersey Governor's office (State of New Jersey Chris Christie 2011), these reforms will substantially lower health benefit costs for local governments, including those at the county, school, and municipal levels, representing another major step forward in providing real, long-term properly tax relief. The reform legislation both secures the long-term solvency of the pension system by achieving a projected funding ratio of 88 percent within the next thirty years while providing over $120 billion in savings for New Jersey taxpayers. Similarly, the reforms to the health benefit system will save New Jersey taxpayers $3.1 billion over the next ten years. The combined savings from these reforms directly translates to real property tax relief for New Jersey families and budget relief for local governments. Similarly, New York Governor Andrew Cuomo has proposed limited pension and health care benefits for new employees including raising the retirement age.

As Edwards (2010) suggests, one of the impediments to enacting reforms is the resistance of the unionized and politically active workforces of state and local governments. Moreover, there are potential economic costs to these reforms as well: lower public employee pay may result in a decline in spending by government employees and a concomitant reduction in local tax revenue; also, potential inefficiencies in government operations due to motivational effects and staffing levels may not be included in the net savings calculations (Dornhelm 2009). However, as unsustainable pension costs drive government budget liabilities, and play an increasingly larger role in deficits (e.g., 20 percent of annual budget liabilities in Atlanta City, Georgia), these costs must be addressed.

Interest in public sector employee benefits and compensation has resurfaced as a result of the economic downturn spurring a wave of actions that may threaten a once secure future of millions of public workers. According to the Pew Center (2010) in the first ten months of 2010, eighteen states took action to reduce then-pension liabilities, either through reducing benefits or by increasing employee contributions and more may do so in 2011 legislative sessions. In 2009, eleven states made similar changes and eight did so in 2008. By February 2010, twenty states had announced or enacted furlough plans that impact over one million employees nationwide (Office of Legislative Oversight 2009).

In February 2011, the University of Michigan Center for Local, State, and Urban Policy found that many of Michigan's local jurisdictions are shrinking the size of their workforce through multiple measures: 23 percent are leaving vacant positions unfilled (including 68 percent of the largest jurisdictions), 22 percent report decreasing their overall levels of hiring (including 79 percent of the largest jurisdictions), and 14 percent report increasing outright workforce layoffs (including 55 percent of the largest jurisdictions). In addition, 12 percent of all local governments in Michigan say they expect to utilize employee furloughs to cut costs (including 47 percent of the largest jurisdictions).

With respect to current employee health care costs, 33 percent of Michigan's local governments plan to increase the share of health care premiums, co-pays, and deductibles paid by their employees. Among the state's largest jurisdictions, this intention increases to 71 percent. Approximately 45 percent of the state's smallest jurisdictions report that they do not offer such fringe benefits to their current employees in the first place, so they have no such costs to shift to employees. In regard to retirement plans, 15 percent of all jurisdictions say they expect to increase the share of retirement plan contributions paid by their current employees (this increases to 38 percent of the state's largest jurisdictions). Approximately 31 percent of Michigan's local governments report that they do not provide retirement packages to their former employees at all (including 43 percent of Michigan's smallest jurisdictions).

According to the National Council of State Legislatures, twenty-five state legislatures enacted significant retirement system changes in 2011 compared to twenty-one in 2010 (Snell 2011). In all, thirty-nine of the fifty states enacted significant revisions to at least one state retirement plan in 2010 or 2011. As of June 2011, pending legislation on pension reform remained before the Massachusetts and Ohio legislatures, and the governors of California and New York had proposed changes that are likely to be considered later in 2011 or in 2012 (Snell 2011). For example, in 2011, five legislatures lengthened the period over which final average salary is averaged to provide the base on which pension benefits are calculated. Eight states made similar changes in 2010. In most cases, the change was from a person's highest thirty-six months to the highest sixty months (three to five years). Florida changed its provision from the highest five years to the highest eight. Such changes applied in all cases to people hired after the effective date of the legislation. Also, in 2011, nine states revised their provisions for automatic cost-of-living adjustments (COLAs), as eight other states had done in 2010. It is hoped that this revision will reduce inflationary erosion of the purchasing power of retirement benefits. In all cases in 2011, as in 2010, state action reduced future commitments. State actions in 2011 affect current benefit recipients in three states, but more frequently were designed to affect people who will retire in the future or (in six states) only people who will be hired in the future. Oklahoma, which does not provide automatic COLAs, enacted legislation requiring future COLAs to be funded at the time of enactment. Other adjustments include changes in (1) deferred retirement option plans, (2) defined benefit plan changes, (3) defined contribution and hybrid plans, (4) divestiture, (5) early retirement incentives, (6) elected officials" retirement programs, and (7) taxation of retirement income.

CONCLUSION: EMPLOYEE IMPACTS AND FISCAL HEALTH RAMIFICATION

With forty-two states and the District of Columbia having closed or working to close $103 billion in shortfalls for Fiscal Year 2012,[2] states' options for addressing them are fewer and more difficult than in recent years (McNichol, Oliff, and Johnson 2011). States will continue to struggle to find the revenue needed to support critical public services like education, health care, and human services for a number of years. Among other impacts, this means that state actions will continue to be a drag on the national economy, threatening hundreds of thousands of private- and public-sector jobs, reducing the job creation that otherwise would be expected to occur. Although governments can raise income through taxation to pay pensions or cut the number of police and teachers, all of these choices have implications to the health of the state and local governments and the communities within which residents reside.

Another result is that consumers who are public employees will have no choice but to alter their behaviors as a result of these benefit modifications. When a person loses his or her job, is forced to work less, or must pay a greater share of their income into their retirement, there may be an immediate impact to that person's standard of living. In the case of job loss, even for those eligible for unemployment benefits and other forms of government assistance (like food assistance), it is often the case that these benefits replace 50 percent or less of their regular income (Simpson 2011). People may also decide to change their spending behaviors and self-provide otherwise purchased goods and services. That means these people are consuming far less than usual. The economic consequences, however, can go beyond reduced consumption. Many people will turn to retirement savings which will result in long-term ramifications.

In addition to the lost spending and tax revenue, there are the costs to the state from service disruptions. Some are obvious, like people taking more time off from private-sector jobs because of longer wait times at public offices like the Department of Motor Vehicles. Then there are other problems, like a truck spill on a Northern California freeway which took twelve hours to clean up because the spill took place on a Friday which was a furlough day. Debacles like these end up costing the state money (Dornhelm 2010) including overtime, contributing to an increase in payroll costs. As productivity falls due to changes in employee motivation or adequate staffing levels, day-to-day operations including delivery of services will take longer: building inspections might not be conducted on the same day and phone calls could take longer to be answered or be returned. Moreover, new and fresh talent entering the workforce will be less attracted to selecting public service as a future career.

However, the fiscal implications are only one part of the story: workforce issues will remain critical as well. Other considerations include the potential ramifications of these changes on workplace productivity, recruitment practices, and general workforce issues for public employees. These changes will have short- and long-run implications for these employees. For government managers, they will likely mean "doing more with less" now and well into the future.

The institutional changes reviewed here or threat of such changes including restructuring collective bargaining rights, unionization, union due collection, and the issues that can be bargained are shifting the playing field for employees and employers in the public sector. Not since the passage of the right to unionization and collective bargaining in the 1960s have such major changes been on the horizon. These changes will have long-standing effects for the public sector including the cost of government, the types of workers attracted to government, and perhaps even the type and quality of services provided. As these changes occur, they provide a rich opportunity for both scholarly research and citizen reflection.

Local Government

By 2012, at least some states were beginning to see light at the end of a very dark financial tunnel. Local governments can see a light too, though it is widely assumed to be an oncoming train rather than a promise of a brighter future. Battered by declining property and income tax revenues, local governments face the end of stimulus dollars from Washington, increased program responsibilities passed on from state governments, restless public labor unions, and another round or two of unavoidably tough budget decisions. As one of the essays in this chapter makes clear, these sorts of problems are literally keeping local officials awake at night.

There are a lot of financial problems at the local level at least in part because there are so many local governments—more than 85,000 of them. This includes all substate governance units, which includes counties, municipalities, and a mind-boggling array of (mostly) single-service special districts that run everything from schools to mosquito control programs to airports. Even though the Great Recession officially ended in 2009, the impact on these governments continues to be felt three years later. The primary sources of revenue for these local governments—mostly sales and property taxes—has yet to return to pre recession levels, and budgets are still being squeezed.

Local governments have less flexibility to deal with these difficult financial issues because, unlike states, they are not sovereign. State governments get their powers and legal authority directly from citizens—this power and authority is codified in the state constitution. Local governments get their powers from the state. What this means is that local governments are not on an equal footing with state governments, and that imbalance can leave local governments vulnerable when budgets do not balance. For example, states can place limits on the ability of local governments to levy taxes. Yet while restraining revenue, states can also require local governments to provide programs and services. States do provide substantial sums of money to local governments like school districts, but those funds often get cut in tight budgetary times.

This vulnerability can be exacerbated as states seek to not only reduce budgets but actually pass on debt to local governments. For example, beginning in 2011, California began experimenting with "realignment." In essence, this term describes a set of state-initiated proposals for state and local governments to swap various funding streams and program responsibilities. The idea is to better align government finances, policy capabilities, and proximity to citizens. As realignment has evolved, however, local governments have come to fear the state passing on expensive program responsibilities without passing on any extra funds. That's a good deal for a state government grappling with a multibillion-dollar shortfall. It's a bad deal for local governments. Not being sovereign, in other words, can lead to a bad budget situation getting worse.

The readings in this section highlight the degree and the depth of the financial problems local governments are dealing with. They also profile some of the officials who are trying to make local government work in spite of these difficult circumstances. The first essay, by Christopher Hoene and Michael Pagano, describes the findings from a national survey of city finance officers. What those finance officers are reporting is the growing recognition of a "new normal" where revenues from property and sales taxes are more likely to move sideways rather than up. Adapting to that new normal is going to be tough, leaving cities less able to meet their financial needs.

The second essay, by Thom Reilly and Mark Reed, takes a look at how local governments are responding to this new normal. According to their data, more than 90 percent of local governments are dealing with budget shortfalls, and in an attempt to fill the gap, they are more likely to lay off people than increase taxes. The third essay, by Kirk Victor, is another look at some of the strategies local governments are pursuing to make the books balance. The problems, and the risks that are being taken to address them, are keeping some officials awake at night.

Finally, Alan Greenblatt profiles Chicago mayor Rahm Emanuel. Like many other cities, Chicago's finances are precarious, and it is also dealing with everything from high murder rates to a declining population. Yet Emanuel is determined to not simply keep his city afloat but move it forward.

28

City Fiscal Conditions in 2011

By Christopher W. Hoene and Michael A. Pagano[1]

The results of a national survey of city finance officers shows the emergence of a "new normal" characterized by flat or declining local government revenues.

T he nation's city finance officers report that the fiscal condition of cities continues to weaken in 2011 as cities confront the persistent effects of the economic downturn.[2] Local and regional economies, characterized by struggling housing markets, slow consumer spending and high levels of unemployment, are driving declines in city revenues. In response, cities are continuing to cut personnel, infrastructure investments and key services. Findings from the National League of Cities' latest annual survey of city finance officers include:

- As finance officers look to the close of 2011, they project declining revenues, with corresponding spending cutbacks in response to the economic downturn;
- The pace of decline in property tax revenues quickened in 2011, reflecting the inevitable and lagged impact of real estate market declines in recent years;
- Ending balances, or "reserves," while still at high levels, decreased for the third year in a row as cities used these balances to weather the effects of the downturn;
- Fiscal pressures on cities include declining local economic health, infrastructure costs, employee-related costs for health care, pensions and wages and cuts in state aid; and,
- Confronted with these pressures and conditions, cities are making personnel cuts, delaying or cancelling infrastructure projects and cutting local services—cuts that have implications for jobs and national economic recovery.

From National League of Cities, September 2011.

MEETING FISCAL NEEDS—A "NEW NORMAL?"

Since 2008, nearly all reflections on the economy and on government fiscal position mention the Great Depression of the 1930s that began with the stock market crash on Black Tuesday, October 29, 1929. "Not since the Great Depression..." is an oft-used prelude to many descriptions of the current period. A similar refrain is heard when policy analysts and citizens discuss cities. In reality, however, the Great Recession that began with the bursting of the housing bubble in 2007 and the sharp drop in stock markets in 2008 did not begin to wreak havoc on cities' revenue profiles until later.

For cities, the collective impact of property values continuing at levels far below their 2007 peaks,

The City Fiscal Condition Survey is a national mail and online survey of finance officers in U.S. cities in the spring-summer of each year. This is the 26th edition of the survey, which began in 1986.

consumer spending slowing, consumer confidence eroding and markets possibly entering a double-dip recession is the worst since the Great Depression. Yet, America's cities are not looking to the past as a guidepost for the future. Indeed, lower property values and declining sales may portend something entirely new, a "new normal."

In 2011, 57 percent of city finance officers report that their cities are less able to meet fiscal needs than in 2010 (See Figure 28.1). City finance officers' comparative assessment of their cities' fiscal conditions from year to year in 2011 improved from their 2010 assessment, when 87 percent of city finance officers said their cities were less able to meet fiscal needs than in 2009, the

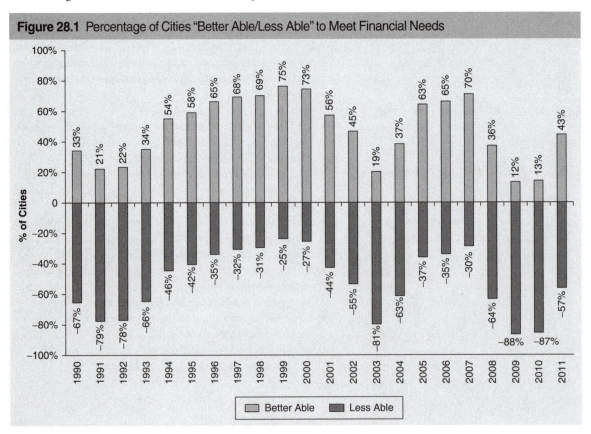

Figure 28.1 Percentage of Cities "Better Able/Less Able" to Meet Financial Needs

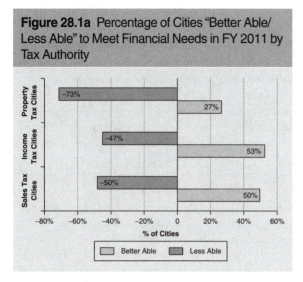

Figure 28.1a Percentage of Cities "Better Able/ Less Able" to Meet Financial Needs in FY 2011 by Tax Authority

officers in cities that rely more upon property taxes (73%)—the most common local tax source—are more likely to say that their cities are less able to meet fiscal needs in 2011 than those in cities reliant upon sales taxes (50%) or income taxes (47%) (See Figure 28.1a).

REVENUE AND SPENDING TRENDS

Cities ended fiscal year 2010 with the largest year-to-year reductions in general fund revenues and expenditures in the 26-year history of the survey.[3] In constant dollars (adjusted to account for inflationary factors in the state-local sector), general fund revenues in 2010 declined -3.8 percent from 2009 revenues, while expenditures declined by -4.4 percent.[4] Looking to the close of 2011, city finance officers project that general fund revenues will decline by -2.3 percent and expenditures will decline by -1.9 percent (See Figure 28.2).

Revenue and spending shifts in 2010 and 2011 portray a worsening fiscal picture for America's cities. The projected decline in 2011 revenues represents the fifth straight year-to-year decline going back to 2007. Over the same period, year-to-year expenditures have declined

highest level in the history of NLC's 25-year survey. The 2011 findings suggest that city finance officers' perceptions are still mostly negative, but they are not necessarily worsening and may reflect a new normal in terms of their assessment and expectations of meeting nearer-term financial needs. Finance

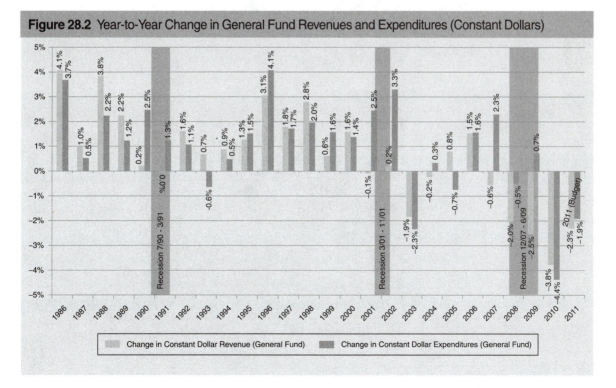

Figure 28.2 Year-to-Year Change in General Fund Revenues and Expenditures (Constant Dollars)

in three of the last four years. In comparison to previous periods, the most recent decade, with recessions in 2001 and 2007–09, continues to be characterized by volatility in city fiscal conditions. With a national economic recovery that has been weak or stalled, and taking into account a lag between economic shifts and the effects for city budgets, it seems very likely that cities will confront further revenue declines and cuts in city spending in 2012.

TAX REVENUES

The fiscal condition of individual cities varies greatly depending on differences in local tax structure and reliance. While an overwhelming majority of cities have access to a local property tax, many are also reliant upon local sales taxes, and some cities (fewer than 10% nationally) are reliant upon local income or wage taxes. Understanding the differing performance of these tax sources and the connections to broader economic conditions helps explain the forces behind declining city revenues.[5]

Property Taxes. Local property tax revenues are driven primarily by the value of residential and commercial property, with property tax bills determined by local governments' assessment of the value of property. Property tax collections lag the real estate market because local assessment practices take time to catch up with changes. As a result, current property tax bills and property tax collections typically reflect values of property from anywhere from 18 months to several years prior.

The effects of the well-publicized downturn in the real estate market in recent years are increasingly evident in city property tax revenues in 2011. Property tax revenues in 2010 dropped by -2 percent compared with 2009 levels, in constant dollars, the first year-to-year decline in city property tax revenues in 15 years. Property tax collections for 2011 point to worsening effects from the downturn in real estate values, projected to decline by -3.7 percent. The full weight of the decline in housing values is now evident in city budgets, and property tax revenues will likely decline further in 2012 and 2013 as city property tax assessments and collections catch up with the market (See Figure 28.3).

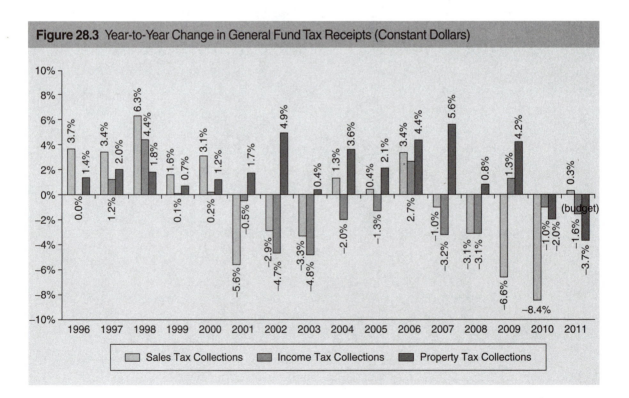

Figure 28.3 Year-to-Year Change in General Fund Tax Receipts (Constant Dollars)

Sales Taxes. Changes in economic conditions are also evident in terms of changes in city sales tax collections. When consumer confidence is high, people spend more on goods and services and city governments with sales-tax authority reap the benefits through increases in sales tax collections. For much of this decade, consumer spending was also fueled by a strong real estate market that provided additional wealth to homeowners. The struggling economy and the declining real estate market have reduced consumer confidence, resulting in less consumer spending and declining sales tax revenues. City sales tax receipts declined in 2010 over previous year receipts by -8.4 percent in constant dollars, the largest year-to-year decline in 15 years. However, in 2011, city sales tax revenues are projected to essentially remain flat (increase of 0.3%) over 2010 levels.

Income Taxes. City income tax receipts have been fairly flat, or have declined, for most of the past decade in constant dollars. Local income tax revenues are driven primarily by income and wages, not capital gains. The lack of growth in these revenues suggests that the economic recovery following the 2001 recession was, as many economists have noted, a recovery characterized by a lack of growth in jobs, salaries and wages. Projections for 2011 are for a decrease of -1.6 percent in constant dollars, as wages and salaries continue to reflect local job losses and with a national unemployment rate hovering around 9 percent.

City finance officers are therefore predicting decline or little growth in all three major sources of tax revenue for cities in 2011. With national economic indicators pointing to continued struggles, and the lag between changing economic conditions and local revenue collections, all indications point to continuing challenges for city budgets in the coming years.

FACTORS INFLUENCING CITY BUDGETS

A number of factors combine to determine the revenue performance, spending levels and overall fiscal condition of cities. Each year, NLC's survey presents city finance directors with a list of factors that affect city budgets.[6] Respondents are asked whether each of the factors increased or decreased from the previous year and whether the change is having a positive or negative influence on the city's overall fiscal picture. Leading the list of factors that finance officers say have increased over the previous year are employee health benefit costs (86%) and pension costs (84%). Infrastructure (79%) and public safety (63%) demands were most often noted as increasing among specific service arenas. Increases in prices, in general, were also oft-mentioned (84%). Leading factors that city finance officers report to have decreased are levels of state aid to cities (60%), the local tax base (53%) and the health of the local economy (42%) (See Figure 28.4).

When asked about the positive or negative impact of each factor on city finances in 2011, at least seven in 10 city finance officers cited employee health benefit costs (82%), pension costs (80%), prices (78%) and infrastructure demands (70%) as negatively effecting city budgets. A majority of city finance officers also cited the level of state aid (58%), employee wage costs (56%) and public safety costs (54%) as having a negative influence (See Figure 28.5).

REVENUE ACTIONS AND SPENDING CUTS

City finance officers were also asked about specific revenue and spending actions taken in 2011. As has been the case for much of the past two decades, regardless of the state of the economy, the most common action taken to boost city revenues has been to increase the levels of fees for services. Two in five (41%) city finance officers reported that their city has taken this step. One in four cities also increased the number of fees that are applied to city services (23%). Twenty percent of cities increased the local property tax in 2011. Since the mid-1990s, irrespective of economic conditions, the percentage of city finance officers reporting increases in property tax rates in any given year has been at about this same level. Increases in sales, income or other tax rates have been far less common, as continued to be the case in 2011 (See Figure 28.6).

When asked about the most common responses to prospective shortfalls this fiscal year, by a wide margin the most common responses were instituting personnel-related cuts (72%) and delaying or cancelling capital infrastructure projects (60%). Two in five (42%) reported that their city is making cuts in services other

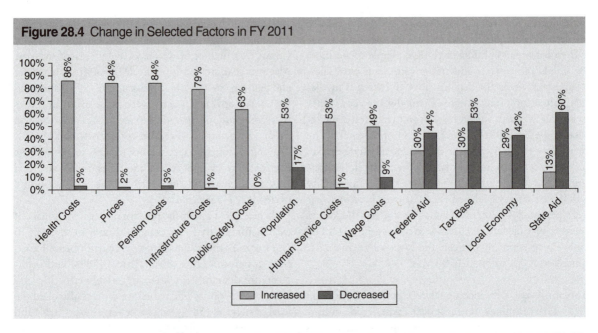

Figure 28.4 Change in Selected Factors in FY 2011

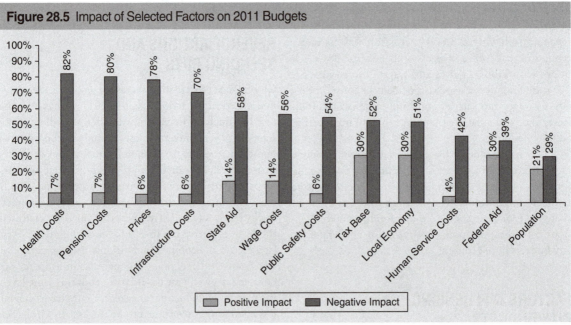

Figure 28.5 Impact of Selected Factors on 2011 Budgets

than public safety and human-social services (services that tend to be higher in demand during economic downturns), such as public works, libraries, parks and recreation programs. One in three finance officers (36%) reported modifying health care benefits for employees (See Figure 28.7).

The 2011 survey also asked about specific types of personnel-related cuts made in 2011 (See Figure 28.8). The most common cut was a hiring freeze (68%). Half (50%) of cities reported salary or wage reductions or freezes and nearly one in three (31%) cities reported employee layoffs or reducing employee health care

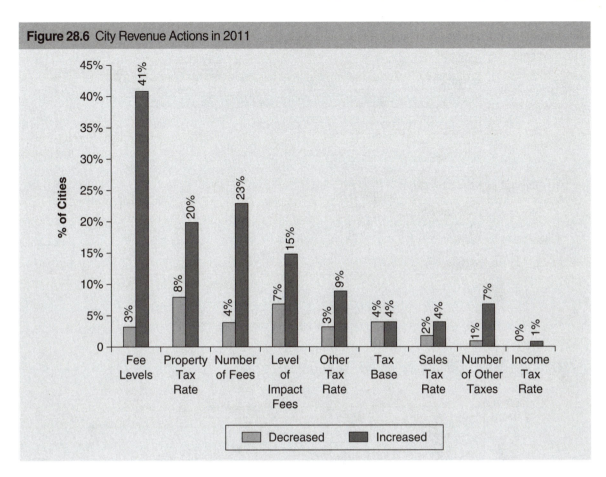

Figure 28.6 City Revenue Actions in 2011

benefits (30%). Other personnel actions included early retirements (25%) and furloughs (19%). Many cities have used some combination of these types of actions in an effort to reduce personnel costs. The combination of these personnel-related cuts is resulting in a significant reduction in the size of local government workforces. In 2010, a separate NLC survey on local jobs projected a total reduction in city and county employment of nearly 500,000 positions from 2009 to 2011.[7] More recently, the U.S. Bureau of Labor Statistics' latest national unemployment numbers, as of August 2011, revealed that total local government employment in the U.S. had decreased by 550,000 jobs from peak levels in 2008.[8]

State Actions

State budgets have also been confronted with several years of shortfalls and constraints. The Center on Budget and Policy Priorities reports that states are facing their fourth year in a row of budget-cutting, with the 2012 cuts being deeper than in previous years.[9] In many cases, the cuts that states are making reduce aid and transfers to city governments. NLC's 2011 survey asked city finance officers about the types of state actions they've encountered since 2009, including cuts in general aid (50%), cuts in state-shared and/or state-collected revenues (49%), revocation or reduction of reimbursement programs or other transfers (32%), cuts in funding for services that cities and other local governments deliver on behalf of state governments (22%) and transfer of state program responsibility (17%). Amid the politics of state budget-balancing, sometimes state actions are also taken that reduce or limit local authority (13%).

This mix of state actions taken by state leaders to balance state budgets adds to the cyclical economic pressures and constraints that cities and other local governments are confronting. Looking across state and

Figure 28.7 City Spending Actions 2009–2011

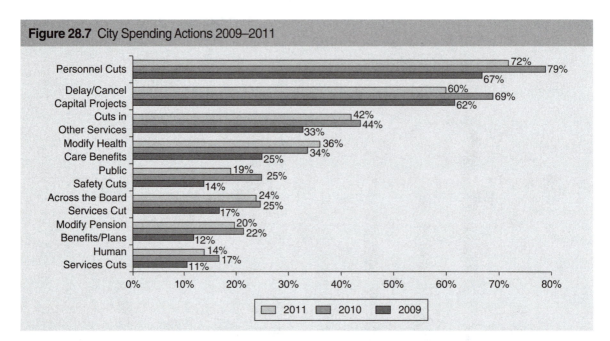

Figure 28.8 City Personnel-Related Cuts 2010 & 2011

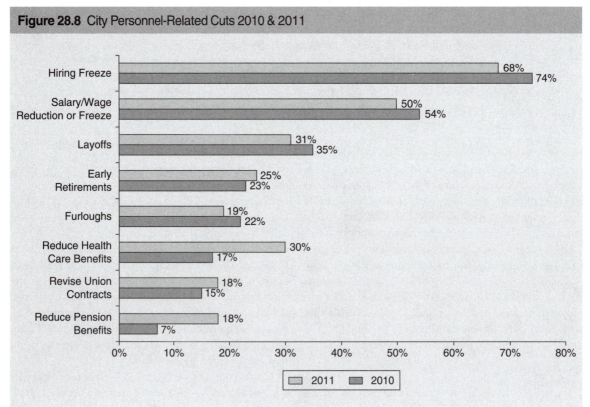

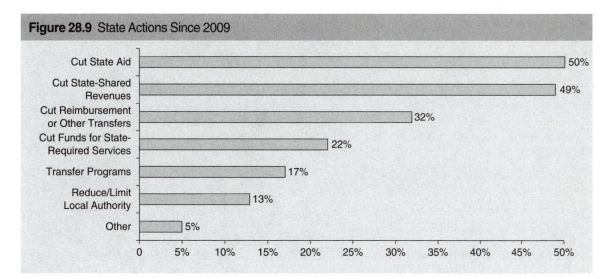

Figure 28.9 State Actions Since 2009

local actions in response to fiscal stress reveals the pro-cyclical nature of state-local fiscal actions—that during economic downturns, the decisions that state and local leaders make to balance budgets often exacerbate the effects of the downturn for other levels of government, for jobs and for the quality of life and well-being of individuals and communities.

ENDING BALANCES

One way that cities prepare for future fiscal challenges is to maintain adequate levels of general fund ending balances. Ending balances are similar to reserves, or what might be thought of as cities' equivalents to "rainy day funds," in that they provide a financial cushion for cities in the event of a fiscal downturn or the need for an unforeseen outlay. Unlike states' "rainy day funds," there is no trigger mechanism—such as an increase in unemployment—to force release of reserves; instead, reserves are available for spending at any time or for saving for a specific purpose. Ending balances, which are transferred forward to the next fiscal year in most cases, are maintained for many reasons. For example, cities build up healthy balances in anticipation of unpredictable events such as natural disasters and economic downturns. But ending balances are also built up deliberately, much like a personal savings account, to set aside funds for planned events such as construction of water treatment facilities or other capital projects. Bond underwriters also look at reserves as an indicator of fiscal

responsibility, which can increase credit ratings and decrease the costs of city debt, thereby saving the city money. Finally, as federal and state aid to cities has become a smaller proportion of city revenues, cities have become more self-reliant and are much more likely to set aside funds for emergency or other purposes.

Prior to the recession, as city finances experienced sustained growth, city ending balances as a percentage of general fund expenditures reached an historical high for the NLC survey of 25 percent. However, as economic conditions have made balancing city budgets more difficult in recent years, ending balances have been increasingly utilized to help fill the gap. In 2010, cities reduced their ending balances to 17.4 percent of expenditures, and in 2011, city finance officers projected ending balances at 15.4 percent of expenditures (See Figure 28.10). If this projection holds, since the high point in 2008, cities will have drawn down total ending balances by nearly 40 percent (from the high of 25.2% to 2011's 15.4%).

BEYOND 2011

2011 reveals a number of continuing and troubling trends for city fiscal conditions. The impacts of the economic downturn are clear in city projections for final 2011 revenues and expenditures and in the actions taken in response to changing conditions. The local sector of the economy is now fully in the midst of realizing the effects of the recession from 2007–2009 and the, to date, anemic

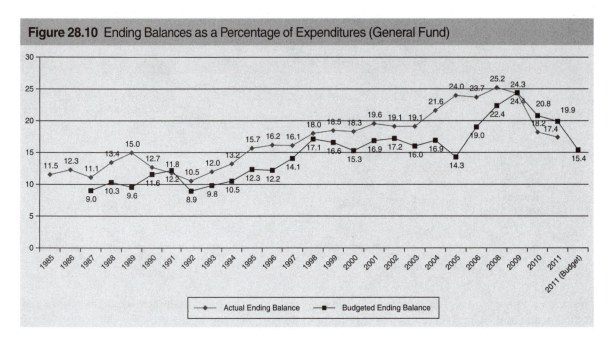

Figure 28.10 Ending Balances as a Percentage of Expenditures (General Fund)

economic recovery. The effects of depressed real estate markets, low levels of consumer confidence and high levels of unemployment will continue to play out in cities through 2011, 2012 and beyond. The fiscal realities confronting cities include a number of persistent concerns:

- Real estate markets continue to struggle and tend to be slow to recover from downturns; projections indicate a very slow recovery of real estate values, meaning that cities will be confronted with declines or slow growth in future property tax collections not just in 2011 but most likely through 2012 and 2013;
- Other economic conditions—consumer spending, unemployment and wages—are also struggling and will weigh heavily on future city sales and income tax revenues;
- Large state government budget shortfalls in 2011 and 2012 will likely be resolved through cuts in aid and transfers to many local governments;
- Two of the factors that city finance officers report as having the largest negative impact on their ability to meet needs are employee-related costs for health care coverage and pensions. Underfunded

pension and health care liabilities will persist as a challenge to city budgets for years to come; and
- Facing revenue and spending pressures, cities are likely to continue to make cuts in personnel and services, and to draw down ending balances in order to balance budgets.

NOTES

1. Christopher W. Hoene is Director of the Center for Research and Innovation at the National League of Cities. Michael A. Pagano is Dean of the College of Urban Planning and Public Affairs at the University of Illinois at Chicago. The authors would like to acknowledge the 272 respondents to this year's fiscal survey. The commitment of these cities' finance officers to the project is greatly appreciated.

2. All references to specific years are for fiscal years as defined by the individual cities. The use of "cities" or "city" in this report refers to municipal corporations.

3. The General Fund is the largest and most common fund of all cities, accounting for approximately 55% of city revenues across the municipal sector.

4. "Constant dollars" refers to inflation-adjusted dollars. "Current dollars" refers to non-adjusted dollars. To calculate constant dollars, we adjust current dollars using the U.S. Bureau of Economic Analysis (BEA) National Income and Product Account (NIPA) estimate for inflation in the state and local government sector. Constant dollars are a more accurate source of comparison over time because the dollars are adjusted to account for differences in the costs of state and local government.

5. For more information on variation in local and state tax structures, see "Cities and State Fiscal Structure," (NLC, 2008) at http://www.nlc.org/File Library/ Find City Solutions/Research Innovation/Finance/ cities-state-fiscal-structure-2008-rpt.pdf.

6. The factors include: infrastructure needs, public safety needs, human service needs, education needs, employee wages, employee pension costs, employee health benefit costs, prices and inflation, amount of federal aid, amount of state aid, federal non-environmental mandates, federal environmental mandates, state non-environmental mandates, state environmental mandates, state tax and expenditure limitations, population, city tax base and the health of the local economy.

7. See "Local Governments Cutting Jobs and Services" (NLC, 2010) at http://www.nlc.org/File Library/ Find City Solutions/Research Innovation/Finance/ local-governments-cutting-jobs-services-rpt-jul10 .pdf.

8. See http://www.bls.gov/news.release/empsit.nr0.htm.

9. See http://www.cbpp.org/cms/index.cfm?fa=view& id=3526.

29

Budget Shortfalls, Employee Compensation, and Collective Bargaining in Local Governments

By Thom Reilly[1] and Mark B. Reed[1]

More than 90 percent of local governments are facing budget shortfalls. That means layoffs but not necessarily higher taxes.

INTRODUCTION: LOCAL GOVERNMENT COMPENSATION RESPONSES TO BUDGET SHORTFALLS

Local governments across the United States are grappling with reduced revenues brought on by the financial crisis and recession. Sales taxes, property taxes, and other forms of local government revenues have been severely curtailed (Boyd 2009; Shubik, Horwitz, and Ginsberg 2009, 3). Most local governments project declining revenues for the next several years and budget shortfalls are actually expected to widen over this period (Hoene 2009; Hoene and Pagano, 2009; Pollack 2009). This drop in revenues, coupled with a faltering economy and increased service demands, has enormous consequences for local governments and their citizens. The large budget shortfalls are jeopardizing the ability of cities and counties to perform core functions (Boyd 2009; Ginsberg and Horwitz 2009). Unlike the federal government, local governments cannot run deficits. To balance their budgets, they must cut spending or raise taxes. Those local jurisdictions attempting tax increases face additional obstacles besides these changes being politically unpopular (Shubik, Horwitz, and Ginsberg 2009, 1). Although cutting services may be a more common fix, there are limits to what citizens will allow in these reductions (Shubik, Horwitz, and Ginsberg 2009,1). Since labor costs make up the largest portion of overall local government spending, reductions in this area are unavoidable. However, with increased unionization of public sector workers, attempts by cities and

From *State and Local Government Review*, December 2011.

counties to reduce benefits and salaries have led to tense labor-management stalemates (Horwitz 2009).

The purpose of this study was to examine how local governments are responding to budget gaps and revenue shortfalls and to explore how compensation practices across the United States are correlated with changes in service delivery and the presence of collective bargaining. Type of government (county vs. city), collective bargaining status, and governing board partisanship were used as variables to explore possible associations with budget shortfalls, responses to these shortfalls, and employee compensation including wages and benefits.

The Effects of Unions on Local Compensation

While union membership has been declining in the private sector for the past several decades, public sector union membership has been rising. Government workers are nearly five times more likely to belong to a union than private workers. The number of union workers employed by government for the first time outnumbered union ranks in the private sector in 2009, the result of massive layoffs that plunged the rate of private-sector union membership to a record low of 7 percent (Bureau of Labor Statistics [BLS] 2009). Local, state, and federal government workers made up 51.5 percent of all union members in 2009.

One major reason cited for the escalation in wages and benefits for public sector workers has been the increase in membership in public sector employee unions. Research has confirmed that public sector unions, via collective bargaining processes, positively inflate employee wages and benefits (Belman, Heywood, and Lund 1997; Johnston and Hancke 2009; Kearney 2003; Llorens 2008; McKethan et al., 2006; Reilly, Schoener, and Bolin 2007). Overall, public sector unions raise nonwage benefits for their employees more than they raise wages (Freeman 1986). Kearney and Carnevale (2001) contend that public sector unions support increasing benefits over wages because the costs are less transparent to the community and can be spread out over time. This is supported by Hunter and Rankin's (1988) compensation model which suggest that fringe benefits have grown substantially in the public sector because they are used as political payments by elected officials and the public rarely is aware of what is being awarded to employees.

The National League of Cities (NLC) recent survey cites the growing costs of employee wages (cited by 83 percent), the health of the local economy (81 percent), and employee health benefits (79 percent) as having the largest negative impact on the financial health of a municipality. Hiring freezes/layoffs (cited by 67 percent) and delay/cancellation of capital projects (62 percent) were cited as the primary responses to budget shortfalls (Hoene and Pagano, 2009). A recent report by the Pew Charitable Trusts (Shubik, Horwitz, and Ginsberg 2009) examining budget decisions in large municipalities, found that rather than raising taxes most cities were attempting to cut services, employ workforce reductions, and freeze salaries. Proposed service cuts included recreation facilities, libraries, and trash collection. Attempts at freezing salaries and successfully obtaining wage and benefit concessions from municipal labor unions have been difficult. A common theme being played out in these large cities is for the mayor to threaten layoffs in order to extract concessions. When these have not materialized, layoffs have been employed; however at levels reduced below those initially discussed (Horwitz 2009).

THE STUDY

The present study seeks to examine whether collective bargaining predicts the responses to budget shortfalls made by local municipalities across the United States. Furthermore, we were interested in examining the effects of collective bargaining on employee benefits within municipalities during a time of economic recession.

Variables were selected based on prior research linking them to budget shortfalls in local governments and public sector wages and benefits. Reilly, Schoener, and Bolin (2007) found county governments tended to have fewer budget shortfalls than city governments most likely due to the fact that counties usually have wider geographical areas and therefore receive tax revenues from more diverse sources than cities which may miss tax revenues from more affluent areas outside the city limits.

The same authors found that local governments with collective bargaining were more likely to see a decline in the number of employees during a budget shortfall. Additionally, Vallenta (1989) and Zax and Ichniowski

(1988) found that local government unionism can increase department and city expenditures. Therefore, we predicted that counties would show fewer budget shortfalls and those local governments with collective bargaining agreements will more likely face budget shortfalls. In addition, as mentioned above, studies have suggested that unionization positively influences earnings for both state and local governmental employees. Accordingly, we predicted that those local governments with collective bargaining agreements in place will result in higher employee compensation.

Finally, we wanted to explore what impact partisan- versus nonpartisan-governing board may have on responses to budget shortfalls and employee composition so we included a partisan/nonpartisan dichotomy in the survey.

METHODS

A survey on public sector compensation and related issues confronting local governments throughout the United States was administered to human service directors in the largest 150 cities (populations more than 160,000) and 150 counties (populations more than 360,000) in September 2009. Respondents were also given the option to respond to the survey online and rigorous follow-up was employed. Data collection ended in December 2009.

The survey instrument addressed questions on the general fiscal conditions of the local government as well as on compensation, benefits, health insurance, retirement, and/or pension plans for four different employee groups: management employees, nonmanagement employees, nonmanagement fire employees, and nonmanagement police employees. Collective bargaining status and partisan make-up of the governing body were also addressed. Respondents were asked to respond to their largest employee union, if there were multiple plans. Analysis of responding and nonresponding local governments can be found in Table 29.1.

Measures

Those respondents who reported experiencing a revenue shortfall in the last two years were asked to indicate how their jurisdiction responded (yes/no) to the shortfall from a list of twelve possible responses (imposed hiring freeze, laid off employees, eliminated vacant positions,

offered early retirement, furlough employees, reduce/eliminate public services, reduce benefits/wages, reduce retiree health care benefits, raise taxes/increase user fees, use reserve funds, borrow funds, or other). Then these responses were combined to form six distinct categories (layoffs, reduce/eliminate public services, raise taxes/increase user fees, workforce reduction, reduction in benefits/wages, and borrow funds).

Respondents completed a similar set of questions corresponding to four distinct job categories within the city/county government: nonmanagement, management, fire, and police. For each job category, the respondents were asked to indicate the amount of cost of living allowance (COLA) given to each job category for the FY 07/08 and FY 08/09 and whether the benefits of the group generally increased, decreased, or stayed the same during this two-year period. Respondents were asked to only include COLA increases and not other forms of wage increases such as merit step increases and longevity. Additionally, the respondents were asked whether the jurisdiction allowed collective bargaining for wages and benefits for this group. Those responding "yes" were then asked whether the collective bargaining agreement had been renegotiated in the middle of its term as a consequence of budget shortfalls.

Data Analysis

Our first set of analyses examined bivariate associations between the variable of experiencing a budget shortfall and the following variables: type of respondent (city or county), elected official partisanship, and allowance of collective bargaining. We then tested the bivariate associations between each of the six categorized shortfall responses and the same variables listed above.

For each job category, we then first tested bivariate associations between the items asking whether benefits generally increase, decreased, or stayed the same and the following variables: collective bargaining for the job category, type of respondent and whether the elective officials in government were partisan. A series of bivariate analyses were also conducted with the same independent variables noted above.

Although we were also interested in examining whether budget shortfalls and employee compensation varied by region, the small cell sizes for the Midwest ($n = 11$) and Northeast ($n = 8$) regions resulted in unstable

Table 29.1 Budget Shortfall by Shortfall Type

Variable	Workforce Reductions		Reduce Wage/ Ben.		Layoffs		Reduce Services		Raise Taxes		Raid Funds	
	%	N	%	N	%	N	%	N	%	N	%	N
Type												
City	94.4	67*	29.6	21	57.7	41	42.3	30	23.9	17	49.3	35
County	82.8	48	25.9	15	56.9	33	31	18	25.9	15	50.0	29
Collective bargaining												
Yes	96.3	77**	31.3	25	63.8	51	43.8	35	26.2	21	60.0	48*
No	79.5	35	22.7	10	47.7	21	27.3	12	25.0	11	34.1	15
Partisan												
Yes	91.0	61	31.3	21	53.3	32	35.0	21	26.7	16	46.7	28
No	90.0	63	22.9	16	61.5	40	38.5	26	21.5	14	53.8	35

*$p < .05$. **$p < .01$.

percentage estimates. Additionally, given that our sample underrepresented these regions (see below), the generalizability of results utilizing this variable would be tenuous at best.

FINDINGS

Budget Shortfalls and Budget Shortfall Responses

Nearly all (95.3 percent) of the county and city respondents reported experiencing a budget/revenue shortfall in the past two years. The most common response to a budget shortfall was to make a workforce reduction (89.1 percent) followed by layoffs (57.4 percent), borrowing funds (48.9 percent), and reducing or eliminating services (37.2 percent). The least common response was raising taxes or fees (24.8 percent) followed by reducing wages and benefits (27.9 percent). Slightly fewer than half of respondents reported having a partisan city or county council while a solid majority (64.8 percent) reported allowing for collective bargaining for wages and benefits. The average COLA for each job category (management/nonmanagement, police, fire) ranged from 2.09 percent to 2.90 percent.[1]

We examined the association between budget shortfalls and the following variables: type of respondent (city vs. county), partisanship of council (yes/no) and

allowance for collective bargaining (yes/no). Bivariate analyses showed a significant association between having a budget shortfall and type of respondent as well as collective bargaining (results not shown). Specifically, a significantly lower percentage of counties reported budget shortfalls (89.7 percent) relative to cities (100 percent), $p < .01$ (Fisher's exact test). Additionally, a significantly lower proportion of respondents without collective bargaining (88.6 percent) reported shortfall relative to respondents with collective bargaining (100 percent), $p < .01$ (Fisher's exact test).

For cities/counties reporting revenue or budget shortfall for the past two years, we examined whether type of respondent, collective bargaining, and partisanship of council was associated with the following budget shortfall responses: workforce reduction, reduce wages/benefits, layoffs, reduce/eliminate services, raise taxes/fees, and borrowing funds. As observed in Table 29.1, workforce reductions were significantly more likely in cities than in counties. The use of collective bargaining was significantly associated with a greater likelihood of responding to the budget shortfall through the use of workforce reductions, reductions in services, and the raiding of funds. The partisanship of the county/city council and type of respondent was not associated to any of these budget shortfall responses (Table 29.1).

Wages and Benefits

In every job unit except management (i.e., non-management, police, fire), a majority of respondents reported that the jurisdiction allowed collective bargaining for these groups. Of those locales with collective bargaining for these job units, less than one-quarter reported renegotiating contacts for the particular job unit. On average, each bargaining unit received a 2 to 3 percent cost-of-living adjustment (COLA) over the 2007–08 and 2008–09 fiscal years. Police and fire employees received the highest COLA while management received the lowest average COLA. Across all job units, respondents reported increases in benefits despite budget shortfalls. Nearly half of respondents reported increases in benefits for police and fire personnel, while fewer than 10 percent of respondents reported decreases in benefits for nonmanagement, fire, and police employees.

Table 29.2 presents the bivariate associations of benefits for each employee unit and the following variables: type of respondent, collective bargaining, and

Table 29.2 Benefit Increases/Decreases by Personnel Unit

| | Nonmanagement | | | | | | Management | | | | | |
| | Increase | | Same | | Decrease | | Increase | | Same | | Decrease | |
Variable	%	N	%	N	%	N	%	N	%	N	%	N
Type												
City	35.2	25	56.3	40	8.5	6	18.6	13	68.6	48	12.9	9
County	37.9	22	56.9	33	5.2	3	22.2	13	68.4	39	8.8	5
Collective bargaining												
Yes	48.6	35	45.8	33	5.6	4**	34.8	8	56.5	13	8.7	2
No	21.8	12	70.9	39	7.3	4	17.0	17	72.0	72	11.0	11
Partisan												
Yes	43.3	26	51.7	31	5.0	3	29.3	17	62.1	36	8.6	5
No	29.2	19	63.1	41	7.7	5	12.3	8	75.4	49	12.3	8

| | Fire | | | | | | Police | | | | | |
| | Increase | | Same | | Decrease | | Increase | | Same | | Decrease | |
Variable	%	N	%	N	%	N	%	N	%	N	%	N
Type												
City	40.0	26	52.3	34	7.7	5	42.2	27	51.6	33	6.2	4
County	43.3	13	50.0	15	6.7	2	41.5	22	54.7	29	3.8	2
Collective bargaining												
Yes	50.0	32	43.8	28	6.2		48.6	36	48.6	36	2.7	2*
No	22.6	7	67.7	21	9.7	4	28.6	12	61.9	26	9.5	4
Partisan												
Yes	51.4	19	37.8	14	10.8	4	45.5	25	49.1	27	5.5	3
No	35.1	20	61.4	35	3.5	2	35.6	21	59.3	35	5.1	3

$*p < .05.$ $**p < .01.$

council partisanship. Collective bargaining was significantly associated with employee benefits for nonmanagement, fire, and police employees. For each of these job units, respondents reporting collective bargaining indicated significantly higher increases in benefits over the two-year fiscal year period. Neither type of respondent nor partisanship was significantly associated with benefits.

Table 29.3 shows the bivariate results of an analysis testing whether type of respondent, collective bargaining, and partisanship were associated with average COLA over the two-year fiscal year period for each job unit. For each job unit, only collective bargaining was significantly associated with average COLA with those respondents reporting the allowance of collective bargaining having higher average COLA values compared to cities/counties without collective bargaining allowances for these job units.

DISCUSSION

The findings that have emerged from this study of public sector compensation practices have produced several important findings. Over 95 percent of the jurisdictions indicated they were facing a budget shortfall which underscores the fiscal crisis facing local governments. In response to their budget shortfall, local governments appear to be reducing their workforces, laying employees off, borrowing and utilizing reserves and reducing or

eliminating services rather than raising taxes and/or reducing current wages and benefits. Raising taxes during a recession is not only politically risky but in many cases almost impossible in many jurisdictions due to state laws, ballot initiatives, and constitutional restrictions that complicate and/or prohibit them from being enacted (Shubik, Horwitz, and Ginsberg 2009). The growing power of politically influential unions in the public sector has made wage and benefit concessions a difficult and challenging path to pursue. In instances where unions have been willing to make concessions, it has been for future employees. Thus, they protect what they have for the existing membership, but sacrifice wages/benefits for those yet to be hired. These responses will clearly exacerbate the ability of local governments to deliver essential services in their communities.

As predicted, both types of government and collective bargaining were associated with budget shortfalls. A significantly lower percentage of counties and those without collective bargaining agreements faced budget shortfalls. However, the overwhelming majority of local jurisdictions reported shortfalls. As suggested earlier, county governments typically encompass larger geographical areas and therefore receive tax revenues from more diverse sources. This may account for this finding.

Even though 95 percent of the local governments responding reported budget shortfalls, each of the four groups reviewed in this study continued to receive

Table 29.3 Average Cola Benefits by Personnel Unit

Variable	Nonmanagement			Management			Fire			Police		
	M	*SD*	*N*	*M*	*SD*	*N*	*M*	*SD*	*N*	*M*	*SD*	*N*
Type												
City	2.67	1.71	63	2.13	1.60	61	2.88	1.85	58	3.01	2.00	56
County	2.34	1.46	54	2.05	1.53	53	2.71	1.36	28	2.76	1.7	48
Collective bargaining												
Yes	2.91	1.53	68**	2.86	1.44	21**	3.20	1.64	61	3.34	1.81	73**
No	1.99	1.55	47	1.87	1.87	89	1.92	1.50	25	1.86	1.59	30
Partisan												
Yes	2.57	1.84	55	1.98	1.54	53	2.94	1.61	25	2.75	1.60	50
No	2.46	1.40	59	2.16	1.61	58	2.76	1.78	50	2.99	2.1 1	52

*$p < .05$. **$p < .01$.

cost-of-living adjustment (COLA) increases averaging between 2 percent and 3 percent for each of the years surveyed. Multiyear contracts may factor in to this. Public safety units had higher COLA than management and nonmanagement. This may be due to public safety enjoying considerable taxpayer and voter support (Boyd 2009), but there were a higher percentage of jurisdictions with collective bargaining agreements for public safety units. The existence of collective bargaining contracts means that these COLA increases will continue to occur during the duration of the agreements unless the city or county is successful in opening up the existing contract for renegotiation. This forces governments to exercise budgetary discretion in other places.

Across all four job units, respondents reported increased benefits despite budget shortfalls. For nonmanagement, fire, and police units, few reported decreases in benefits (approximately 7 percent). Clearly, existing collective bargaining agreements in some jurisdictions reduce the ability to unilaterally reduce wages and benefits. However, the fact that less than a quarter of collective bargaining units in each of the four job units reported renegotiating existing contracts is a contributing factor as well. In addition, decision making on how to respond to budget problems at the local level can take considerable time and involve multiple actors. The time period for the data collection for this study may not capture new collective bargaining or employment agreements with workers and any renegotiation that ultimately may take place.

As predicted, collective bargaining was significantly associated with employee benefits for nonmanagement, fire, and police units. For each of these units, jurisdictions reporting collective bargaining indicated significantly higher increases in benefits during the two-year period. Additionally, for each of these units, collective bargaining was associated with higher COLAs compared to local governments where collective bargaining does not exist. Finally, the use of collective bargaining was significantly associated with a greater likelihood of responding to a budget shortfall through workforce reduction, borrowing funds, and reduction in services. Where bargaining is strong, local governments were more likely to reduce the labor force rather than decrease salary and benefit levels. This interaction may lead to inefficient outcomes during the recession, with local government employees receiving above-market wages and benefits, and, in turn, citizens facing reduced service capacity.

The local governments that responded to the survey had workforces that were more unionized than the latest figures from the BLS on local union membership. This higher rate of unionization could be a result of surveying larger local governments where collective bargaining practices may be more common. Additionally, some respondents may have included supervisors in their managerial ranks which may have inflated the number of unionized management employees.

Compensation increases for state and local government employees have been trending upward for the last several years and have been substantially higher than those for workers in the private sector from 2005 to 2008. Given local government responses to budget shortfalls in this survey (as well as others), there appear to be fewer regional and municipal workers and less capacity to deliver core services. This study did not capture any additional wage increases that local government employees may have received during this survey period such as merit increases, step increases, and/or longevity pay. While it is reported that benefits have generally increased during this survey period, this may or may not be a result of more generous benefits being extracted. Rising health care costs are a major budgetary drain on local governments and paying for these may account for significant compensation increases.

In light of this discussion, it is important to consider limitations to this study. First, data collection methods in this study relied on self-reports that may be susceptible to response bias. Second, the survey focused on the largest county and city governments. The extent to which smaller local governments have similar or different experiences and practices is not clear. Finally, the survey did not capture the size of the budget shortfall, and this may have influenced the choice regarding some responses. Despite these limitations, this research offers important insights into public sector compensation practices in the United States.

CONCLUSION

The fiscal stress on local governments is projected to continue for the next several years; and the choices available for cities and counties appear to be limited. The workforces of local governments are becoming increasingly unionized. As a result, wages and benefits have been increasing; even during tough economic times. The inability (or unwillingness) of many jurisdictions to raise taxes and the reluctance of public sector unions to agree to wage and benefit reductions will leave many state and local governments with limited options and make it increasingly difficult to offer the same level of services in their jurisdictions.

As more media attention is focused on public sector compensation as well as the high levels of unfunded liabilities for pensions and OPEB benefits such as retiree health care (and a real or perceived inequity with private sector workers), there is a limit to the reduction in essential services and requests for additional revenue that taxpayers will accept. The most effective measure public managers can employ is to insist on increased transparency in all aspects of public sector wages and benefits. This includes more public discussion and deliberation on employee wage and benefits packages, collective barraging agreements, and long-term financial commitments that may affect future generations. COLA increases during tough economic times and increases that exceed inflation need to be publicly justified. Finally, local governments need to be prepared to explain why wage and benefit reductions are not being considered when dealing with budget shortfalls.

30

Struggling Cities Strike Deals to Solve Fiscal Problems

By Kirk Victor

Financial problems at the local level mean developing new strategies and taking some risks. They also mean sleepless nights for local officials.

Julien X. Neals doesn't sleep well at night. Even when Newark, N.J.'s business administrator nods off, it is, he says, "on a surface level where you are thinking, 'OK, how are we going to tackle this problem tomorrow?'"

The fitful nights are understandable. Newark faces fiscal challenges that are extraordinary. When Neals was sworn in more than a year ago, Mayor Cory Booker said he was counting on the new administrator to help guide Newark as it faced "one of the worst economic crises in our city's modern history."

Newark is hardly alone. The litany of economic woes are a fearsome foursome: persistently high unemployment, soaring pension and health-care costs, dwindling property values that have robbed cities of revenues, and cutbacks in federal and state assistance that have further eroded the revenue available to the cities.

The magnitude and depth of the problems are daunting. Several mayors have likened it to a generational event where local officials can't look back and say, "We've dealt with this before." It has been decades since anything like this has happened.

Faced with this reality, it's not surprising that city leaders may be open to new ways to finance their fiscal challenges. Some of these solutions may be brought to their attention by investment bankers who come to the table armed with an array of exotic—and often difficult-to-understand—financing tools.

That combination of cash-strapped local government leaders and aggressive dealmakers has produced a situation in which the inadequacy of the usual means of balancing the budget meets the risky road to immediate access to capital. That was at the heart of

From *Governing*, March 2012.

two of today's high-profile municipal struggles—Harrisburg, Pa., and Jefferson County, Ala. "So often politicians do not look long term; they are just looking to push the buck or the can down the road until they won't be responsible," says Daniel Miller, the city controller of Harrisburg, which is struggling with fallout from the unfortunate financing of an incinerator deal that left the city with a $317 million budgetary hole.

Even when the cutting-edge deal stems from a genuine try at solving long-term fiscal issues, experts in municipal restructuring say they worry that city leaders don't have the knowledge base to analyze the deals sufficiently. The lack of sophisticated investment analytical abilities puts them and their cities at risk of making ill-informed decisions or even of being taken to the cleaners. The level of sophistication when city leaders and Wall Street bankers come to the table is "wildly asymmetric," says David Johnson of Chicago-based ACM Partners, which advises a range of clients, including municipalities and their bondholders. As he describes it, when bankers and city managers sit down together, the bankers may face a city manager who has been doing municipal finances for 20 years, and possibly doesn't have an MBA. Meanwhile, the city manager is probably sitting across the table from three bankers who have a combined 500 transactions behind them. "I would never bet on the city manager in that case," Johnson says. "Not that city managers aren't good at what they do, but there is so much asymmetry. [They need help] to get through these complicated transactions."

While the terms of a deal can be highly technical, complicated and confusing, sometimes the deal-making leads to illegal conduct. For example, Jefferson County's municipal bankruptcy was precipitated by a combination of aggressive Wall Street bankers and local leaders on the take. At issue was a complex financing deal to modernize the sewer system.

An investigation by the Securities and Exchange Commission (SEC) of the sewer deal revealed bid rigging, bribes and other misdeeds. The SEC settled charges with J.P. Morgan Securities, which forked over $750 million for illegal payments that it had steered to influential people in the county to help the firm win the bond deal. Some 20 city employees were convicted of bribery and conspiracy.

Part of the Jefferson County story is about corruption, but another part centers on the failure of leaders to understand the deals being pushed by aggressive Wall Street pitches. "When there is a need, the investment banking community will figure out a product to match it," observes David Hooks, chief of staff to Jefferson County Commissioner Jimmie Stephens. Stephens was elected in 2010 after the illegal conduct had occurred and is trying to clean up the mess as head of the Finance Committee. Hooks points out that city leaders often simply fail to ask questions when they don't understand the ins and outs of a deal. "Elected officials," he says, "never want to get embarrassed by looking like they don't know what they are doing."

It's a sentiment echoed by William Brandt, chair of the Illinois Finance Authority. Brandt, having talked with a number of people involved with the deal, reports that "there were too many meetings where nobody understood the true nature of the securitization, and there was a lot of illusionary language about what was going to occur that didn't."

Misunderstandings may stem less from the lack of a deep knowledge of the deal than from an eagerness for a quick fix. In late 2008, Chicago leased its parking meters to a Morgan Stanley–led partnership. Then-Mayor Richard Daley was trying to close a budget hole, and the deal called for Morgan Stanley to hand Chicago $1.16 billion in exchange for a 75-year agreement to lease and manage the meters. The transaction has since provoked outrage among residents who were subsequently hit with repeated hikes in parking fees.

The thinking of city leaders, says Brandt, was that the public-private partnership deal to lease the city's parking meters would gain the city a bundle of money. If that meant the folks who leased the parking meters were to triple, quadruple and, in some cases, quintuple the rates, so be it.

To Brandt's way of thinking, the parking meter situation could have been handled in a far better way if the mayor had the political will to raise the parking meter rates himself. Politically, "there would have been hell to pay," Brandt says, "but the city wouldn't have had to quintuple the parking rates. It could have tripled them and then sold that revenue stream into revenue bonds and probably come out in the same place and still owned the damn parking meters."

Subsequent reporting by Bloomberg News revealed that the Morgan Stanley partnership will receive at least

$11.6 billion for the parking concession over the course of the deal, or 10 times what it paid. As to Chicago, Brandt says "it doesn't appear that the analysis on a best-practices basis or cost-benefit basis is getting done."

Not every deal is a bad deal. Even critics of privatization deals don't necessarily rule them out as an option. But they caution that privatization must be done smartly and transparently. Deals should not be cut behind closed doors.

Transparency, Newark's Neals argues, is the course his city has taken. Newark worked with New York–based Class Green Capital Partners, a firm that is a member of the U.S. Conference of Mayors Business Council. It is a specialized municipal advisory firm that helps cities get low-cost capital through real estate and infrastructure properties that then undergo energy retrofits to make them more efficient. At the end of the 20-year lease, when the structures are returned to the city for $1, the projects are more valuable—and the cost of maintaining and running them is less.

In the sales-leaseback transaction with the Essex County Improvement Authority, Newark sold 16 buildings, including the courthouse and police and fire stations, to the improvement authority. The authority then issued a $73 million tax-exempt bond, with the buildings as collateral. Newark used roughly $40 million of the bond proceeds to plug the budget, $20 million to retrofit the buildings and do an environmental clean-up, and the remainder to pay down existing debt and transactional costs. "This not only preserved vital city services and jobs," Neals says, "but reduced by more than half an otherwise significant property tax increase."

It was not, of course, free money. Newark now has to take on an additional budget item: paying back bondholders.

Neals concedes that if the economy had not crashed, the city probably would not have done the deal, "but it was the best of some pretty bad alternatives." The new reality in the public sector, he argues, is that with rising health-care and pension costs "if municipalities didn't do something to plug budget holes as a bridge to try to cure structural deficits, they would go out of business."

The deal is one part of Newark's balanced approach that includes cutting city jobs and raising property taxes—a combination that has reduced the deficit from roughly $175 million in 2009 to $80 million at the start of 2012.

Class Green's co-founder and chief executive John Hirschfeld notes that the firm is in talks with about 20 cities that are interested in pursuing a similar course.

Not all budget mavens are sold on these kinds of one-shot deals in which city leaders sell or lease assets to cover a budget shortfall and saddle the city with debt for years—even with the advantage of the energy retrofit. "I wouldn't say no one-shots ever. You would like them to be financially and programmatically sensible," says Don Boyd, executive director of the Task Force on the State Budget Crisis, a group evaluating the fiscal situation in five big states. "In general, the extraordinary pressure to do something other than raise taxes or cut services makes it very attractive to do things that don't make financial sense. Taxpayers ought to be wary."

Providence, R.I., like Newark, worked with Class Green and leased buildings used as collateral for bonds that generated $35 million, $30 million of which went to close its budget gap while about $5 million was earmarked for energy efficiency upgrades to the buildings. That deal prompted Rhode Island's revenue director, Rosemary Booth Gallogly, to raise concerns similar to Boyd's. "I am certainly not saying they should never be done," she says. "I just think when possible, they should be avoided, and when used, they should be part of an overall long-term plan."

The problem with the deals is that, though they solve a short-term problem, they push the bill for the solution down the road, says ACM Partners' David Johnson. When leaders earmark the capital for one-shot budgetary fixes, "they are selling the family silver," he says. "You need to use that to change your structure and not to just fill a one-time budgetary hole. Next year could be just as bad, and then what do you do?"

But Class Green's Hirschfeld counters that his firm encourages cities to devote a large portion of the proceeds of transactions to energy upgrades. By so doing, they can blunt, if not eliminate, the criticism that the transaction is primarily deficit financing. His company suggests that cities spend 50 percent or more of the proceeds of each transaction on actual upgrades to produce efficiencies and lower the net effective cost of capital of the entire transaction.

The lesson in all of this is that there are no magic financing techniques. Put another way, Johnson says, his advice to hard-pressed municipal leaders is: "Just because someone is coming to you with a bag of money doesn't necessarily mean the deal is in your favor."

31

Rahm Emanuel Takes on Chicago

By Alan Greenblatt

A former White House chief of staff follows his own path in taking on some big problems in Chicago.

Rahm Emanuel came up with a useful catch phrase when he was White House chief of staff for President Obama. With the new administration facing challenges that started with two wars and a recession of vast proportions, Emanuel declared, "You never want a serious crisis to go to waste." The phrase took on a life of its own—at least in Washington.

Now Emanuel is bringing it home to Chicago. With good reason. Chicago's finances are a wreck, murder rates in parts of the city are among the highest in the country and infrastructure has been long neglected. In addition, foreclosures and unemployment have exacerbated the traditional disparities between the rougher south and west sides of town and the still-glittering downtown. It's a set of problems on which Emanuel, who was sworn in as mayor on May 16, fully intends to bring his crisis-exploiting mentality to bear.

"This is the opportunity to do things you couldn't do before because it was too politically hard," Emanuel says. "The change is going to be significant, and it's going to be equal to the challenges we face."

For those who have not been following Chicago politics closely, it may come as something of a surprise that Emanuel has inherited a raft of problems. He is following in the footsteps, after all, of Mayor Richard M. Daley, who not only served for a record 22 years, but also earned an international reputation as one of the most successful and innovative mayors this country has ever seen.

Daley was fearless in addressing many of the intractable difficulties of the city, taking formal control of perennial problem areas such as management of the school system and public housing. Unlike many other former industrial cities in the Midwest, Daley

From *Governing*, June 2011.

helped Chicago adapt to a post-manufacturing economy long after it ceased being the hog butcher for the world and suffered the shutdown of the massive U.S. Steel plant along the lakefront. "Chicago stands out in the industrial heartland," says Minneapolis Mayor R.T. Rybak, "as being the best example of repositioning your city for the post-industrial economy."

Daley's emphasis on quality-of-life issues—not just the climate change and green roof campaigns that were widely copied by his peers, but his promotion of parks, colleges and cultural institutions—have helped spruce up a downtown that remains a magnet for tourists and corporate headquarters. The downtown Loop area, which might have had 10,000 residents 10 or 15 years ago, now is home to 150,000. Daley helped change the notion that cities were the sick centers of regional doughnuts, showing instead that they could be places that create wealth. "A lot of cities didn't protect their downtown areas," says Alderman Bob Fioretti. "That's when they got in trouble."

But for all his clear victories, Daley punted some fiscal problems into his successor's hands. The recession that Emanuel and his old boss, Obama, couldn't fully lift is still affecting Chicago. The city is dependent on help from a state that will begin its new fiscal year next month more than $8 billion in arrears in scheduled payments to municipalities, school districts, hospitals and other service providers. The city's budget shortfall will be at least $500 million; the school district's will easily exceed that. Chicago, which managed to defy the population-loss trend in other major cities in the 2000 Census, has over the past decade lost nearly 200,000 residents, slipping back to a population level not seen since before 1920.

Emanuel intends to address all that and more. His ambitions may yet exceed his grasp—and the tough decisions ahead of him will make for an exceedingly short honeymooon period. But to the extent that Emanuel can right Chicago's wrongs, he may provide a more useful guide to his peers in how to steer through tough times than even Daley would have, had he stuck around for yet another term.

Emanuel recognizes that his job description now requires not only putting the fiscal ship back right but ensuring that Chicago doesn't slip up in the ways that Daley managed to prevent during his long time in office. "The decisions we make in the next two or three years

will determine where we are in the next 20 to 30 years," Emanuel says. "If we make the wrong decisions, we could veer off. We could become a Cleveland."

Emanuel is famous not only for his catch phrase, but also for a few personal quirks. He studied ballet throughout his youth and then served as a civilian volunteer on an Israeli army base during the first Gulf War. What he's best known for, though, is his swearing.

Emanuel is known to have cursed not only at White House underlings, but at presidents and prime ministers too. (He served as a top aide in the Clinton White House before winning a seat in Congress in 2002, which he gave up to work for Obama.) When as a teenager he sliced his middle finger—he lost part of it—Emanuel developed an infection so bad that his parents worried it might cost him his life. After he checked himself out of the hospital, his mother worried the fever "might have affected his mentality or his intellect," as she once told a reporter. "But the first time he woke up, I realized he was cursing, and it was, 'He's going to be OK.'"

That kind of reputation might harm a mayoral candidate's image in many places, but not Chicago, which likes its leaders to be strong. "The more they said things about Rahm being tough and not necessarily a nice guy, the stronger his support became," says Paul Green, a veteran observer of the city's politics and a political scientist at Chicago's Roosevelt University.

Emanuel has a tough-guy gaze but also a high-pitched laugh. His personality seemed to undergo a bit of a shift as he made the rounds of school auditoriums and "L" train stops during his campaign. He may have always used swearing for emphasis—"even when he has a temper and says [the F-word], he is not out of control," says Marilyn Katz, a media and public policy consultant who has known him for years—but throughout the campaign, he swore it off. When confronted about his foul language at a forum a couple of weeks prior to his inaugural, Emanuel said, "I would like the record to show—have I done that in seven months?"

There are still reports leaking out about Emanuel cursing during private meetings with aldermen, but his public demeanor has become G-rated and perfectly calm. The sense of discipline he's displayed has helped him, says Larry Bennett, a political scientist at DePaul University and author of *The Third City*, a recent book about Chicago. During the long, heated battle about whether

Emanuel met the city's residency requirements to run for mayor, he remained composed in the face of considerable baiting. "It allowed him to be the embattled figure who was the victim of small-minded Chicago ways," Bennett says. "It was tremendous for him. He was the calm public servant, just waiting for the opportunity to serve."

Chicagoans are deeply proud of their city. In contrast to his opponents, who often seemed unable to look beyond the city's fiscal problems and endemic economic divides, Emanuel managed to convey a sense of Chicago's continuing promise—if it can get such problems under control, he always emphasized. "For as long as I've known him, 20 years, he's been a person who wasn't afraid to push to make things happen, and voters like that," says Avis LaVelle, a consultant and Daley's first mayoral press secretary. "I don't think voters chose Rahm Emanuel to keep doing the same things and not ruffle the nest. They like the get-it-done attitude of the new mayor."

Emanuel's appeal apparently transcended racial lines, something he has in common with his predecessor. Daley may not have been known for it nationwide, but in Chicago one of the main accomplishments people speak of in discussing his legacy was his success in calming the city's racial tensions. Chicago was known as "Beirut by the Lake" during the 1980s tenure of Harold Washington, the city's first black mayor, who was undercut by a racially divided council that frequently came down 29-21 against his proposals. His opponent's theme song in the 1983 mayoral election was *Bye, Bye Blackbird*.

But where Washington entered office after winning just 13 percent of the white vote, Emanuel had the support of 53 percent of the city's African-Americans.

LaVelle recounts being approached by an African-American man at an inner-city McDonald's who told her he would be supporting Emanuel, despite the attempts of other candidates to divide the vote along racial lines. Emanuel pulled together a coalition resembling Obama's in 2008, winning the support of affluent white liberals and African-Americans alike. Emanuel avoided a runoff, carrying 40 out of the city's 50 wards. "I'm going with Rahm," the man at the McDonald's told LaVelle, "because we don't want a nobody for mayor, and we don't want a mayor that nobody knows."

Emanuel may have proven popular among black voters, but he did less well with Hispanics, and some of the relatively few wards he lost had been reliably Democratic since the days of mayors who predate even Daley's father's time in City Hall.

The reason is that Emanuel lacked support from public employees, who share a great deal of unease that he will become yet another contemporary executive setting out to cut their salaries and benefits. "There is no way he can go and attack the deficits of $500 million to $700 million without going after pensions and health care," says Roosevelt University's Green. "He lost wards that have been Democratic since [Mayor] Anton Cermak [in the 1930s] because city workers know what's coming."

Last year, Daley filled a budget hole of $650 million without raising property taxes, but he did it primarily through the use of one-time funds. Daley drained dollars raised through leasing parking meters and a highway. That means the city has already used up in six years some 80 percent of the money raised by 75- and 99-year leases. He also bought labor peace by inking multiyear contracts—written in more prosperous times, when 4 percent annual pay raises seemed like a reasonable idea.

In addition to the operating deficits, the city's four major pension funds are more than $12 billion short of full funding. As a result, over the past decade Chicago has not only lost population, but also seen the share of unfunded pension liability increase from $827 to $4,340 per resident. "A recent Daley commission I served on found that the city is $710 million short annually in pension contributions," says Laurence Msall, head of the city's Civic Federation, a nonpartisan government research organization. "Making this up would require that the city more than double its annual property tax levy."

Emanuel had no trouble winning applause during the campaign by promising not to double property taxes. He devised a variety of ideas to tackle the city's financial problems, from charging nonprofits for water use to instilling competition in such areas as garbage pickup. He has even, like many other soon-to-be disappointed elected officials before him, talked up the idea of lowering the sales tax but broadening the base to capture more of the economy, including services.

The main thing, though, is that he wants public employees to recognize that they will have to help make up the gap in areas such as pension funding. Emanuel says he's open to ideas about how to achieve the savings he needs, but he also says he won't vary from his goal in terms of dollar amounts. "Nobody—business, labor, people in the administration—can come to me with the attitude of defending the status quo," he says. "The status quo does not work, and I've got $500 million in problems to show you that."

The public employee unions, which did not support his candidacy, say that while Emanuel talked a good game about consulting them during his transition, they have yet to see evidence of his willingness to work with them. "Some people, their idea of collaboration is to say, 'Here's our plan, and we want you to endorse it. If you don't endorse it, you're an obstacle to change,'" says Henry Bayer, executive director of American Federation of State, County and Municipal Employees Council 31. "I don't think someone is being an obstacle to change if they don't want to rubber stamp every idea the mayor has."

Emanuel is fond of pointing out that the unions didn't support him—but he won anyway. Even before being sworn in, he successfully lobbied the Illinois Legislature to change work rules in the Chicago schools, which he frequently complained have the shortest term of any major city's district, as well as school days that run 90 minutes shorter than most other metropolitan districts. "We can't run from these problems any longer," he says. "I want a debate about how we're going to use that hour and a half, not how we're going to get compensated for it."

Daley managed to convince not only Chicago residents, but also businesses that expended millions at his behest that it was worth investing in what had been a miserable public school system. Daley put billions into school construction and helped pave the way for a host of reform ideas that are now being promoted nationally by his former schools chief, Arne Duncan, Obama's secretary of education. "If Daley hadn't changed the tone about what could be accomplished, there would have been a taxpayer revolt," says Alderman Patrick O'Connor.

As in many areas, Emanuel not only wants to build on what Daley has done in education, but to move things a few steps further. Chicago public schools, though much improved, remain a disappointment, with a dropout rate of about 50 percent. Emanuel supports a broad panoply of education changes—not just lengthening the school day and school year, but more aggressive use of charters, a limit on teacher strikes, and changes to tenure and merit pay for administrators as well as teachers. "Rahm is going to take on what Daley couldn't—the unions and longer school days," says Chuck Bernardini, a former alderman. "What's going on countrywide will probably be helpful to Rahm. Everyone sees what's happening in other states, and that has to bring some realism to the unions."

Emanuel may be convinced that he is going to have to restructure the services the city can deliver—and reduce the size of the workforce that delivers them. But within the school district, as in other areas of government services, Emanuel is going to have to confront forces that aren't convinced his ideas are necessarily the best, or even politically tenable. Bernard Stone, who served for 38 years on the City Council before being ousted in April, notes that his opponent—who was backed by Emanuel—received significant financial support from unions. The question Stone asks is, "What loyalty does she owe?"

One-fourth of the 50 City Council members are newly sworn in, along with Emanuel. The vast majority are inclined to support his positions, but many will be looking to establish their own power. Despite being a city that's long been known for its mayors, Chicago actually has a weak-mayor form of government by law. "Daley didn't start with a council that gave him unanimous votes for everything," says LaVelle, the consultant. "He had to earn that."

But the fact that the council is so sprawling makes it difficult for it to stand on equal footing with the mayor—particularly one with the star power Emanuel has shown. "The problems of the city are so great, and 50 aldermen have such narrow interests," says Green. "Only the mayor can provide a citywide solution."

Emanuel starts out as mayor with the ear of the president, and the personal Rolodex and fundraising ability to chart his own course. He has already attracted top talent from around the country, not relying on the usual coterie around Chicago City Hall. His pick to run the school system, Jean-Claude Brizard, helped raise graduation rates from 39 percent to a much-improved though still miserable 51 percent during three years in the same job in Rochester, N.Y. Garry McCarthy, his pick for police chief, comes from Newark, N.J., where he helped drive down crime rates—especially for violent crime—repeating a trick he'd pulled off as a deputy commissioner in New York City. "He's attracting talented people from inside and outside the city," says Msall, the Civic Federation president.

Not everyone has applauded Emanuel's picks. A group of black aldermen complained that the faces of the mayor's public safety team are too white. The Chicago Teachers Union is more than a bit unhappy that he chose a schools CEO who had just received a vote of no-confidence from the union in Rochester. How Emanuel's administration is ultimately judged, of course, will depend on how close he can come to making good on his promises to address Chicago's problems.

But because of his prominence and the independence his political celebrity buys him, some Chicagoans even dare to hope he'll run an administration that won't be hampered by the same sort of corruption that the city has long been known for. As media and public policy consultant Katz notes, when Steven Spielberg handed Emanuel a check, he wasn't hoping to land a city contract.

Mostly, Chicagoans hope that Emanuel will not only bring new ideas, but also the drive to push them past what is likely to be considerable resistance. This is not the time for a wimpy mayor. Emanuel took the risk during the election of saying he was going to take on the city's most difficult problems, and he won a big victory. So he starts, at least, with a strong hand. If the person taking office after Daley was someone "who people felt was a step down, Chicagoans would be nervous about their future," says Alderman O'Connor. "But I don't think that's the case."

IX

Budgets and Taxes

For the past five years, the budget news for state and local government has pretty much been all bad. The news is no longer all bad—just most of it. For many states, revenues have still not returned to their pre recession level, unemployment remains stubbornly high, and all policy debates continue to be defined by the brutal realities of a gap between income and proposed expenditure. Yet there are, finally, some shafts of sunlight cutting through the budgetary gloom. Revenues may not be reaching historical highs, but they are climbing northward from historical lows. Unemployment is higher than anyone would like, but hiring is on a cautious upswing. In a few states, economic expansions are even in full-throated swing.

The Great Recession's stubborn financial hangover is still being felt in many places because of its unusual triple whammy on state and local finances. The three primary revenue sources for subnational governments are income, sales, and property taxes. During economic downturns, it is not unusual for income and sales taxes to take a dip, but property taxes are usually a bit more stable because property prices historically have been less volatile. Not this time. High unemployment reduced income taxes, sales taxes plummeted as people cut back spending, and property values declined—in some states they went off a cliff. In some states and localities, tax receipts dropped by 20 percent or more, and unlike their federal counterparts, the vast majority of these governments are legally obligated to balance their books. In other words, they could not borrow and spend money they did not have. That left three tough choices: (1) raise taxes, (2) cut spending, or (3) do both.

Even slashing public services and engaging in massive layoffs was not enough (state and local governments have been shedding 10,000 or more employees a month for *years*). Pretty much the only thing that stood between state and local governments and bankruptcy for the past couple of years has been the federal government, which became the single largest source of state and local revenue as it pumped billions in stimulus dollars through subnational agencies. That money, though, is drying up. States and localities are going to have to learn to stand on their own financial feet in the next year or two.

The readings in this section suggest that state and local governments are going to be able to do just that, but it is not going to be easy. The first essay, by Daniel Vock, takes an overview of state finances and finds there are some things to cheer about. Manufacturing is picking up. Property values have stabilized. People are buying again. A handful of states are actually enjoying economic boom times. The net result is a steady increase in revenue for state governments—not enough to bring coffers up to pre recession levels but enough to allow a firm step or two away from the financial abyss.

While traditional sources of revenue are picking up, the second essay, by Donald Kettl, examines the federal debt and its potential impact on state and local government. Kettl argues that moves to constrain the national debt means all federal aid to state and local government—not just special stimulus programs—has become increasingly vulnerable. There are many reasons to predict this development, but they all spring from the same basic problem: Federal government finances are, if anything, in worse shape than state and local finances. While the

federal government does have the enviable power of being able to print money, most recognize that it must rein in its spending. That means cutting vulnerable discretionary programs and, especially, entitlement spending. That is worrisome news for subnational governments that get a lot of dollars from discretionary programs like federal community development grants and especially for state governments that help fund entitlement programs like Medicaid.

The final two essays look at two ways in which state governments are trying to raise revenues. First up is an essay by Kirk Victor that looks at state efforts to collect Internet sales taxes. Sales tax codes have not kept up with the steady shift of commerce to the Internet, and the billions in tax receipts that are being lost because people are increasingly buying stuff from Amazon rather than brick-and-mortar stores is a big concern. Amazon, however, is fighting efforts to make it collect sales taxes.

Lastly, an essay by John Gramlich takes a look at a revenue-raising option that will hit college students and their parents particularly hard: tuition hikes. Even before the onset of the Great Recession, some states were progressively reducing their share of the costs of higher education. That progression tipped into free fall during the past few years; there have been serious proposals to cut state appropriations to higher education by as much as 50 percent. That has left public colleges and universities with few options; even after making deep cuts, they need to find income to replace at least some of the lost state revenues. That means higher tuition, which in some states is jumping as much as 10 percent per year.

32

At Last, a State Budget Year When the Sky Is Not Falling

By Daniel C. Vock

The financial news is not all good for state and local governments, but it is financially not all bad either. That is a big improvement over the past few years.

D uring the depths of the Great Recession, states had to do many unsavory things to balance their budgets. But few things left a more bitter taste than Arizona's decision to sell off the office space of its state Capitol complex. It helped lawmakers close a gap in one year's budget, even though it meant taxpayers would essentially have to pay rent on the property for the next two decades.

Now, Arizona's budget outlook is showing some improvement: For the first time since 2006, the state finished its last fiscal year with a surplus, which came as a surprise to state financial forecasters. Governor Jan Brewer told lawmakers where she wants to spend some of the $600 million windfall: buying back the state's buildings from its landlords. "Together," the Republican said during her state of the state speech on Monday, "we can celebrate the burning of that mortgage."

No one is saying Arizona's boom days are back. Its 8.7 percent unemployment rate is slightly higher than the national average and its housing industry is still struggling. Roughly $1 billion of Arizona's annual revenue will disappear next year when a temporary sales tax expires, an event lawmakers are calling "the cliff." But for the first time in five years, the legislature is in a position to put money toward its top priorities rather than cut, cut, cut.

And that is a pretty good assessment of where a lot of states are, as they head into a new budget season. According to the Rockefeller Institute of Government, at least 45 states saw their revenues increase over the past year. After a four-year run during which states had to close budget gaps of historic proportions, the term "surplus" is finally making a modest comeback in capitals. Whether they

From *Stateline.org*, January 2012.

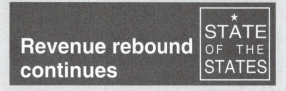

Revenue rebound continues

STATE OF THE STATES

State tax revenues have grown for seven quarters in a row. However, revenues plunged so deeply in 2008 and 2009 that many states have yet to return to their pre-recession levels.

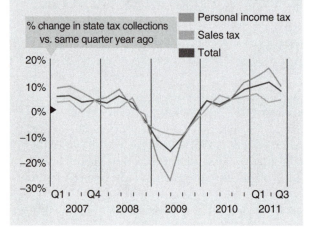

% change in state tax collections vs. same quarter year ago

- Personal income tax
- Sales tax
- Total

Source: Rockefeller Institute of Government, December 2011.

slashed K–12 education during the budget crisis, closed state parks or cut doctors' rates for treating poor patients, many states will start reversing the most painful of their recent cuts in 2012.

There are asterisks on all this positive news, of course. One is that while state revenues are generally up, they fell so far during the recession that most states have not caught back up to where they were before. "Eight quarters of growth is a good trend," says Rockefeller's Robert Ward. "The problem is that states were down so deep that they effectively have lost three years worth of growth."

Another point of caution is the economy. Joblessness continues to place huge demands on the social services states provide. The housing market remains soft, and there is a real threat that a European recession could have spillover effects in the United States.

But overall, enough economic vital signs are headed in the right direction that the mood in most states is encouraging. In its most recent survey of legislative fiscal directors, the National Conference of State Legislatures reported that more states were "cautiously optimistic" or "positive" about the fiscal outlook for the rest of 2012 than "concerned." The number of fiscal directors who said they were "pessimistic" was zero.

"The odds of a double dip (recession) have certainly diminished," says Sujit CanagaRetna, a tax and budget expert at the Council of State Governments. But, he adds, "we really cannot afford to have any more of those hiccups in our recovery programs."

AN UNEVEN COMEBACK

Just as the recession did not spread its pain evenly, the economic recovery is not appearing in equal force in every state. Generally speaking, the states can be sorted into three groups.

First are the states that never really felt the brunt of the recession in the first place. North Dakota is the most obvious example, with its recent oil boom. But many of its neighbors, with economies dependent on minerals or agriculture, are doing well, too. North Dakota is one of a small number of states that anticipates ending this fiscal year with enough money in the bank to cover a tenth of its yearly expenses, according to the National Association of State Budget Officers. The others are Alaska, Delaware, Iowa, Montana, Nebraska, Texas, West Virginia and Wyoming.

On the opposite end of the spectrum are states still wrestling with major budget shortfalls, whether that is because revenues are rising too slowly or because spending demands are rising too quickly. In Washington State, lawmakers met in a December special session to try and close a $2 billion hole that had developed in their current budget. They only managed to fill about a third of it. And California continues to struggle. The state has a budget gap of $9.2 billion through the end of its next fiscal year. Democratic Governor Jerry Brown wants voters to approve hikes in income and sales taxes. Otherwise, he says, the state must make painful cutbacks in services, including shortening the school year by three weeks.

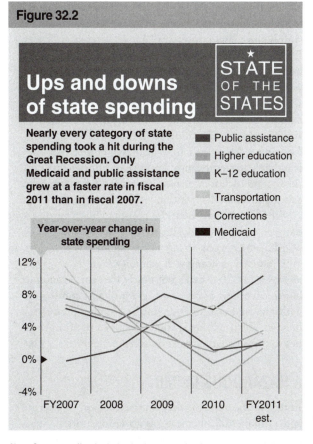

Figure 32.2

Note: State spending includes both general fund spending and federal funds.

Source: National Association of State Budget Officers.

On the Democratic side, New York Governor Andrew Cuomo says a $2 billion hole in next year's budget should not preclude spending $1 billion to revitalize the city of Buffalo and to build bridges and improve state parks. In Minnesota, Governor Mark Dayton wants to take advantage of a newfound surplus to support a round of construction projects. And in West Virginia, which also is projecting a surplus, Governor Earl Ray Tomblin wants to reduce property taxes while stashing away money for infrastructure projects.

While the healthier revenues most states are seeing is a positive development, revenue is only one part of the budget equation. According to an analysis by the Pew Center on the States (*Stateline*'s parent organization), Illinois is one of the three states that has surpassed its previous high-water mark on revenues (North Dakota and Vermont are the others.) However, Illinois only got there with an infusion of cash from a major income tax increase, and the state still owes close to $7 billion in unpaid bills.

The left-leaning Center on Budget and Policy Priorities says there is no reason to celebrate the states' current fiscal situation. Its report issued this week painted a more pessimistic budget picture than recent analyses by other groups monitoring state finances. By CBPP's count, more than half of all states face budget gaps for the year to come or have already closed them. The end of the federal stimulus program, along with increasing K–12 enrollments and escalating Medicaid costs, are still putting massive strains on states. "Even though the revenue outlook is trending upward," the report says, "states are still addressing large budget shortfalls by historical standards."

"IT FEELS DIFFERENT"

Even some of the states that have had the worst budget struggles, however, are seeing upbeat economic signs.

In Washington State, for example, as lawmakers wrangle a budget deficit in Olympia, Boeing is boosting production—and hiring workers—to catch up on a backlog of orders for 4,000 aircraft, or eight years' worth of work. Microsoft, the state's other marquee employer, is adding jobs, too. Unemployment claims, while still high, are falling.

Even long-struggling Michigan finally has good news to talk about. After nearly a decade of headlines about

By and large, most states lie somewhere in between the two extremes. They made it through the worst of the fiscal crisis, and now face more manageable deficits than they have in recent years, or even modest surpluses. And like Arizona, they are pondering which of their recession-era cuts they want to undo, especially in education.

In Virginia, Republican Governor Bob McDonnell has said he wants to raise the state contribution to higher education this year, a break from five consecutive years of state cuts. Idaho Governor C. L. "Butch" Otter, also a Republican, is calling for a $32 million boost for public schools and another $21 million increase for colleges and universities.

job losses and a retrenching auto industry, manufacturing is picking back up. The state's revenues have improved along with its economy in small but noticeable ways. Tax collections for the state's two biggest accounts were up 8.6 percent in the last fiscal year. "It feels different for people," says David Zin, the chief economist for Michigan's Senate Fiscal Agency. "The changing signs have a pretty significant psychological effect."

Recent changes in Michigan's tax laws mean the state will likely see less money in the current year than last year, Zin says, and the revenue increases are not keeping up with inflation. The bigger concern is over how long the economy will take to get into a higher gear. Consumers still worry about their future, preventing them from buying big-ticket items. And when they have been spending, they had to borrow to get the money. "We are expecting the economy to grow in 2012 and 2013," Zin says, "but a lot less than it did in 2011."

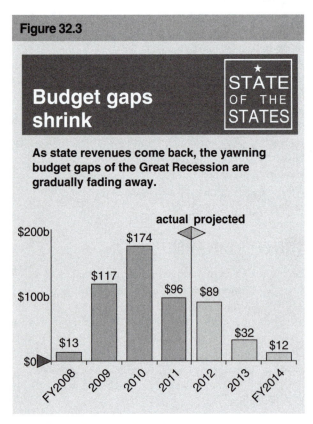

Figure 32.3

Budget gaps shrink

★ STATE OF THE STATES

As state revenues come back, the yawning budget gaps of the Great Recession are gradually fading away.

Source: National Conference of State Legislatures.

The collapse of the housing market also continues to weigh down the economies of some states. There are simply too many houses available or, alternatively, too few buyers. Florida officials say the amount of unsold houses on the market there continues to grow, because of persistent unemployment and foreclosures. "The state will need significant time to work off the current excess—at least two years in the optimistic scenario, likely longer," the Florida Economic Estimating Conference wrote last fall. "The overall Florida economy is unlikely to significantly improve until new construction comes back to life, and that won't happen until the existing inventory is reduced."

Far from the Sun Belt, the housing glut is putting a damper on the economic recovery in Oregon. Mark McMullen, Oregon's acting state economist, says the logging industry is doing well when it comes to shipping logs overseas. "But that's not nearly the same economic boost as you get from running a mill and coming up with plywood or timber or finished lumber products," he says. "That market is still reeling as a result of their ties to the broader national housing market."

A HAZARDOUS CLIMB

Ironically, the other big drag on the economy in Oregon and a number of other states is government itself. State governments shed 5,000 jobs between October and November; local governments lost another 11,000 jobs, more than half of which came from schools. Layoffs by state and local governments are exacerbating unemployment. Normally during an economic recovery, Oregon adds 350 public sector jobs a month. Last year, Oregon lost 615 public sector jobs a month.

State economists also are keeping their eyes on Europe. The U.S. economy is closely linked with Europe's, so a recession there could have an impact in states with the greatest exposure. An analysis by Wells Fargo Securities noted that Utah's economy benefits from gold exports to Britain; four cents of every dollar in the West Virginia economy is tied to Europe through coal exports; and Alabama and South Carolina have close economic ties to Europe because of their automobile factories.

"The greatest threat to the U.S. economy remains the European sovereign debt crisis," wrote Washington state forecasters in a December update to the legislature. "If the sovereign debt crisis degenerates into a full-blown banking crisis, it will spread to the United States because of our banks' exposure to European banks. A U.S. banking crisis will push the U.S. back into recession."

The current downturn is unlike most that have come before it in key ways that makes it hard to predict how long and how fully it will take states to recover. Oregon's McMullen points out that the sheer numbers of people who have been unemployed for years is something his state has not seen in recent memory. The recession in the early 1980s put similar percentages of people out of work, but they were not there as long as today's job seekers. It is an important consideration for state lawmakers and budget writers, he says, because the long-term unemployed demand a lot of social services.

For Washington State, the nature of the recession and the state's heavy reliance on sales taxes combine to make this downturn especially difficult. In the recession of the early 2000s, Washington residents kept building houses and buying cars, says Arun Raha, the chief economist for Washington State's Economic and Revenue Forecast Council. So the state fared relatively well. But the state's lack of a personal or corporate income tax means it must wait until people and companies start spending again to shore up its finances.

But CanagaRetna, from the Council of State Governments, says many signs point to an economy that is near recovery. People are shipping more goods through package companies like UPS and FedEx than they ever have before. Companies have amassed $2 trillion in cash, a higher percentage of the total economy than any time in the last half century. CanagaRetna says that means they will be poised to spend it soon, either on capital improvements or on hiring new workers.

"For the first time in three or four years, I'm a little optimistic on where the economy is going," he says, "but with the cautious note that states still have some sizable challenges to deal with."

33

2011 May Mark the End of Federal Aid

By Donald F. Kettl

Moves to rein the national debt may reshape federalism as aid to states and localities becomes a ripe target for budget cutters.

W hen Congress finally staggered to the finish line in August with its debt deal, the financial markets weren't the only players who recoiled. State and local government officials worried they were about to get slammed.

And when Standard & Poor's voted no-confidence in the deal by downgrading the federal government's debt, the worries grew. New Jersey found itself knocked down a notch, joining Kentucky and Michigan at Fitch's AA-, just ahead of California and Illinois. Manassas Park, Va., a small Washington suburb, fell five notches in the Standard & Poor's rating.

But a careful examination of the situation by Josh Goodman of Stateline.org showed that the debt deal wasn't nearly as bad for state and local governments as everyone feared—at least in round one. Grants for entitlements (mostly for Medicaid, the Children's Health Insurance Program, welfare and food stamps), which constitute two-thirds of all federal aid, are off the table. Congress's new bipartisan "super committee" has to find more cuts, but heavy betting is that programs for the poor will escape in this round. The result is likely to be far less damaging to federal grants.

In the long run, however, 2011 will probably join 1978 and 1987 as one of the major post–World War II turning points in federal aid to state and local governments.

First, let's look at 1978 and what made it a turning point. In the two decades prior, discretionary grants tripled from 1958 to 1968, and then tripled again by 1978, even after accounting for inflation. President Richard Nixon may have been one of the best friends that state and local governments ever had, with his "new federalism"

From *Governing*, October 2011.

programs that created block grants for job training, health, social services and community development. In 1972, the feds even created a general revenue-sharing program that relocated Vietnam War military spending to state and local governments to spend with very few strings attached. The Ford and Carter administrations maintained the momentum.

Those were the salad days. The 1978 budget, in fact, was the high-water mark of discretionary federal aid, not matched since (except by the short-term infusions of cash through the stimulus program). Since the late 1970s, federal aid has been the story of rising spending for entitlements and declining support for everything else.

That made 1987 the next important point in federalism: It was the first time federal grants for entitlements exceeded discretionary grants. Congress snuffed out general revenue sharing in 1986, and the remaining block grant programs were either killed or far more tightly regulated. Meanwhile, spending for Medicaid grew rapidly, as the program began covering more items and nursing home expenses soared, with more seniors unable to afford the enormous cost of long-term care. With this shift, intergovernmental finance changed forever.

Remember these years: 1978, the high-water mark for traditional federal grants, and 1987, the crossing point for entitlement grants. To these benchmarks we can now add 2011, a debt deal that puts federal aid on the block.

There are three reasons for this. First, as Congress combs through the budget, the long list of federal discretionary grants will be ripe targets. Federal aid for community development, housing, job training, social services and similar programs has been under attack for a long time. Faced with inescapable pressures to protect other discretionary programs like air traffic control, airport security, food safety and defense, these programs are more vulnerable than ever. The automatic trigger would nick them if the super committee fails to agree on spending cuts; if the super committee avoids the trigger, the cuts are likely to be far greater. There doesn't seem any way discretionary grants can escape, especially as we roll forward toward the big targets looming down the road.

Second, all roads to a long-term deficit solution run through entitlements and, especially, health care. There is overwhelming consensus that we need to rethink Medicaid and the underlying federal-state deal for funding it. Medicaid escaped in the first round, but it can't remain on the sidelines for long. Some state officials are proposing a grand deal in which the feds trade a pot of money for state control of the program. They think they can make the program work better without federal regs and oversight. Looking down the road at the soaring cost of the program, the feds might eagerly take that deal. But there's no escaping fundamental—and painful—decisions on just how we're going to rein in costs for health care and nursing homes.

Third, the massive economic instability that aggravated this most recent round of budget battles will likely be with us for a while. State and local governments have largely been collateral damage, with growing responsibilities for services supported by a tax base weakened by plunging real estate, uncertain consumer sales and stagnant wages. The 2011 debt deal will make it far harder for the feds to step in with help during future economic downturns.

We've faced tough economic challenges before, and we've faced big shifts in intergovernmental grants. State and local governments have never had to tackle both together. This time, they're increasingly likely to find themselves on their own.

34

Who's Winning the Amazon Tax Battles?

By Kirk Victor

A battle between bricks and clicks increasingly pits state governments against big Internet retailers. State governments want those retailers to start collecting sales taxes. The big gorilla in this fight is Amazon, and it is not interested in what the states want.

From *Governing*, November 2011.

When Texas state Rep. John Otto found out that Amazon was challenging a $269 million bill for uncollected state sales taxes, he was surprised. Several states have been trying to force the Internet retailer to collect the tax on sales to its in-state customers, but Amazon's physical presence—or nexus—in those states has been disputable. In Texas, it is clear. Amazon has a large facility in Irving that it uses to distribute the books, electronic devices and other items it sells from its website.

What Otto couldn't figure out was how that facility did not fall under the "nexus standard" that a 1992 Supreme Court case, Quill Corp. v. North Dakota, set for requiring a remote seller—such as an Internet or catalog company—to collect sales taxes.

So Otto dialed up the state comptroller. He asked her what tools she needed to collect the $269 million that had been accruing for four years. "I told her, 'To the average citizen, this company has physical presence here.'" What the comptroller told him was that Amazon claimed it was not in Texas as a retailer, that the Irving facility was a "distribution center." Moreover, it claimed that its plant was a subsidiary—and thus, a separate entity.

As Otto saw it, the Quill decision doesn't draw such distinctions. It speaks only to physical presence. So he introduced legislation that insisted that Amazon had an obligation to collect and remit the taxes. "If you have a subsidiary, control 50 percent or more of it and it has physical presence in the state," Otto says, "then you should collect our sales tax." Although it led to a showdown with the governor, Otto considered his bill a very conservative approach. "I wasn't trying to push the envelope," he says.

But other states have been. And for good reason. Uncollected Internet sales taxes—whether they're from sales on Amazon.com, Overstock.com or any number of other Internet-only retailers—are a big deal. A study published by the University of Tennessee estimates sales tax losses on e-commerce will be $11.4 billion next year. The total estimated loss between 2007 and 2012: $52 billion.

The impetus to collect that money is fed in part by the revenue losses states have experienced during the Great Recession and which continue today. But there is also a frustration that this is money that is due the states. It's not a new tax after all, states argue. If the retailer does not collect the tax, consumers are supposed to report their purchases on their state tax returns and pay the tax themselves. They rarely do, however, because most don't know they are required to do so or how to do it.

States have been coming up with a variety of ploys—some conservative, others more radical—to get Internet retailers to collect the tax. Their efforts range from a handful of states claiming nexus via in-state affiliates that sell on the big-name websites to a 24-state compact to streamline sales tax systems. At the same time, states that levy sales taxes have come up with new allies in the fight to get the U.S. Congress to redress the collection issue and undo Quill. These allies include not just small mom-and-pop stores on Main Street but also giant retailers such as Target and Wal-Mart—retailers with robust Internet sites that do collect the sales tax because they have nexus in almost all states.

At every turn, Amazon has gone to great lengths to block state collection efforts. In states that claimed nexus because Amazon affiliates were located there, Amazon ended relationships with those businesses and, in turn, pursued litigation in the state. In states where it had facilities, it threatened to pull them out, thereby raising the specter of eliminating jobs. And where Amazon wanted to open facilities, it insisted on a free pass on tax collection. Amazon declined interview requests for this story.

Its pugnacious ways have paid off in some states, where the company was given the green light not to collect sales taxes for years—so long as it kept or built a facility in the state. But those ways have left bruised feelings, especially among legislators. In Tennessee, where legislators have been rethinking a deal Amazon struck last year to build distribution warehouses in return for not collecting the tax on goods shipped from those facilities, state Sen. Randy McNally likens Amazon lobbyists to take-your-lunch-money bullies. "They are making demands on the states that if a smaller business came in and tried to do, we'd laugh at 'em."

This fall, however, there was what may be the biggest breakthrough on the Amazon tax front: California's settlement with the company. After fighting legislation that would require out-of-state online retailers to collect sales taxes if they had affiliates, offices, workers or other ties to the state, the company ponied up millions of dollars to put the issue to taxpayers via a ballot referendum. It also cleansed its website of California-based affiliates. Then, the company suddenly backed down—in part because the damage to its reputation was growing. The online retailer struck a deal with the state that will require it to begin collecting sales taxes in California after a one-year grace period. In September, Gov. Jerry Brown signed the agreement into law.

The California deal suggests that Amazon may be changing its game plan. If that's so, it would probably bring the rest of the Internet retailers into the fold as well. (Amazon recently made a similar deal with Tennessee.) Meanwhile, the states battle on, with legislators contending with the lobbying power of a giant—juggling the need for revenue versus promises to bring a few jobs to the state.

In Texas, Otto ended up with his hands full. His bill was not well received by Amazon, which tried to persuade him to drop it. "They held out enticement of jobs and everything else," he recalls. "They started at 3,000 jobs. By the time we were done, they were up to 6,000." Otto estimates the distribution center in Irving employs about 200 people. He is scratching his head over the number of distribution centers that Amazon would have to build to employ an additional 5,800 people.

But the jobs offer wasn't enough to turn him around. "I like a level playing field," he says. "We have companies in Texas who already collect taxes on Internet sales—like Target, Wal-Mart, and Bed, Bath and Beyond—because they are physically here. How do you allow a company like Amazon that puts a distribution center in your state to argue they are not physically present?"

Ultimately, Amazon threatened to close the distribution center and pull out of the Lone Star State. That threat got Gov. Rick Perry's attention. He told Otto he would veto the measure if it passed. It did, with overwhelming approval, and the governor vetoed it on the last day of the session in May. When lawmakers returned for a special session, they struck back. Perry had no alternative but to allow it to become law, even though he saw the law, his deputy press secretary says, as containing "risks of significant unintended consequences, including a loss of Texas job opportunities and weakening of our state's competitive advantage."

A similar battle played out differently in South Carolina. Outgoing Gov. Mark Sanford struck a deal with Amazon last year that offered incentives for the company to build a facility in the state and create some 1,200 jobs. The deal included property tax reductions, job tax credits and a five-year exemption from collecting the sales tax. That exemption was not, however, binding on the Legislature.

When Nikki Haley became governor, she complained that the deal was "bad policy" and gave Amazon an unfair advantage over its competitors. However, Haley added that if the Legislature voted to allow the exemption, she would let it become law as she felt bound to honor the deal between Sanford and Amazon.

Initially, the state House rejected the exemption. Amazon reacted swiftly, threatening to cancel $52 million in procurement contracts and eliminate job postings from its website. It also offered some carrots, boosting its offer with a promise to create 2,000 jobs and to increase its investment in a million-square-foot building by $35 million.

Some legislators saw the issue purely as one about jobs since the state struggled with one of the highest unemployment rates in the country. "We had the votes to pass it even though the governor was vehemently opposed to it," says state Sen. John M. "Jake" Knotts Jr., who backed the bill. "And then the big boys came in, like Wal-Mart, and said the bill to give a sales tax exemption was against small businesses, and they felt it was wrong." The South Carolina Commerce Department estimated the exemption would create a net gain of $232 million in the first year and $1.7 billion over 10 years.

South Carolina state Sen. Larry Grooms filibustered against the sales tax exemption because he opposed the government picking out one particular retailer for a special benefit. Grooms, a Republican, suggested that the state should either refuse to extend the special sales tax exemption to Amazon or extend it to every online retailer that has a presence in South Carolina. "Amazon wasn't interested in the sales tax exemption being expanded to all online retailers—just themselves," Grooms says.

As the fight over the exemption dragged on, Amazon's supporters upped the ante. They suggested that the firm would move to Georgia and still make sales in South Carolina without collecting the tax. To which Grooms replies, "I don't know how folks in Georgia could look their existing online retailers in the eye and say, 'Yeah, but these guys are special and y'all are not.'"

Though Grooms' filibuster failed, several ameliorating amendments passed, including one to require Amazon to send a statement to its customers, reminding them to remit the sales tax on goods they purchase on its website and providing a link to the state revenue department.

In the end, Amazon was a big winner. It gained a five-year exemption from collecting sales taxes in return for following through on its jobs and investment pledges.

In California, the fight started out being even bloodier. After the law to force certain online retailers to collect the sales tax was enacted, Amazon spent $5 million to collect signatures for a referendum to overturn it. As in South Carolina, Amazon also dangled the possibility of opening a half-dozen distribution centers and creating 7,000 jobs—if its sales tax exemption was preserved until 2014.

California state Assembly Majority Leader Charles Calderon worried that the referendum Amazon was collecting signatures for "would be a difficult political fight" for the bill's backers. Still, lawmakers stood firm. California has been losing $1.2 billion a year in sales and use tax collections from e-commerce, Calderon says, and Amazon does about $4 billion of business in the state. Amazon also threatened to litigate the state's claims about what constitutes nexus. "We had a pretty good chance in court, but of course nothing is certain when you go to court," Calderon says. "So the stage was set for some kind of compromise that placed the decision in our hands—Amazon and the state—not in the hands of the electorate or the courts."

Meanwhile, Bill Dombrowski, president of the California Retailers Association, lobbied hard against Amazon interests. The brick-and-mortar retailers found it maddening, he says, that people come into electronics stores, check out expensive flat-panel TVs and then buy from an online retailer. "You can save a couple of hundred bucks if you are not paying sales tax on a TV like that. It is a huge issue and it had to be addressed."

Amazon offered to collect the sales tax after two years. Calderon called that proposal a "nonstarter." Ultimately, both sides agreed to a one-year moratorium in tax collections after which Amazon would collect the taxes—unless federal legislation is enacted. If Congress does not enact legislation, the company would have to start collecting California taxes next September.

Even as it fights the states over the issue, Amazon is supporting a national solution. Legislation introduced in July in Congress, the Main Street Fairness Act, is the latest effort to begin a much-needed simplification of tax laws, but it has not won Republican support this year as it has in the past.

Scott Peterson, executive director of the Streamlined Sales Tax Governing Board, which seeks a settlement on a national basis, is upbeat about the measure's prospects. The legislation would give the 24 states that have signed on to the streamlined sales tax agreement the authority to require retailers to collect sales tax while also simplifying tax collection for the sellers.

Noting that Senate Majority Whip Richard Durbin, a Democrat, is a sponsor of the bill, Peterson says, "We are extremely optimistic, and all the negative things being said are proof that we are close to actually getting something done."

But a Senate Democratic staffer said that with no Republican support, "it's not likely to move." Given the fierce partisanship on Capitol Hill, a safe prediction is that this measure is a long shot for passage this year—or in 2012, an election year.

Instead, look for battles to continue to be waged from state to state. Take New York, which is litigating whether the nexus requirement is met when an affiliate business in the state has a link on Amazon (or other out-of-state retailer) and receives a commission on sales after a consumer clicks on the link. New York says that affiliate relationships create a "presence" so that Amazon must collect sales tax. The state won in lower court, but Amazon is appealing—and collecting the sales tax as the litigation proceeds. As it pursues its case in New York, Amazon has terminated affiliate programs in such states as Illinois, North Carolina and Rhode Island.

In surveying the states' varied actions, Michael Mazerov, a senior fellow with the Center on Budget and Policy Priorities, applauds Texas and California for standing firm. "If states want to solve this problem, they have to hang together and not be picked off," he says. "I understand that state officials want to do what they can to create jobs, but the situation in California seems to indicate that when push comes to shove, [Internet retailers will] go ahead" and do business in the state anyway.

For now, Mazerov, who started working on this issue in 1990 at the Multistate Tax Commission, says he is "very supportive of these state-specific approaches, but they can only chip away at the problem; they can't solve it comprehensively. Federal legislation is the only way to do that."

When does he see an end to this protracted battle? "Here we are in 2011, and we are still fighting," he says. "I don't expect to see this resolved anytime soon."

35

Coming This Fall: Big Tuition Hikes

By John Gramlich

When state governments seriously consider cutting higher education spending by 50 percent, there's no question that tuition is going up. The only question is by how much.

For a telling example of the money troubles facing public colleges and universities, consider Pennsylvania. On June 30, Governor Tom Corbett signed a state budget that slashes funding for higher education by 19 percent, and school officials smiled with relief.

For universities, it could have been much worse. In March, Corbett introduced a budget proposal that called for a 50-percent cut to higher education. But improving state revenues and a public backlash against the proposal led lawmakers to pare back the governor's plan. In the end, Pennsylvania's 14 state-owned universities walked away with a painful but manageable cut that will result in tuition increases of 7.5 percent this fall.

Students elsewhere will not be so fortunate. Double-digit tuition increases await public university students in Louisiana, Tennessee and Nevada, all as a result of reduced state funds. In New Hampshire, lawmakers followed through on what Pennsylvania only talked about doing: cutting higher education funding in half. A 48-percent funding reduction has the University System of New Hampshire warning that it will face its most challenging academic year ever, and students and parents will feel the pain in the form of tuition hikes of up to 9.7 percent.

New Hampshire's cut came as a "major and unanticipated shock," says Matt Cookson, a spokesman for the university system, "especially in light of the traditionally low level of financial commitment to higher education" that the state has shown in the past.

At least half the states cut funding for higher education in their recently concluded legislative sessions, according to the National

From *Stateline.org*, July 2011.

Conference of State Legislatures. In most cases, higher tuition will be the inevitable result. Some of the most dramatic increases will come in the biggest states. The 240,000 undergraduates in the Florida public university system will see 15 percent tuition hikes for the third consecutive year. In California, where 530,000 undergraduate students attend public universities, tuition hikes of up to 12 percent are coming after state funding reductions of more than 20 percent. This follows a 32-percent tuition hike at the University of California system just two years ago, which produced such discord that administrators had to be escorted onto campus by security personnel.

But the year's most dramatic example of collegiate sticker shock will likely come in Washington State. There, the budget that lawmakers approved this year imposes a 24-percent cut in state funding. Tuition will go up 20 percent as a result.

WHY HIGHER EDUCATION?

Lawmakers do not like cutting money for higher education. Voters depend on it and the private sector wants an educated workforce. But higher education is a target because it is one of the few discretionary program areas left for state lawmakers to cut.

After K–12 schools and health care, higher education is the largest item in state budgets. It is usually easier to cut than the others because funding is not enshrined in state constitutions or complicated by matching federal grants, as is the case for public schools and Medicaid, respectively. Deep cuts to corrections, another major category of state spending, can carry public safety implications that lawmakers often want to avoid.

Higher education, notes Patrick Callan, president of the National Center for Public Policy and Higher Education, is a common target for another reason. Because a university can raise tuition, "it has a revenue source of its own. You can't charge people on public assistance and you can't charge people in prison." The added political benefit, he says, is that students and the public often don't connect tuition increases with what happens in state legislatures. Instead, they fault the universities themselves.

"State legislatures and governors," Callan says, "can do this in a way that doesn't leave their fingerprints on it."

ALTERNATIVE APPROACHES

Big tuition increases at public universities are nothing new. According to The College Board, in-state tuition has risen at 5.9 percent above the rate of inflation over the last decade, and that trend has grown more pronounced during the last few years of economic stagnation. In the 2010–2011 academic year, the average tuition at public, four-year schools increased by 7.9 percent.

While state support for higher education has been declining during the recession and its aftermath, enrollment continues to rise. More people—many of them unemployed—are attending public universities, which are usually far cheaper than their private counterparts. Yet another strain is the expiration this month of about $23 billion in federal stimulus funds for higher education. The combination of pressures has left many universities with few alternatives but to raise tuition substantially.

Some states are trying to blunt the effects of tuition sticker-shock. New York's recently passed budget includes a significant cut to higher education, but it has also resulted in a five-year plan in which the State University of New York will raise tuition by a steady 5.5 percent each year. While students and parents are unlikely to celebrate a consistent hike in tuition, predictable funding is important for university administrators, and Wall Street likes it, too. An analysis by Moody's Investors Service this month hailed the move as "game-changing" legislation that will "free the state's public universities from a history of erratic tuition setting and political control."

In Michigan, Governor Rick Snyder has taken a tougher approach, signing a budget that cuts higher education by 15 percent and threatens bigger cuts if universities raise tuition by more than 7.1 percent. In effect, Michigan is ordering universities to find savings without calling on students and parents for extra revenue, forcing schools to tighten their belts even more than they have. In Missouri, Governor Jay Nixon used a similar tactic, cutting funds for some universities more than expected because they exceeded the 5-percent cap on tuition increases that he wanted.

Lawmakers elsewhere are cutting back on scholarships and grant programs they created during good times, hoping to avoid more generalized cuts that would affect the entire student population.

Public university students in Georgia will see only a modest 3-percent increase in tuition this fall, but that doesn't mean lawmakers didn't aim the budget knife at higher education. They just aimed it at a specific part of higher education: the HOPE scholarship program, which previously allowed any Georgia high school student with a B average to attend a four-year public university in the state for free. This year, Georgia lawmakers cut back the program by reducing the state grant to about 90 percent of the costs of a four-year education.

John Millsaps, a spokesman for the Georgia Board of Regents, says his state's support for higher education has declined by $1 billion over the last decade, forcing some colleges into huge tuition increases. Georgia State University, for example, raised tuition by 46 percent between 2007 and 2010, according to a tuition tracking website recently developed by the U.S. Department of Education.

This year, Millsaps says, lawmakers simply made an extremely generous state scholarship program a little less generous. "Had HOPE never existed before and the governor announced a plan to provide 90 percent of college costs (to any eligible high school student in the state)," he says, "there would have been parades in every town in Georgia."

Policy Challenges

The big policy challenge for state and local governments remains unchanged for a fifth consecutive year: figuring out how to keep conducting the business of governance while keeping revenues and expenditures on roughly equal terms. As Part IX highlighted, balancing the books is the overwhelming policy priority for many state and local governments. Yet it is worth remembering that the purpose of government is not to simply keep the public checkbook in the black. Money management is critical, but it is the means, not the end, of government.

State and local governments have always been expected to tackle a breathtaking array of enormous policy responsibilities. Education, law enforcement, infrastructure, public transportation . . . the list goes on and on. Increasingly added to this list are high-profile issues like health care and illegal immigration. Governments cannot avoid dealing with the ever-growing list of expectations piled on them because of a financial crisis. Indeed, financial crisis has created a whole new set of expectations—not just on what governments should do but how it should be done.

The readings in this chapter examine some of those new expectations and also provide a reminder that, regardless of economic and policy challenges, governance is busily evolving. In contrast to the readings in Part IX, which were mostly about how economics influences government decisions, the first essay, by Louis Jacobson, is about how government decisions might influence economics. Can state governments really do anything to increase employment? Historically, states have focused on creating jobs by poaching them from other states through policies like tax breaks designed to lure companies into relocating. Some states are starting to think more about creating that poaching. These innovative approaches might help, say economists, but you cannot simply cut or spend your way to business growth.

The second essay, by Ryan Holeywell, takes a look at a radical new development in governance. In Michigan, a new state law is stripping power from financially distressed cities and giving it to outside financial managers. Once appointed, these managers have broad authority over local government affairs; they can hire, fire, create the budget, and issue ordinances. This *dictator law* is in strong contrast to traditional notions of how local governments should be run. Supporters argue it is necessary to meet the challenge of cities that are incapable of solving their own existential financial problems. Opponents say it is creating a new and disturbingly undemocratic form of government—cities run by unelected state appointees with unilateral powers over local government.

The third essay, by Russell Nichols, takes a look at a new and innovative financing model for government. Massachusetts is experimenting with social impact bonds. First developed in the UK, these allow social programs to be funded with limited risk—if they do not work, the state does not pay for them.

The final reading is by Bruce Perlman, and it reminds us that the policy challenges faced by state and local governments are more than dealing with expenditures and revenue. Many governments are now experimenting with social media as a tool of governance. This means more than setting up a Facebook page. For example, some local governments are using Twitter as an emergency communication tool and websites as a means to involve citizen participation in multiple levels of local government. This essay also shows how new communications technology is in some ways globalizing local government; successful use of social media by local governments in one nation can rapidly diffuse to other nations.

36

Jobs Crisis

By Louis Jacobson

States cannot cut and spend their way to stimulating business growth. Innovative policy approaches, though, might help create a few more jobs.

Everyone who's been paying attention to national politics knows how polarized the fight over job creation has become. Last fall, President Obama and congressional Republicans continued to slug it out over who has the best vision for the economy. The president proposed the American Jobs Act—a mix of targeted tax cuts, funds to keep state and local workers on the payroll and to build infrastructure projects, and an extension of unemployment insurance—only to see it stall in Congress. The president then took to the hustings to decry inequities in the tax code between the super-rich and the middle class.

Republicans attacked Obama's proposed tax hikes on wealthier Americans, describing them as an all-out assault on the nation's job creators.

Where the economy, taxes and the budget are concerned, the two sides today are on different planets, a split that is echoed in legislatures across the country.

"The president's plan is the best one I've heard so far," says Assemblywoman Maggie Carlton, a Democrat from the economically hard-hit Las Vegas area. Her state is staggering under an unemployment rate that was at 13.4 percent in October, the highest in the nation. "We need to get very serious in Nevada, where unemployment in the construction trades is over 50 percent."

But Republican Senator Paul G. Campbell Jr. of South Carolina argues temporary tax cuts aren't the best way to help businesses. Decisions on "shovel ready" projects risk being made for political reasons, not economic ones, he says. "The president's proposal doesn't make a bit of sense."

From *State Legislatures*, January 2012.

169

With the federal government paralyzed over how best to spur job growth, what can states do? A range of economists who specialize in economic development agree there are things states can do to improve the nation's jobs outlook, but there are plenty of pitfalls, too.

Most experts agree the states' role in job creation is limited because they have less capacity to jolt the economy than the federal government and they're facing severe fiscal constraints.

Promoting job creation "is really a task for the federal government," says Jeffrey A. Frankel, a professor of capital formation and growth at the Harvard University Kennedy School of Government. Only the federal government has the tools to increase consumer demand and the availability of credit on a large scale, says Roger Noll, an emeritus economics professor at Stanford University.

In addition, states historically have devoted a big chunk of their economic development efforts to luring factories and other types of businesses to relocate within their borders, sometimes with lavish tax breaks and other incentives. Always controversial, such efforts not only have become more spendthrift than ever before, but are also damaging to the national economy since they merely shift employment and do nothing to create new jobs for the nation as a whole.

States are still "trying to attract jobs from other states," says Jon Shure, director of state fiscal strategies for the Washington, D.C.–based Center on Budget and Policy Priorities. "Many states still feel that, by offering lower taxes and higher subsidies, they can grow their economies. It is not a long term-strategy, but states still do it. And companies still play states off against each other, asking for the best deal and then leaving when they get a better one someplace else. It's a sucker's game for states, but no one wants to unilaterally disarm."

INVESTMENTS VS. INCENTIVES

In Connecticut, efforts are underway to take a different course. Governor Dannel P. Malloy received bipartisan backing from the legislature on two measures aimed at creating new jobs, not just poaching them from other states.

The first, Bioscience Connecticut, calls for investments in the state's flagship public university and its health center to promote high-tech investment nearby, providing—in the estimates of its sponsors—3,000 jobs annually between 2012 and 2018.

"We need to find what can be our future, and moving aggressively into biotech and research can be that future," Senate Majority Leader Martin Looney said when the bill was passed. "It requires us to make this investment today because this is the specific opportunity that has presented itself in this time frame and now is the time to do it."

The second measure is a $626 million economic development package that includes cuts in regulations favored by GOP lawmakers and supports worker training advocated by Democrats. There are financial incentives for each job created and even larger benefits for companies that hire veterans, disabled people and the unemployed.

"States are recognizing the importance of organic growth," says Martin Shields, a regional economist at Colorado State University. "Fostering entrepreneurship is increasingly recognized as an important source of growth. The importance of innovation and creativity, and the supporting role that institutions can play in this, is evident in policy initiatives, such as clean energy, biopharmaceuticals and the like."

Yet, Shields acknowledges the limits to such policies, especially the possibility that governments will create a revenue-wasting "industrial policy" rather than letting the free market work its magic.

> *"Fostering entrepreneurship is increasingly recognized as an important source of growth."*
> Martin Shields, Colorado State University

"At the end of the day, it's very hard to plan economic development," Shields says. "It's hard to pick winners. It's hard to identify and seed 'the next big thing.'"

IS GREEN GREAT?

The recent implosion of Solyndra—a politically well-connected solar energy equipment company that received

$535 million in federal stimulus money from the Obama administration—has only fueled criticism of efforts to "pick winners," whether it's at the federal or state level.

Joel Kotkin, an author and fellow at Chapman University in southern California who specializes in the future of urban areas, says there may be valid reasons to support "green" industries, but job creation isn't one of them. The jobs created, he said, simply cost too much in taxpayer money to represent a good investment.

"The idea that going green would be economical in the short- to medium-term is off," he says. "It's one thing to say we need to do this for other reasons, but to pretend it's an economic policy is disingenuous."

When Michigan tackled changes to its tax code earlier this year, the governor and Legislature took a broader approach. They reduced taxes on an entire class of businesses—limited-liability corporations, many of which are smaller—from 23 percent to 6 percent while also simplifying the rules for deductions.

"We call it economic gardening," says Representative Mark Ouimet, who represents a portion of Ann Arbor. Even though Michigan is best known as the headquarters of the Big Three automakers, "we feel it will be small business that will lead us out of the economic challenge we're in," he says.

Plethora of Policies

Policies that help create jobs, some targeted and some more holistic, can help states pull out of the prolonged labor slump, experts say.

Efforts to improve workers' skills and advise companies on everything from how to expand locally to how to break into foreign markets are beneficial, as long as the programs are well run, says Ryan Sharp, director of the Center for Strategic Economic Research in Sacramento, Calif.

Ernie P. Goss, a regional economist at the Creighton University College of Business in Omaha, Neb., urged quicker processing of payments to state vendors and expediting state and local projects that may be on hold because of a lengthy approval process. "And pray for favorable factors, such as good weather and no natural disasters," he says.

Another option for states are work-sharing programs that allow employers to reduce a worker's hours so those employees then can receive partial unemployment insurance benefits while continuing to work part time, says Dean Baker, an economist and co-director of the Center for Economic and Policy Research in Washington, D.C. The federal government lets states run such programs even when the employee has exceeded the 26 weeks of state unemployment and is tapping into extended benefits during which the federal government pays a larger share.

"This would encourage employers to cut workers' hours rather than lay them off," Baker says. "Twenty states already have work-sharing programs, but the take-up rates are very low. This is because most employers don't even know about it, and because the program tends to be overly bureaucratic. However, if a state could get more widespread use of work sharing, it could be an effective way to bring down its unemployment rate."

"Do No Harm"

Of course, the easiest way for states to prevent job losses is to refrain from cutting state workers. Nationally, private sector payrolls have been increasing, at least modestly, for the past year and a half. It's been government payrolls that have held back employment growth overall. State governments have shed 125,000 jobs since 2008, and local governments have cut another 525,000 over the same period, according to Bureau of Labor Statistics. That's both an enormous drag on the monthly employment numbers and a wallop to the larger economy from lost wages and lower consumer spending.

"One of the best things states can do is not lay off public sector workers," says Shure of the Center on Budget and Policy Priorities. "I'd say, 'first, do no harm.'"

Low interest rates are the silver lining for states in the current economy, Shure says. They allow states to borrow for infrastructure repairs and maintenance that can put people to work.

But the most important strategy may be the least hands-on—that is, just providing the kinds of fundamental conditions that allow businesses to thrive.

"In general, the key to job creation is understanding that governments don't create jobs," says Michael Pakko, an economic forecaster at the Institute for Economic Advancement at the University of Arkansas at Little Rock. "They only provide an environment that is conducive—or not—to job growth."

Both Sides Bring Value

The good news for those craving bipartisan solutions to the jobs crisis, economists agree, is that both liberal and conservative ideas have something to offer. Liberals can take comfort that smart investments in education, research and general infrastructure are important. Conservatives can relish that efforts to eliminate needless regulations and counterproductive tax policies can help.

"What it comes down to is doing things to make sure the environment is positive for business growth," says Mark Schill, vice president for the Praxis Strategy Group.

"We understand certain regulations are for the public good. We don't want to have no regulation. But you need timely answers, more streamlined processes, agencies not competing with each other," he says. "We call it fighting 'DURT'—delays, uncertainty, regulation and taxes."

"Policymakers should ensure that their [state's] tax system is competitive with that of its neighbors," says Creighton's Goss. "This means the tax code should not be cluttered with special cutouts and incentives for a narrow slice of firms and individuals. For long-term, sustained development, policymakers should reduce tax rates at the same time they widen the tax base. Special incentives do the opposite."

Even the most business-friendly environment, however, won't help if your state skimps on shelling out for basic amenities. Carlton, the Nevada legislator, notes her state ranks high nationally for business friendliness but low in education spending. In fact, an Education Week comparison published in 2009 found Nevada ranked third from the bottom of the 50 states in expenditures per pupil when adjusted for local costs.

Carlton says when courting prospective employers, falling short in education "is one of the first things that gets you taken off the list. We really found that out when the recession hit."

Schill emphasizes any solution has to be balanced. "You can neither cut nor spend your way there," he says.

With educational attainment increasingly important for securing good jobs, "focusing so much on cuts is not healthy," Schill says. "It doesn't mean you just throw more money at the problem, but you have to have adequate levels of investment in your workforce."

One of the biggest challenges of enacting a balanced approach to job creation is the nature of politics itself. One obstacle is overindulgence to entrenched interests. Kotkin emphasizes a promising agenda is impossible to accomplish if it bends too much to powerful interest groups, whether they be unions, environmentalists or real estate developers.

Another obstacle is deeply ingrained partisanship. Vicious fights over a few fundamental issues lead to demonization of the other side, which, in turn, makes cooperation on more mundane—and historically bipartisan—issues that much more difficult. "State officials often get caught up in the national debate, whether by choice or not," says Colorado's Shields.

Ultimately, however, voters cannot escape blame entirely, says Noll of Stanford. "Most pundits blame it on weak leadership, but I think that is a cop-out," he says. "We elect them, probably because we like strong personalities and simple, home-spun solutions to complex problems."

"The problem with 'growing your own' jobs," Goss says, "is that it takes longer, and thus is less politically viable for elected officials who have very short time horizons."

37

Emergency Financial Managers: Michigan's Unwelcome Savior

By Ryan Holeywell

In Michigan, the state is appointing outsiders to run financially distressed cities. Whether these managers are saviors or dictators depends on whom you are talking to.

An outsider's first visit to Pontiac, Mich., feels a bit like Alice's first glance at Wonderland. Everything seems upside down. City Council meetings last for hours, but there is nothing on the agenda. The city has a mayor, but he doesn't have any authority. There are workers inside City Hall, but they aren't employed by the city. And the man at the head of the table is an exceedingly charming 74-year-old who might be destroying his hometown, or who might be the only person willing to save it.

Thanks to a law championed by Republican Gov. Rick Snyder and passed by the Michigan Legislature early last year, that man, Lou Schimmel, has almost unilateral authority to run the government in this city of 60,000 that state leaders have deemed to be in the midst of a fiscal emergency. That law, known as Public Act 4 (PA4), is the same one that state leaders held over Detroit officials as they threatened a state takeover (the two sides eventually agreed to a more limited type of oversight).

In Pontiac, Schimmel oversees the city's day-to-day operations. He hires and fires employees. He forces major changes to labor contracts. He sets the budget. He creates ordinances. He sells city property. His critics call the policy that put him in power the "dictator law."

Pontiac isn't alone. Five other local governments in Michigan have emergency managers who make decisions that, until now, have been under the purview of democratically elected local officials. In those communities, locally elected officials have virtually no decision-making power. It's a trend that's not limited to Michigan. More than half the states in the country have provisions that allow them to exercise some degree of financial supervision over distressed localities, and it's

From *Governing*, May 2012.

173

clear they're willing to exercise it. In places like Harrisburg, Pa.; Central Falls, R.I.; and Nassau County, N.Y., state-appointed officials are making decisions that were once decidedly local.

But nowhere in America do local officials have less control—and state appointees more—than in the financially distressed communities of Michigan. Republican leaders here say that's no accident, and that they intentionally crafted a mechanism for outsiders to swoop into a troubled community, assess the financial damage and fix it—all without being beholden to local political interests. They argue that if a locality declares bankruptcy, taxpayers statewide could be left holding the bag. Preventing such a situation is a paramount concern. "You don't want to go through municipal bankruptcies and pay the debts of these communities," says state Rep. Al Pscholka, the sponsor of PA4, which vastly expanded the power of state-appointed fiscal overseers established in a previous law. "We have to have protection for taxpayers." On the surface, it's a statement that's hard to argue with. But it also raises a more fundamental question: Can democracy become too expensive?

In 1986, a circuit court named Schimmel the receiver for Ecorse, a small city just outside of Detroit, and told him to put the city's fiscal house back in order. With that assignment, Schimmel believes he became the first person in the country to hold what's becoming an increasingly frequent position in local government: emergency financial manager. In 2000, the state again tapped him to take over Hamtramck, a financially distressed city surrounded by Detroit. Now, he's on his third dance—and he insists it will be his last. But he's not the typical outsider this time. Pontiac is his hometown, the place he was born and raised. It's a job that few would be interested in taking, given the track record of Pontiac's previous two emergency managers. Both encountered harsh resistance from local officials, both resigned after little more than a year and neither is spoken of favorably here. For Schimmel, it's clear that part of the job's draw is the immense challenge it offers, as well as the rare opportunity to see what could be realized if a manager were given total control without political interference. "It's a sense of accomplishment when you take something that's broke and fix it," says Schimmel, who, despite the seriousness of his job, almost always wears a smile and constantly cracks jokes.

Critics of the law that put him in power are doing everything they can to get it taken off the books. A campaign to repeal the law, supported by the National Association for the Advancement of Colored People and the labor community, among others, has likely gained enough signatures to force a statewide vote later this year. In the interim, PA4 will be suspended, but it's unclear what that means for the five emergency managers. In addition, the law is the target of several lawsuits, one of which—at least briefly—got the emergency manager in Flint removed from office. (After a successful appeal, he's back on the job for now.) What's unclear is whether the legal and political challenges will mean the end of emergency managers in Michigan, or simply a return to the earlier version of the law, which still gave the state significant oversight over troubled localities.

Regardless of the outcome, some believe the debate is moot: Pontiac residents elected a mayor and council to run the city. The state gave them Schimmel instead. Schimmel isn't accountable to anybody in Pontiac. He answers to the governor and an appointed state treasurer. Yet Schimmel disputes the premise that democracy has been subverted in Pontiac. "The law I'm operating under was passed under a democracy," Schimmel says. "It wasn't a law handed down by a king. It was passed by a legislature."

For some, that point offers little consolation. The debate about PA4 in Pontiac is bitter and discussed in overtly racial terms. The majority of Pontiac's population is black. All three emergency managers—not to mention the governor, treasurer and legislator who sponsored PA4—are white. Democratic blogger Chris Savage generated national attention when he noted in December that, if you included Inkster and Detroit, two cities that were on the verge of emergency management, more than half of the state's black population could soon lack full-fledged local democracy. Fred Leeb, Pontiac's first emergency manager, says that some people in Pontiac tried to promote the sentiment that he was "the master sent from Lansing to control the plantation." Indeed, at a recent City Council meeting, one black resident thanked an elected official for tying to protect "field negroes" like him from "carpetbaggers" like Schimmel.

Pontiac got into fiscal trouble when the automobile industry, which once had manufacturing plants throughout the city, began its decline. A boomtown in the first half of the 20th century, Pontiac's population peaked around 1970 at 85,000 and then declined dramatically in subsequent decades. Today, it has 30 percent fewer residents than it did at its height. More than a third of those residents live in poverty, including nearly half the city's children. For decades, its unemployment rate has exceeded the national average. Right now, it's at 22.5 percent—second worst in the state. "When we were affluent, we didn't diversify," says City Councilman Kermit Williams. "We married GM instead of dating around, and when the divorce happened, it was brutal." General Motors plants, which were once the economic driver of the city, are being demolished, and their rubble is carried away by freight trains. The process gives residents the unusual opportunity to watch their city disappear before their eyes.

As Pontiac's population and economy declined, so too did property values and tax revenue, along with its share of state revenue. That caused deficits to mount in the short term; in the longer term, debt from projects that might have been profitable in better times is climbing. Meanwhile, the city faces an unfunded liability for retiree health and life insurance of nearly $270 million. For officials in the state capital of Lansing, it became clear in 2009 that Pontiac needed professional help, so then-Gov. Jennifer Granholm picked Leeb as her man for the job.

Two managers later, Schimmel is in charge. He's not only Pontiac's first emergency manager appointed under Snyder, a Republican, he's also Pontiac's first emergency manager appointed under PA4. Schimmel says critics shouldn't blame him for his work. "I'm not the one who made the appointment," he says. "The law is what it is." But Schimmel himself is being modest, as his work may have helped inspire key aspects of the law. In 2005, Schimmel wrote a piece for the Mackinac Center for Public Policy, an influential conservative think tank in Michigan, that detailed reform he thought the state should make to its existing emergency management law, which he believed lacked the tools needed to enact a serious municipal turnaround. He recommended that emergency managers be given immunity from lawsuits, the authority to assume powers held by the mayor and city commission, and the ability to cancel labor contracts. All those provisions made it into PA4, and today Schimmel is able to take full advantage of them.

Schimmel's focus in Pontiac has been on cutting costs. He ripped out the city's parking meters when he realized it cost more money to collect parking fees than the city was taking in. He consolidated 87 separate city employee health plans into one to save $5 million annually. And he's launched a major effort to sell city property. But what's generated the most controversy is an aggressive campaign to outsource as many city services as possible. He can rattle off a list of city services that are no longer performed in-house: building permits, water and sewer operations, income tax collection, payroll, trash pickup, IT and cemetery operations, among others. Indeed, walking through City Hall (which Schimmel might sell, by the way) is an unusual experience. The city's payroll has been reduced from about 600 to 60 employees. The building is largely empty, and those who remain perform city work but get their paychecks from the private-sector companies that employ them.

Schimmel's predecessor closed the local police department and outsourced law enforcement to the Oakland County Sheriff's Office in a move expected to save $2.2 million annually. Schimmel took a similar step and used his authority to outsource the fire department service to neighboring Waterford Township. The Pontiac firefighters' contract wasn't set to expire until June 2013, but Schimmel was set on the move. So when Pontiac firefighters resisted, he essentially gave them an ultimatum: agree to a deal—and get some modicum of job security—or risk getting laid off completely. "Without Public Act 4," Schimmel says, "I couldn't do that." In the end, firefighters reluctantly agreed to a provision in which all but a handful received early retirement or new jobs with Waterford, albeit on a lower pay scale. The changes, Schimmel says, will save Pontiac $3 million annually.

While he says these decisions are critical to an effective and quick turnaround of a city, his critics are skeptical. They view his 2005 article and subsequent job at Mackinac as evidence that ideologically driven Republicans are using Pontiac as a testing ground to see if a model based on outsourcing can be reproduced in other cities. "It's just an experiment to see if privatization works," says Williams, the city councilman.

Moves like the firefighter deal aren't popular in a city that's down on its luck and views the fire department as one of the few remaining sources of local civic pride. That's part of the problem, says Mayor Leon Jukowski, who has no authority as mayor but is a paid member of Schimmel's staff. "That sort of emotional attachment to an institution is part of what's dragging the city under at this point," he says.

"I'm a Democrat," Jukowski continues. "People in my party say it's union busting. To a certain extent, it is. The dilemma is, how do you send someone in and say, 'I want you to fix this problem, but you can't touch 80 percent of what's under the hood?'" Douglas Carr, a professor at nearby Oakland University, says the firefighter situation illustrates the dichotomy facing the city: Nearly everybody recognizes its financial challenges, but few people like the way that Schimmel's changes are affecting them personally. Those who support the actions of Schimmel and other emergency managers argue that labor contracts have long offered generous terms to public employees and were a ticking time bomb ready to wreak financial havoc on localities at the first sign of a downturn in revenue. Labor supporters say that in the wake of the recession, municipal workers have been unfairly scapegoated when larger economic forces are to blame.

What's clear is that, whoever is right, techniques like the one Schimmel used are being reproduced elsewhere. In nearby Ecorse, emergency manager Joyce Parker recently cross-trained police officers and firefighters, reduced their numbers and combined what was left into a single public safety unit. In Central Falls, R.I., state-appointed receiver Bob Flanders slashed the pensions of emergency responders in a move critics call draconian. Flanders isn't apologetic. "Of course your contracts are being destroyed. That's what it's all about," says Flanders, a former state supreme court justice. "It's tough luck, but that's the way it is."

"If you're a taxpayer, you probably want to nominate me for sainthood," Flanders continues. "If you're a municipal worker, you probably think I'm the devil incarnate."

Meanwhile, the Michigan model is drawing praise from many conservatives, who maintain that labor unions are threatening the finances of cities across the country and believe laws that give officials the authority to blow up those contracts may be the only way to solve the problem. "Over time, what you build up ... is a set of contracts and work rules that are restrictive like a boa constrictor," says Eric Kriss, who served in former Massachusetts Gov. Mitt Romney's cabinet and was involved in state takeovers of the cities of Chelsea and Springfield. Without a change in the law—like Public Act 4—"no administrative effort can break through it."

But others question whether Schimmel's methods will be enough to save Pontiac. As Schimmel focuses on cost cutting, the other side of the ledger is in jeopardy as tax revenue continues to fall.

"There's no question and no debate that a lot of cities are under serious financial stress," says state Rep. Tim Greimel, who represents Pontiac. "The question is: Is an emergency manager likely to improve things and make it better? Just because one way is bad doesn't mean another is better. It may be worse."

No other state centralizes its oversight of distressed localities as tightly as Michigan. Even the decision of when it's time for Pontiac to emerge from its status lies largely with Schimmel himself. In Pennsylvania, a state that has experienced a similar decline in manufacturing, financial oversight plans are developed in concert with localities. Harrisburg—while generating headlines for its problems—is the lone case in which the state has taken the onerous step of appointing a one-man receiver. In neighboring Ohio, when a city falls under emergency status, the state includes local officials on the oversight commission. "It's not one person coming in with a 'hail Caesar' approach," says Dave Yost, Ohio's state auditor.

That's the central question for many here in Pontiac: Does it make political sense to have one person in charge? Many civic leaders in Pontiac say they believe in Schimmel and are even fond of him. Still, they think he has too much authority. "I have a lot of respect for Lou," says Douglas Jones, a pastor in Pontiac who has helped convene an association of business and civic leaders to address the city's challenges. "I think he wants the best for the city of Pontiac, and his heart's in the right place." But too much power in one person—even Schimmel—is problematic. "I've still got to report to God," says Jones.

Others say there are more practical considerations. "If you put in an emergency manager that only acts unilaterally, at some point in time, that person leaves and then what happens?" says John Filan, vice president of DSI Civic, which specializes in government restructuring. Schimmel recognizes that the City Council can undo much of what he's done, and it's not lost on him that Ecorse—the place where he got his start in municipal restructuring—is once again under an emergency manager. Williams, the city councilman, says that upon Schimmel's departure, he expects local officials to start in-sourcing some of the city services that have been privatized.

Nevertheless, critics' skepticism may be warranted, given the city's track record. At the end of last fiscal year, more than two years after Pontiac received its first emergency manager, the city had a positive fund balance of $1.7 million, according to financial statements that Schimmel filed with the state shortly after taking over. But it achieved that largely by failing to make payments into employee pension and benefit funds, and opting against putting aside money for a property tax refund it owes GM. Those liabilities still exist, and if the city had paid them, it would have had a $12.5 million deficit instead.

Some even blame Michigan for inflicting some of the pain Pontiac and other distressed cities are now experiencing. In early 2011, while promoting PA4, Snyder simultaneously advanced a budget eliminating one-third of the state revenue sharing set aside for localities—about $307 million. That was on top of the $4 billion in state revenue that localities had lost over the last decade. While Pontiac struggles, the state ended last fiscal year with a reported $457 million surplus. That disparity has prompted some residents and elected officials to openly question whether Snyder's budget, in concert with PA4, is an attempt by state leaders to systematically dismantle urban communities and promote a regionalized approach that favors counties. Schimmel's immediate predecessor, Michael Stampfler, had suggested that the city consider filing for bankruptcy or being absorbed by Oakland County. The idea infuriated many residents, who viewed it as the state giving up on Pontiac.

Ultimately, however, critics don't buy the oft-repeated argument made by Schimmel and others that local officials aren't willing to address the problem. In 2009, Pontiac residents elected a new mayor and replaced all but one member of the City Council. "I'm 29 years old," Williams says. "Some of the problems we have in Pontiac were created before I was alive." In addition to the City Council losing its power, it's also suffered symbolic affronts. Council members don't get paid, they don't have the keys to City Hall and because they don't have power, the City Council meetings are essentially meaningless.

Members of the City Council say Schimmel tries to keep them in the dark, and even Schimmel admits that while he has an open door policy with locally elected leaders, the relationship isn't great. "My agenda is so different from theirs," he says, "that it became obvious there was nothing to be gained by either side" by trying to work together.

Still, Schimmel says he's making the most effective reforms he can. As fiscal 2013 approaches, he expects the city will have no shortfall as a result of a multimillion dollar deal in which the city will sell excess sewer system capacity to a county comission. (He wryly jokes it's a move that even his critics should like. By helping to shore up the city's finances, the deal will help expedite his departure from Pontiac.) Schimmel also says local officials aren't giving him credible alternatives. He may have a point. Williams says instead of outsourcing the fire department, Schimmel could have simply laid off enough of the existing personnel to keep fire protection in-house. But that plan would have caused an even larger furor over lost jobs. Or, Williams suggests, Pontiac could have generated revenue by absorbing Waterford's department. But that plan would have increased long-term labor expenses.

Williams does make a salient, larger point. "The bottom line is if your city gets poor enough, they can strip your democracy."

The greatest criticism of Michigan's law is that it does little to ensure a long-term turnaround of the state's most troubled cities. The problem, say local officials in Pontiac and elsewhere, is that the state has failed to build up business and encourage urban renewal. Schimmel is candid that his primary concern is not economic development. That duty, he says, is "beyond my purview."

In Schimmel's defense, economic development is a process that takes years, and neither he nor local leaders want him to stay in Pontiac for that long. But it's hard to imagine a strategy based primarily on cuts will do much to change the underlying factors that have caused 20 percent of homes to remain vacant and thousands of residents to remain out of work. As many observers note, people who can afford to pay taxes have a choice of where they can live, and right now, it doesn't seem they have much incentive to move to Pontiac.

But Schimmel also believes people won't move to a town that's in a fiscal crisis either. He's trying to fix the backbone of the city and put it on a successful path. "I've done it before," Schimmel says. "We'll get there. I hope to work myself out of a job by the end of this calendar year."

Others are more skeptical. "The one thing people seem to agree on in Pontiac is that it's a disaster," Leeb says, "and that is unfortunate."

38

Governments Experiment with Risk-Free Financing

By Russell Nichols

Massachusetts borrows a financing model from the United Kingdom designed to fund only programs that work.

S ince 1988, she's been running a nonprofit operation in Chelsea, Mass., designed to keep young people off the streets and out of jails. They're between 14 and 24 years old, and her programs teach them how to get a job and succeed in society. Over a two-year period, she observes patterns and tracks growth to see what's working and what's not. But in her world, she says, success doesn't always reap rewards.

"We have big social problems and they cost a lot of money, and we don't apply the same type of thinking we do to for-profit businesses," says Baldwin, the founder and executive director of Roca Inc. "I could go find 200 more kids on the street, but that doesn't mean they come with money."

When it comes to funding new program models, state and local governments aren't exactly big-time, put-it-all-on-the-table gamblers. In many cases, agencies tend to focus on inputs rather than outcomes. As a result, defective programs can persist for years on end, while successful organizations that focus on issues like homelessness, recidivism and youth violence don't get the money they need. "If you're busy piecing together money all the time," Baldwin says, "you don't get to put all the effort into what the program is."

But what if there were a different financing model, one that pumps dollars into social programs the government can monitor over time without paying a single dime up front? It may sound like an ad for a pyramid scheme, but the United Kingdom is in the middle of a pilot program based on just such a model, known as a social impact bond. In Massachusetts, Gov. Deval Patrick's administration is taking steps to become the first state in the country to use this strategy.

From *Governing*, December 2011.

Here's how it works: Investors (charitable foundations, wealthy individuals, monied families) put up the initial investment for the expansion of a nonprofit program. The nonprofit must agree to meet specific benchmarks within a certain period. A government agency signs off and oversees the progress. If the program meets its benchmarks, the government refunds the investors. There is also the possibility of a profit if the program exceeds expectations. In theory, the government wins either way. If the program succeeds, the government saves money. (Reducing recidivism, for example, cuts incarceration costs.) If the program fails, the government owes nothing.

With the ever-increasing strain on public revenues, governments may look at this new model as a risk they can afford to take. The approach appeals to Massachusetts for its potential to address homelessness, adult corrections, juvenile justice and several other areas where the state hopes to improve certain outcomes, according to Jay Gonzalez, Massachusetts' secretary of administration and finance. The state is exploring the idea now, consulting with experts and soliciting feedback. The goal is to identify the top areas that would benefit from the social impact bond model and contract with providers by the end of the year.

"We're never going to be quite in the same place we were before the recession," Gonzalez says. "In order to deal with this new fiscal reality, we need to find new ways of doing business. This is a concept that typically isn't the way government works, but it's a direction we need to go under this new rubric."

In the U.K., 60 percent of short-term offenders are back in jail within a year of their release, turning the prison system into a revolving door, according to Social Finance, an independent investment bank intermediary.

Social Finance wanted to reverse that trend. The organization pitched a pilot scheme to help 3,000 short-term inmates from a prison in Peterborough, England, find jobs, housing and counseling by securing $8 million worth of social impact bonds. The funds were raised and the program launched last fall. If the program manages to reduce the prison's recidivism rate by 7.5 percent in six years, the British Ministry of Justice agreed to give the investors their money back. If it drops more than that, the return could be even greater.

"In a successful scenario, all the parties win," says Tracy Palandjian, the CEO of Social Finance's U.S.-based arm. "The government only pays for what works. Investors get their returns, and nonprofits are given scaled capital to do what they're good at doing."

The U.K. pilot still has five years to go before the results come in. But President Obama is already sold on the concept of the government only paying for what works. In his 2012 budget proposal, he asked Congress to set aside $100 million for seven "pay-for-success" projects that target job training, education, juvenile justice and children with disabilities, to name a few. In the U.S., state and local agencies deliver social services. The various agencies and disparate accounting could make potential U.S. models slightly more complicated than in the U.K., Palandjian says, but it also gives investors more diverse opportunities.

For all their noted benefits, social impact bonds also have potential problems that need to be worked out in advance, according to Jeffrey Liebman, a professor of public policy at Harvard's Kennedy School of Government. In a report published by the liberal Center for American Progress in February, Liebman wrote that this funding model will only work if proven programs have high net benefits for investors, outcomes that can be easily measured, a well-defined treatment population and credible impact assessments. In addition, shutting down a failing program shouldn't cause damage to the targeted group.

The U.S. can use social impact bonds to overcome barriers to social innovation, Liebman says, but the government must take steps to identify promising areas, assess the investor market, and establish "a neutral authority to measure outcomes and resolve disputes, independent of both the government and the bond-issuing organization." He also mentions the importance of organizations that can act as go-betweens, connecting private investors with public agencies and service providers.

"Innovation is a crucial characteristic of how we're going to solve social problems," says Antony Bugg-Levine, managing director of the Rockefeller Foundation, which invested $500,000 in the U.K. pilot. "These bonds will offer a new way to mobilize for-profit investments. Investors can come in and fund ideas at a time when there's more risk involved and governments are less inclined."

As with any investment, risk plays a critical role. Although in this case, the stakes are the highest for private investors, not the governments. To increase the chances of seeing a return, Bugg-Levine says, investors should put their chips on programs that have already proven successful.

Regardless, risk comes with the nonprofit territory. And even though many innovative programs have had trouble securing public funds because governments considered them high-risk, social entrepreneurs like Baldwin believe desperate times call for different measures.

"I don't want to watch kids die in the street or go to prison, and the potential of social impact bonds allows us to look at things in a different way," Baldwin says. "I like the idea of getting the government on the hook for outcomes instead of trying to rub nickels together."

Social Media Sites at the State and Local Levels: Operational Success and Governance Failure

By Bruce J. Perlman[1]

New social media should be helping to transform the business of governance in states and localities. Is it?

INTRODUCTION

It is opportune to discuss Social Media Sites (SMS) in these pages, given that their possibly most notable icon, Facebook, has only recently opted for an initial public offering that is estimated to net it billions of dollars in capital (Raice 2012). In addition, another key player on the SMS field, Google, has recently issued a new privacy policy, from which users may not opt out, that ties together its various offerings to more closely track users' preferences and make their experience more satisfying and productive across its products (Ohsumi 2012). These social media platforms are becoming increasingly important for many citizens in the roles they play in their daily lives as friends and consumers: it is in fact impossible to access some commercial Internet products or services without using them. These tools are being used extensively in local governments as well. At least one survey by the Public Technology Institute found that 72 percent of responding Chief Information Officers claimed to be using or planned on using Facebook or Twitter in outreach efforts (Trenker 2010).

However, as these programs have become ubiquitous, the study of their place in and impact on our lives has grown but not apace in the effects on governance. Because of the relative recentness of widespread participation in social media technologies, research on social media use in government has been limited. Specifically, the study of and commentary on their effective use in state and local government has increased, but only in some areas. It is the purpose of this essay to review what do know about the effective use of social media at the state and local levels of government and to

From *State and Local Government Review*, April 2012.

examine what we do not know and need to know as well. It is this latter area that highlights the focus of this regular section of the State and Local Government Review: Governance.

Accordingly, this essay opens with a working definition of SMS in the context of computer supported networking. It then proceeds to an examination of successful SMS use in government at the state and local levels as well, discussing some challenges to that effective use. After that, the essay examines the limited research on use of SMS for governance tasks at the state and local levels. Finally, it closes with some conclusions about the two foregoing areas and a call for further research on SMS related to state and local governance.

SMS: A WORKING DEFINITION

Social and Market Media (SMM) is a Computer Mediated Communication (CMC) that allows users to connect for both social and market exchanges. Unlike other familiar CMC instruments, for example e-mail, SMM tools focus on connections made by a site and the distribution of information, goods, and services rather than on messages or statements. Mirroring the non-CMC world, these exchanges may be purely social or may be market based. SMM includes both SMS and Market Network Sites (MNS). MNS are web-based services used by individuals to qualify, offer, or purchase goods and services with other users connected to the sites and to guarantee delivery and payment when necessary. The most notable and well-known example of an MNS is E-bay, but it includes others such as Craigslist or Anglie's List.

The focus of this essay is SMS. SMS are web-based services used by individuals to construct public or limited profiles within a defined system which list the other users that share connections to the site (Boyd and Ellison 2007). This allows users to do two things. First, users can see and navigate their own list of connections. Second, depending on the permissions given by other users, they may see and navigate the lists of other users within the system. SMS focus on the network of connections made by a site and the distribution of and access to information. The most notable examples of these are Facebook, Twitter, and Google, but they

include others as well such as reddit, LinkedIn, flier, and even MySpace.

SUCCESSFUL SMS USE IN STATE AND LOCAL GOVERNMENT OPERATIONS

Increasingly SMS are being used, or at least experimented with, in the day-to-day tasks of state, regional, county, and municipal governments. Most of this use is for operations: the communications, direction, and coordination of service delivery and the numerous specific tasks and activities that make it up. Successful use has been reported in three key operational areas: public safety, transportation, and infrastructure and environmental management.

Public Safety

Innovative and successful uses of SMS have been reported across several areas of public safety, including police-citizen communications, firefighting, and emergency management. These uses go beyond the most common method of hosting a Facebook page and collecting "Likes" for an agency or program. Some examples of innovative and effective use are from the United States while others are from the United Kingdom.

Police and the Community

For example, Crump (2011) has reported the growth in the use of Twitter by U.K. police forces since 2008. By analyzing network structure and message content, his paper presents how U.K. police have employed one particular SMS platform, Twitter, as reinforcement for existing means of communication to collect information from citizens and to alert them to incidents. However, he concludes that the constraints of police culture have led to a limited and cautious one-way use of Twitter making it effective for sending information, but dampening the potential for innovation and its being used only warily and in a controlled manner.

The U.K. Association of Chief Police Officers has attempted to promote the use of SMS as a way to engage uninvolved citizens in conversations about local policing and in consideration of local priorities for policing. Their goal is to increase public participation in crime reduction and encourage it as a shared responsibility as well as enhancing public trust in the police. Unfortunately, this has not been a wholly successful endeavor most probably due to the hierarchical, command, and control nature of police organizations: they are less able to take advantage of the possibilities for user-created content and the freely networked nature of SMS as opposed to a more traditional "push-pull" model of Internet communication.

Disaster and Emergency Management

Emergency communication at the county and city levels has seen the effective employment of SMS. This is especially true in the transmitting of information to the public about emergencies, although the use of SMS in collecting information about the epidemiology of disease has also been reported. An International City/County Management Association (ICMA) report by Chavez, Repas, and Stefaniak (2010) presents six cases of U.S. local government SMS use for emergency communication: Evanston, Illinois; Fort Bend, Texas; Johnson County, Kansas; City of Moorhead, Minnesota; City of Philadelphia, Pennsylvania; and Alexandria, Virginia.

The City of Alexandria used both Twitter and YouTube for citizen emergency communications during the H1N1 influenza outbreak; the epidemiological use of Twitter for tracking disease was particularly notable and innovative. Also, that city has used Twitter for citizen communications in severe winter weather emergencies and to track and route the operation of snow plows during such winter emergencies. Philadelphia has employed SMS for communicating with citizens during critical power outages, although the dependence of SMS on electricity makes this a somewhat counterintuitive example. During the Red River Flood, the City of Moorhead, employed SMS effectively and Johnson County, Kansas, uses both blogs and podcasts to keep citizens informed about tornadoes and the methods for coping with them.

In addition, SMS has been employed by the public in local emergencies in less structured and more emergent ways. SMS use in disaster management outside of official sites is an example of emerging communication networks that have yet to be reflected in state and local operations and in actual organizational arrangements for emergency response. As the U.K. police example illustrates, local agencies themselves may not be able to exploit these networks effectively until they have greater experience with and integration of the SMS tools available. When they do

they may become better managers of the tools and forge more effective communication with the public. However, it is clear that hierarchy, control, and trust will continue to be impediments.

One example of emergent rather than structured network use of SMS is found in the 2007 Southern California wildfires. In this case, SMS for local communications was not led by but emerged as complementary to the operations of local governments. As one study suggests (Sutton, Palen, and Shklovski 2008), SMS sites expanded public participation during this wildfire disaster that crossed multiple jurisdictions. Public participants were able to post, exchange, and update information in a timely way that led to public fears being allayed and public order more effectively preserved. In this instance, it was not the use of SMS by authorities that was effective, but rather the use by citizens: through the use of "backchannel" communications community information resources were mobilized by SMS. The result of these broad, cross jurisdictional interactions was the generation of information that was not always readily available to citizens through official sources.

As would be expected, some concern has been expressed by public safety officials about the accuracy of such emergency information shared through public networking and its potential for creating problems or panic. Nevertheless as Klang and Nolan (2011) point out, if SMS-based disaster communication efforts are hampered by municipal regulations, this risks dampening one of the most effective uses of SMS: citizen networking. Put baldly, the trade-off may be between the desire of local public safety officials for procedural regulation and the saving of lives.

Transportation Management

SMS has been widely used at the state and local level to facilitate transportation both in the United States and abroad. Transportation does not include the maintenance of road infrastructure which is discussed in the third section below. However, it does include two key components of transportation management: Highway Safety and Traffic Management.

Highway Safety

U.K. and Australian state and local agencies have embraced social media approaches in the effective promotion of road safety and injury prevention, specifically the use of YouTube and the targeting of youth through the use of games (Murray and Lewis, September 1–2, 2011). In some cases, like the "Embrace Life" seatbelt campaign from the Sussex Safer Roads Partnership in the United Kingdom, road safety–related campaigns have been devised specifically for dissemination through SMS, in that case, a YouTube commercial targeting seatbelt use. That video and the accompanying campaign attracted worldwide notice (Osocio 2010).

Similarly, in Australia, a video montage of television commercials produced by the Victorian Transport Accident Commission (TAC) was launched in late 2009 on YouTube and also on broadcast television; the TAC's YouTube channel became the third most viewed sponsored channel on YouTube postcampaign (Campaign Brief 2010). Further, the Queensland Department of Transport and Main Roads developed the CityGTiPhone application 4 designed to look like a regular driving game and not a road safety campaign. It was ranked in the top three "hottest Apps" on iTunes, and was one of 2009's most popular free Apps on the Australian iTunes store (Australia 2011).

Traffic Management

Arlington County, Virginia, government has maintained a Facebook page since early 2010. A content analysis of the posts and responses (comments) from the public during a two-month period (August–September 2010) revealed that the most common posts by the County on the Facebook page were about traffic (e.g., conditions, closures, metro outages). The public comments were predominantly related to traffic as well, followed by miscellaneous events (i.e., events that do not fall into other "event" categories, such as food, exercise, music, and film). Interestingly, other related exercise events (city-sponsored bikes and walks) that have an impact on traffic also generated the next most frequent number of comments from the public (Kavanaugh and Nastev, March 11, 2011).

Infrastructure and Environmental Management

One area in which SMS has been effective in pulling information from citizens to monitor government services and operations has been for reporting infrastructure that needs either repair or maintenance and for reporting environmental lapses. This is a key part of citizen participation in government functioning and a source of valuable service and maintenance information. It is an underpinning to the movement to create "smart" cities wherein citizens and their mobile devices are transformed from civic participants only into "sensors" for local government infrastructure and environmental management systems (Ratti and Townsend 2011). These arrangements facilitate a "just in time" delivery of repairs that makes the maintenance of infrastructure more efficient.

"Apps" have been developed for smart phones that allow citizens of local governments to report highway and road infrastructure failings such as potholes directly to public works departments and to have work orders generated to fix them. These applications combine the ubiquity of smart phones and their internal GPS with the ability of the phones to communicate directly with SMS over the Internet to both report and locate needed repairs. Along these lines, other smart phone enabled SMS interactions have been developed such as noise pollution monitoring that makes use of the ability of the phone to "hear," measure, and report (Participatory noise pollution monitoring using mobile phones, 2010). Another useful application of the smart phone SMS link at the local level has been the reporting of graffiti to removal teams making use of the smart phone's camera, as well as its GPS facility and Internet connectivity (Jayakanthan 2011).

GOVERNANCE AND SMS AT THE STATE AND LOCAL LEVEL

As the first part of this essay makes clear, SMS have been employed throughout the world and effectively used to improve the delivery of services by getting information to and from citizens about problems, emergencies, and maintenance. Service delivery and the usefulness of SMS is a component of state and local governments' relationship with their citizens that has been well studied and, in some areas, found to be highly effective and admitting of even greater promise. Nevertheless, there is another element of state and local government for which the promises of SMS—greater connectivity among citizens themselves in the coalescence of policy preferences, faster iteration and communication of these preferences between citizens and representatives, and higher citizen participation in representative forums—have been touted but not yet delivered or well studied. That is the second "building block" of state and local government which this essay examines: the use of SMS in "governance" rather than operational arrangements.

Citizen Engagement and Participation

One arena in which there has been some experimentation in and great hope for the broad connectivity offered by SMS is in the potential for increasing public participation in the formulation of public policy at the state and local levels. The ease of use and connectivity of SMS has implied a route to alleviating the physical difficulties and time pressures of travel, crowds, and fixed hours for participation in traditional public meetings at which policy and policy changes are hammered out. In addition, the leveling factor of lateral connectivity among citizens seems to imply the possibility of a less hierarchal approach to their participation in decision making at the state and local level.

Citizen Engagement and Power Sharing

Only a little study has taken place of the impact of SMS on citizen engagement in policy and allowing for expressive input on important policy framing matters (Lyons 2011). However, at least one study has looked at the power dynamics of the use of Facebook pages in this regard. Hand and Ching (2011) examined the usefulness of Facebook pages as a way to connect citizens with each other (many-to-many) for policy input versus the utilization of those SMS to transmit to and receive from government to citizens (one-to-many) in a more authoritative manner. What the authors encountered in their exploratory study in the Phoenix area is that the city governments studied use Facebook to maintain power relations and inform citizens about their views (speaking-from-power) rather than using the platform for the sort of connectivity for which it was intended: that is flat, egalitarian networked communications or even iterated and critical feedback (speaking-to-power) exchanges.

Citizen Engagement and SMS Usage Policy

SMS can be seen as a resource for increased interaction between municipal authorities and citizens. However, as authorities attempt to employ SMS, they may become trapped by their own traditional regulatory frameworks that emphasize openness and transparency rather than citizen interaction. Rather than being a largely innovative endeavor that attempts to extend public participation, provide an alternative to other mechanisms, or replace traditional local government forums, SMS use at the local level may be challenged by existing constraints and legal frameworks.

A study of the SMS policies of twenty-six Swedish municipalities is interesting in this regard. It reveals that these SMS regulatory polices do not take a united view on the usefulness of SMS and some treat it as a problem rather than a possibility. In general across the municipal policies examined, the tendency was to take a "command and control" stance and to establish clear goals and routines for SMS use and to discipline activities to adhere to this order. Moreover, the authors offer that such an approach does not merely err on the side of transparency instead of citizen interaction, but that it most often explicitly disallows activity that promotes local government innovation and adaptation to citizen needs (Klang and Nolin 2011).

This focus on regulating and the controlling innovation in using SMS to engage citizens in policy formulation seems to be found in the United States as well. In a recent study designed to help fill the gap in what is known about social media policy in U.S. government, the Center for Technology in Government undertook a content review of SMS policies. The study was a "best practices" effort designed to produce a new resource to guide government social media policy development efforts. The study found that there are eight core elements of local government social media policy in the United States: (1) employee access, (2) account management, (3) acceptable use, (4) employee conduct, (5) content, (6) security, (7) legal issues, and (8) citizen conduct (Hrdinova, Helbig, and Peters, May 2010). It is not surprising that nearly all of these elements are restrictive and concerned with regulation of conduct and content, and that they do not speak to the issues of SMS innovation, use in policy networks, or citizen participation.

Elections and Electoral Campaigns

SMS have been used for voter participation, mobilization, and fund-raising in various national elections. Some have credited them with a significant role in the

2008 U.S. Presidential victory of Barack Obama. However, other research has cast some doubt on this premise (Kushin and Yamamoto 2010). Also, in the 2010 national elections in the Netherlands, politicians with higher SMS engagement got relatively more votes within most political parties. However, SMS did not significantly influence voting behavior during the 2010–2011 local elections (Picazo-Velazquez n.d.). Other studies of local SMS roles played in state and local elections have not been forthcoming.

Another component of elections, campaign financing and candidate wealth information, has been affected by SMS-like applications if not by SMS themselves. Most states in the United States, many counties and municipalities, and similar jurisdictions in other countries, for example Mexico, use some sort of Internet-based platform for the collection and publication of electoral financing. In many cases, these sites receive only financial information inputs from the campaigns of candidates who must post them. However, most often the information posted is "crowd sourced," that is, accessible to anyone who cares to access it. In some states, this includes digitized affidavits, brochures, receipts, or other documents. In addition, most election results down to the precinct level are available online, post election.

CONCLUSION: THE UNDELIVERED PROMISE OF SMS FOR STATE AND LOCAL GOVERNANCE

SMS are all the rage today: the staple of daily communication and commerce for many; the source of new fortunes for a few. In state and local governments throughout the world, they have played a significant role in helping to put the eyes of citizens on operations that range from filling cracks in the sidewalk to tracking the money collected by local officials in their runs for office. Like other technological innovations in the commercial world from the steamroller to the personal computer, SMS has changed the way government does its business: new tools for private business mean new business and operations and this always means the same for the public sector as well as new regulatory responsibilities (Dadashzadeh 2010). After all, as Allison points out, the two sectors are just alike in all "unimportant respects" (Allison 1979).

Conversely, it is in these "important respects" of state and local government—citizen engagement and participation, policy input, elections, and representation; the stuff of local governance if not government—where SMS has not played a noteworthy role (Lampe et al. 2011). Furthermore, this is an area where some hope might be held out for its development as a tool specifically of government and not business: replacing real town halls with virtual ones; tracking citizen policy preferences in real time (Mentzas et al. 2011); issue-based coalition formation and dissolution among networked citizens rather than interest group formation as the norm; enhanced citizen connectivity (Taylor-Smith and Lindner 2010). Virtual business is a reality, but virtual government is not.

Obviously, this sort of SMS use would be transformational and thus not without transaction costs, risks, and difficulties of fitting technology to task (Lampe et al. 2011). Replacing the old with the new is never costless and the regulatory frameworks that we have now present both cost and risk in the widespread use, availability, and archiving of SMS and the records they generate. This is why the preponderance of the articles on the topic of SMS use for government are about either using them as tools in current operations or controlling them: strategies for use, best practices and policies, or rules for effective employment (Mergel 2010).

Clearly then, what is lacking in the study of SMS at the state and local level is examination of their effective use in governance. How can we successfully employ SMS to link citizens together and with business and with government? How to make the "governing" part of government easier and more connected in order for citizens to engage in it and not just government operations? How to link business more effectively with government and vice versa? What is needed is further research, building on the successful research conducted already, in at least four areas:

- Making the actual virtual: What are the ideas, experiments, and efforts to reinvent local forums, meetings, and other essential gatherings using SMS to better and more easily connect citizens with local government in the formulation of public policy? This includes the discussion, design, and testing of policy and not just comments on proposals.

This is not merely a suggestion for more research into the already commonly used broadcast or collection of information by local governments.

- Best transformational practices: What are state and local governments doing to promote innovative use of SMS in governance and to reduce the risks, opportunity costs, and transaction costs for SMS adoption? Some of this research should focus on who is innovating, where, and in what in SMS supported governance arrangements at the local level. Other parts of this research should focus on the legal aspects of innovative SMS use possibly examining proposals to differentiate networked communications from standard ones governed (and limited) by transparency and other strictures that make them too costly and risky for local government. Other research in this area might focus on the way to incentivize or at least remove disincentives for SMS use in governance innovation.

- Emergent-cies: What are citizens doing with SMS to communicate about local government policy, representation, and service that local government can learn from and employ? One of the tenets of SMS is connectivity and one of the tenets of this is "laterality," the notion that there is no hierarchy in effective networks. If SMS is to be used to engage citizens in their governments, especially in a nonhierarchical way, some of the best ideas may emerge from the practices of citizens themselves. This is one of the ingredients least studied by political scientists, students of public administration, and practitioners because they tend to study stable government institutions and not emergent citizen-driven ones.

- Electoral connections: How can SMS be used to more effectively mobilize citizens at the state and local levels to participate in the selection of their representatives, communicate with them, and increase their satisfaction with this process? Again, this is not the mere automation of existing processes and procedures in e-government, but their lateralization and transformation. It includes studying the use of SMS in all aspects of elections to improve the willingness and ability of citizens to volunteer to support candidates, or to participate in poll watching or registration, or other local electoral tasks and activities.

These suggestions may not exhaust the areas in which SMS research on state and local governance needs to be carried out. However, they are a start that is based on the perceived holes in current research. One hopes that the pages of the State and Local Government Review will be an outlet where some of this new research is debuted. Certainly, one hopes also that it will be one of the places credited with spurring it.

Text Credits

Chapter	Credit
1.	Peter Harkness. January 2012. "What Brand of Federalism is Next?" Governing. http://www.governing.com/columns/potomac-chronicle/gov-col-what-brand-of-federalism-is-next.html. Accessed February 12, 2012.
2.	Pamela M. Prah. January 10, 2012. "Washington and the States: A Year of Uncertainty and Foreboding." Stateline.org. http://www.stateline.org/live/details/story?contentId=623722. Accessed January 20, 2012.
3.	Alan Greenblatt. April 2011. "States Handing Off More Responsibilities to Cities." Governing. http://www.governing.com/topics/mgmt/States-Handing-Off-More-to-Cities.html. Accessed October 6, 2011.
4.	Lisa Soronen. 2012. "States' Rights at Center of Trilogy of Cases Before Supreme Court." Capitol Ideas. March/April: 44-45. Printed with permission from The Council of State Governments.
5.	Excerpted from Wendy R. Weiser and Lawrence Norden. 2011. Voting Law Changes in 2012. New York: Brennan Center for Justice at NYU School of Law.
6.	Edward P. Smith. December 2011. "Policy, Politics and Population." State Legislatures. http://www.ncsl.org/legislatures-elections/redist/policy-politics-and-population.aspx. Accessed January 24, 2012.
7.	John Gramlich. January 9, 2012. "After a Contentious Political Year, Republicans May Moderate Their

Approach." Stateline.org. http://www .stateline.org/live/details/ story?contentId=623384. Accessed January 20, 2012.

8. John Gramlich. June 13, 2011. "In An Era of One-Party Rule, Republicans Pass a Sweeping State Agenda." Stateline.org. http://www.stateline.org/live/details/ story?contentId=580741. Accessed January 20, 2012.

9. Alan Greenblatt. July 2011. "Are the Unions Winning the Fight?" Governing. http://www.governing.com/topics/public-workforce/are-unions-winning-the-fight .html. Accessed January 20, 2012.

10. Alan Greenblatt. December 2011. "ALEC Enjoys A New Wave of Influence and Criticism." Governing. http://www .governing.com/topics/politics/ALEC-enjoys-new-wave-influence-criticism.html#. Accessed March 21, 2012.

11. Louis Jacobson. 2011. "Welcome to the Tea Party." State Legislatures. September: 12-15.

12. Peggy Kerns. 2011. "Do Ethics Laws Work?" State Legislatures. July/August: 43.

13. Judy Nadler. October/November 2011. "Blog, Tweet and Post: Proceed With Caution." State Legislatures. http://www .ncsl.org/legislatures-elections/ethicshome/ blog-tweet-and-post-proceed-with-caution .aspx. Accessed April 5, 2012.

14. Alan Greenblatt. November 2011. "Can Redistricting Ever Be Fair?" Governing. http://www.governing.com/topics/politics/ can-redistricting-ever-be-fair.html. Accessed January 20, 2012.

15. Josh Goodman. January 27, 2012. "Why Redistricting Commissions Aren't Immune From Politics." Stateline.org. http://www .stateline.org/live/printable/ story?contentId=627668. Accessed March 30, 2012.

16. Mary Branham. 2011. "Washington Governor: 'Set Your Partisanship Behind You, Now It's Time to Govern.'" Capitol Ideas. July/August: 34-35. Printed with

permission from The Council of State Governments.

17. John Gramlich. January 26, 2012. "In Kansas, Governor Sam Brownback Drives a Rightward Shift." Stateline.org. http:// stateline.org/live/details/ story?contentId=627000. Accessed January 25, 2012.

18. John Gramlich. August 9, 2011. "After Years Away, Comeback Governors Try to Rekindle Their Power." Stateline.org. http:// www.stateline.org/live/details/ story?contentId=592757. Accessed January 24, 2012.

19. Alan Greenblatt. March 2012. "Kris Kobach Tackles Illegal Immigration." Governing. http://www.governing.com/ topics/politics/gov-kris-kobach-tackles-illegal-immigration.html . Accessed April 9, 2012.

20. Daniel J. Hall. 2011. Reshaping the Face of Justice: The Economic Tsunami Continues. Williamsburg, VA: National Center for State Courts.

21. Emily Badger. January 20, 2012. "Private Prisons Can't Lock In Savings." Miller-McCune.com. http://www.miller-mccune. com/business-economics/private-prisons-cant-lock-in-savings-39230/. Accessed January 20, 2012.

22. John Gramlich. April 4, 2011. "California Shrinks Its Prisons, But Overcrowding Persists." Stateline.org. http://www.stateline .org/live/printable/story?contentId=564291. Accessed March 9, 2012.

23. Richard Williams. 2011. "The Cost of Punishment." State Legislatures. July/ August: 55-56.

24. Steven Walters. 2011. "Showdown in Madison." State Legislatures. July/August. 20-23.

25. Ben Wieder. January 12, 2012. "Unions Adapt to New Rules, Even As They Fight to Reverse Them." Stateline.org. http://www .stateline.org/live/details/story?contentId= 624407. Accessed April 18, 2012.

26. Emily Badger. March 2, 2011. "Bargaining and Budget Shortfalls: Are They Linked?" Miller-McCune.com. http://www.miller-mccune.com/politics/bargaining-and-budget-shortfalls-are-they-linked-28798/. Accessed April 18, 2012.

27. Helisse Levine and Eric Scorsone. December 2011. "The Great Recession's Institutional Change in the Public Employment Relationship: Implications for State and Local Governments." State and Local Government Review. 43(3): 208-214.

28. Christopher W. Hoene and Michael A. Pagano. September 2011. "City Fiscal Conditions in 2011." Research Brief on America's Cities. National League of Cities.

29. Thom Reilly and Mark B. Reed. December 2011. "Budget Shortfalls, Employee Compensation, and Collective Bargaining in Local Governments." State and Local Government Review. 43(3): 215-223.

30. Kirk Victor. March 2012. "Struggling Cities Strike Deals to Solve Fiscal Problems." Governing. http://www.governing.com/topics/finance/gov-struggling-cities-strike-deals-to-solve-fiscal-problems.html. Accessed April 9, 2012.

31. Alan Greenblatt. June 2011. "Rahm Emanuel Takes on Chicago." Governing. http://www.governing.com/topics/politics/rahm-emanuel-takes-on-chicago.html. Accessed April 23, 2012.

32. Daniel C. Vock. January 13, 2012. "At Last, a State Budget Year When the Sky is Not Falling." Stateline.org. http://www.stateline.org/live/details/story?contentId=624742. Accessed January 20, 2012.

33. Donald F. Kettl. October 2011. "2011 May Mark the End of Federal Aid." Governing. http://www.governing.com/columns/potomac-chronicle/2011-may-mark-end-federal-aid.html. Accessed April 25, 2012.

34. Kirk Victor. November 2011. "Who's Winning the Amazon Tax Battles?" Governing. http://www.governing.com/topics/finance/whos-winning-amazon-tax-battles.html. Accessed January 20, 2012.

35. John Gramlich. July 13, 2011. "Coming This Fall: Big Tuition Hikes." Stateline.org. http://www.stateline.org/live/details/story?contentId=587120. Accessed April 30, 2012.

36. Louis Jacobson. January 2012. "Jobs Crisis." State Legislatures. http://www.ncsl.org/issues-research/labor/jobs-crisis.aspx. Accessed May 4, 2012.

37. Ryan Holeywell. May 2012. "Emergency Financial Managers: Michigan's Unwelcome Savior." Governing. http://www.governing.com/topics/mgmt/gov-emergency-financial-managers-michigan-municipalities-unwelcome-savior.html. Accessed May 7, 2012.

38. Russell Nichols. December 2011. "Governments Experiment With Risk-Free Financing." Governing. http://www.governing.com/topics/health-human-services/governments-experiment-with-risk-free-financing.html. Accessed January 20, 2012.

39. Bruce J. Perlman. April 2012. "Social Media Sites at the State and Local Levels: Operational Success and Governance Failure." State and Local Government Review. 44(1): 67-75.

⑤SAGE research**methods**

The essential online tool for researchers from the world's leading methods publisher

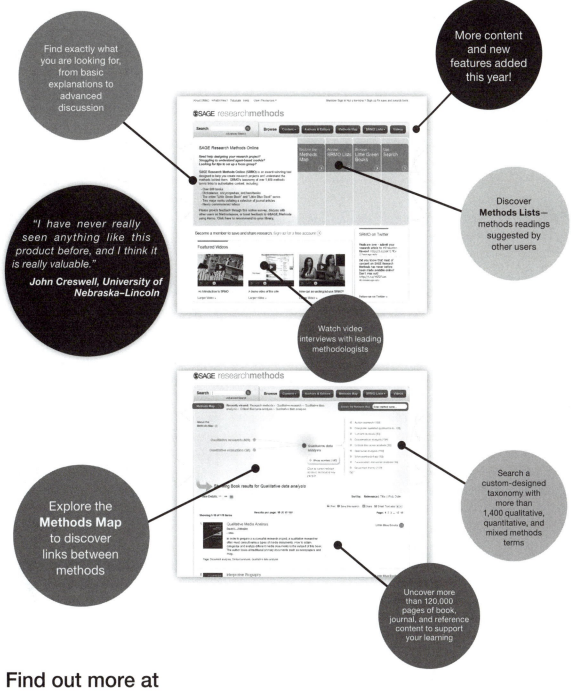

Find exactly what you are looking for, from basic explanations to advanced discussion

More content and new features added this year!

"I have never really seen anything like this product before, and I think it is really valuable."

John Creswell, University of Nebraska–Lincoln

Discover **Methods Lists**—methods readings suggested by other users

Watch video interviews with leading methodologists

Explore the **Methods Map** to discover links between methods

Search a custom-designed taxonomy with more than 1,400 qualitative, quantitative, and mixed methods terms

Uncover more than 120,000 pages of book, journal, and reference content to support your learning

Find out more at
www.sageresearchmethods.com